Footprints, Harbours and Colours

Ria Wiid

ISBN: 1507540817
ISBN-13: 978-1507540817

DEDICATION

To Joseph
who taught me to fly.

CONTENTS

ACKNOWLEDGMENTS

Each and every person I met on my journey has enriched my life in some way or another. Without them my story would simply not be the same. I have changed the names of a number of them in order to preserve their anonymity.

My family for their endless support and patience during the lengthy writing and editing process.

Kissed Off Creations (www.kissedoff.co.uk), Worcester for creating the cover.

Tony Held (www.tonyheld.com) for giving the content a once-over.

PART 1: AFRICAN CLAY

When you start on your journey to Ithaca,
then pray that the road is long,
full of adventure, full of knowledge.
Do not fear the Lestrygonians
and the Cyclopes and the angry Poseidon.
You will never meet such as these on your path,
if your thoughts remain lofty, if a fine
emotion touches your body and your spirit.
You will never meet the Lestrygonians,
the Cyclopes and the fierce Poseidon,
if you do not carry them within your soul,
if your soul does not raise them up before you.

K. P. Kavafis (C. P. Cavafy), translation by Rae Dalven

Beginnings

I grew up in Apartheid-era South Africa – the youngest of four children in a conservative Afrikaans home. The announcement of my imminent arrival came as a surprise; when my mother went to see her doctor in search of a cure for her menopausal symptoms, she was sent home to buy knitting needles. I slipped into the home as a full-stop to the family.

My birth happened in 1961, the year South Africa became a Republic and Queen Elizabeth II was stripped of her title "Queen of South Africa". For most of my school years I was labelled a 'Republic baby' and every year on Republic Day, the 31st May, I became part of a fancy dress parade in honour of the founding father of the nation, Jan van Riebeeck. On this day all the students born in 1961 would take part in a re-enactment of the arrival of our forefathers. European settlers who, in 1652, established a resupply station at the Cape of Good Hope. It was a story about their hunger for expansion and control; and one about slaves who were brought in from Indonesia, Madagascar and India to work for the colonists. Finally, it was also a story about the British occupation of the Cape after the Napoleonic Wars, and about a band of Boers (aka Voortrekkers) who trekked inland for a better life and away from British control. A trek which resulted in many conflicts with native tribes such as the Zulus as the Boers sought dominance over the interior of South Africa. For the powers that be there was something special about being a Republic baby, as if I represented some milestone. It tried to colour me, and growing up I had no inkling of what it was all about.

I came into this world as a "blow-in" – with the DNA of my Danish, Dutch and German forefathers like mini footprints in my blood. I arrived into a world of privilege; my skin was white, my parents educated, and this meant endless opportunities. However, I had arrived in an unnatural world, a place held together by artificial beliefs, systems and structures. I arrived in Pretoria a little out of place. Pretoria (also known as Jacaranda City due to its large number of Jacaranda trees), one of the capitals of South Africa, started as a centre for Afrikaners, and it is home to the Voortrekker Monument – a massive granite structure built to commemorate the Great Trek that took place during the 1830s and 1840s. The monument was supposedly built as an altar to a God who created a new civilisation inland; one that somehow ignored the inhabitants that were already there. I arrived in a world that appeared stable and solid; a world with the taste of paradise, but one with segregation based on skin colour at the core of its fabric.

As the youngest of four children, I fell into the slipstream of my three older siblings and somehow just grew up. Armed with a compass, boundaries and tenacity, I had to work things out for myself. Independence was highly valued from an early age. My mother was always very proud of the fact that I simply got on with it; apparently seamlessly.

I don't remember much about my early childhood. My first memories are from my Grade One school year in Summerstrand, Port Elizabeth: the wind, learning to ride my first bike, winning an egg-and-spoon race at a school sports day, and a box of 36 Croxley crayons. I spotted the crayons in the window of our local pharmacy - the box had all the shades of the rainbow plus three silver and gold crayons. I remember walking past the shop window many times, dreaming about the colours, and working out a plan of how to save my pocket money until I had enough to buy them. As a six-year-old I imagined a life with silver and gold.

When I was between six and seven years old we moved to Johannesburg, where my father was involved in setting up a new university.

We stayed in a big old house in Auckland Park until our new house was built. It was a sombre house with a dark wooden staircase and walls that had absorbed the stories of many people who had lived there before us. Somehow the house knew its days were numbered and that as soon as the first sod for the new university was dug, it would be demolished. Living there was like being in the presence of a brooding widow wearing black mourning clothes. Here I met death for the first time when our sausage dog was run over. Death was not something that was discussed openly; it happened in silence, behind a veil, somewhere else where words had no sounds. I never wanted to know the spot in the garden where our dog was buried.

I witnessed our new house taking shape in a cul-de-sac in Randburg, a neighbouring town of Johannesburg and at the time still on the edge of urban sprawl. There was something special about entering the foundation, and following the long passage into each of the rooms as if for the first time. Standing in the unfinished spaces allowed me to imagine what the finished rooms could look like. In a yet-to-be-built room there are no limits; anything is possible: colour, texture, furnishings, ambiance, and dreams. Although there were no walls yet, I always entered through the doorway. The house in Randburg was to be our home for almost two decades.

Carefree

My childhood was carefree and happy; there were no upheavals or dramas, no scenes or tragedies. It was as if everything was held together with the precision of a Fibonacci sequence. From an early age I was introduced to music: singing hymns around the piano on a Sunday evening; the sounds of my siblings' violin, recorder and guitar playing; operas and symphonic orchestra performances in the city hall; and beautiful classical music on Sundays. Sound was very important to my father and he always invested in top-end hi-fi systems. He even custom-built two massive speakers and they stood in our lounge like two maître D podiums waiting to hold a speech. The hi-fi system was holy, and growing up we were not allowed to use it. When I was finally old enough to play a record I was nervous every time I tried to line up the needle with the beginning of a track on the LP record. I was very aware that the two massive speakers would bellow a missed target, and that scared me.

For us children there was a portable turn-table, mostly occupied by my older teenage sister. Sometimes she would host us our own hit parade. I adored listening to her stream of popular grown-up songs. During her hit parades it was difficult to score *"Morning has broken"*, *"Hey Jude"*, *"Me and Bobby McGee"* and *"Don't forget to remember"* on our hit list. There was such excitement to find out which of our songs made it to Number One.

There were also piano lessons. I cycled the four or so kilometres to my weekly piano class. My bike was black, second-hand and had thick tyres. It was not a bicycle I was proud of, or one I was keen to make stand next to the other Raleigh bikes in the neighbourhood. But it was faithful and took me up and down hills to various places. I loved playing the piano but didn't like my piano teachers; for some reason they were all always moody and angry, and would lash out at the slightest finger mistake. For them there was no joy in the teaching experience; instead they used our interaction to make uninspired comments, as if they were sergeant majors in a piano teachers' army. These teachers drained my love for the piano and by the time I left school the music scales and notes had died down.

Our home in Randburg had a swimming pool. I remember it taking shape. A digger arrived and dug a big hole in our front garden. There was something special about feeling the hollow of the concrete space before the water filled it, and trying to imagine the depth and feel of the water. Our swimming pool was not constructed by a pool company, but instead took shape under the watchful eye of my father. At first the walls were concrete grey, and without white or sky blue to colour the water, our pool looked more like a dam. Until the walls of our pool changed from dull to sparkling, it felt less than the other swimming pools in the neighbourhood. But then again our pool had an extra deep deep-end – when it came to diving, my father would have nothing other than nine feet of depth. We spent endless hours in our pool.

My father had a passion for nature: our garden was beautiful. With the help of a gardener he tended a big rockery with aloes, shrubs, rare cycads and Namaqualand daisies in the front garden; and indigenous trees, bougainvillea, vegetable patch, peach trees, flower beds and a big avocado tree in the back. The lawn consisted of sheep's grass and was always perfectly manicured. Our garden was big enough to hold a game of netball and cartwheels. In summer the flower beds would burst with the colours of sweet peas, daisies, pansies, petunias, azalea and roses; and in the winter months California poppies. There were always fresh flowers in the house. Putting poppies in a vase required a ritual and it was often my job to burn each stem over a candle so they could last longer before I put them in a vase.

Both my parents were educators and we were privileged with a number of holidays a year: summer at the south coast of Natal, winter at the Drakensberg and Easter at my grandparents' farm near Haenertsburg (aka Mpumalanga). The farm was big with hills and valleys; a stretch of eerie woodland; cows and sheep; a big dam and a windmill; messy farm yard with a car wreck or two; outside loo; small community school; azalea and fuchsia in many shades; and an old milking parlour. We spent hours pottering around the place – there was so much to discover. The roots of the tall

Alhambra tree provided the perfect world for our matchbox cars: sweeping driveways and an intricate road network for our miniature Hillman Minx, Triumph and VW Kombi. And the big oak tree gave a supply of acorns, which became our eggs in their own little egg cups. We boiled them and pretended we had a restaurant.

We'd make our annual trip to the local co-op store in the back of a pickup-truck. The store stocked everything from a needle to a coffin; sweets in glass jars; brooms and mops; and had the smell of paraffin and linoleum. I always left with a little brown paper packet with Wilson's toffees, gobstoppers, Aunty Alice's apricot sweets and pink cachous.

We stayed in the out building with two bedrooms – the four of us in one big room. My oldest sister always got to choose her bed first, and then my two brothers would pick and I always got the smallest bed in the corner next to the door to my parents' room. My sister had the privilege of a screen around her bed that separated her from us. At night when the gas lamps went out it would be pitch black. Growing up I was sure there was no moon over Haenertsburg. It scared me, and I couldn't wait for the morning so that I could see the outlines of my hands. There were the dark nights spent with pee pots under our beds, the customary sheep slaughtering; the smell of offal cooking on the Aga stove, soap boiling in a cast iron pot under the oak tree, the cold sitting room, and the flea bites that itched for weeks afterwards. I was the only one who attracted the bites – my experience with fleas coloured my time on the farm. At some level I always felt conflicted over wanting to be there, and dreading the horrible insect bites. We often spent Christmas there, and I wondered how Santa Claus knew where to find us.

December was the time for our summer holidays. At first we frequented a high-rise apartment block in Amanzimtoti, and then moved further south to Hibberdene and Uvongo. I remember the holiday atmosphere, the sun and sea of bright umbrellas and swimming costumes, beach full of people, huge waves, life-savers, daily ice-cream treat, and the energy of the Zulu dance performance. We laughed a lot. Getting there was a process; my mother started baking weeks before our departure and she'd fill tins with cookies from a cookie press. My father packed the car with precision, limiting each of us to one small piece of hand luggage. We'd leave at four or five o'clock in the morning. In the dark each of us would sneak an extra something or two into the car, and the four of us would end up like sardines squashed into a tin. When my older siblings were too old to join us, I took my walking doll along. Pretending she was real, I'd sit her in the middle seat like a little sister. Her face was scary and she never really walked.

There was always a tree at Christmas. Our parents warned us not to get up too early on Christmas morning to open our presents. It was difficult to go to sleep with an empty pillowcase at the end of my bed and excitement swirling in my belly like little fizzy bubbles. I always waited until at least five o'clock before I dared to inspect the pillowcase full of shapes. I felt such pleasure in trying to trace the outlines of the surprises inside. Each time the girls' Lucky Dip delivered a thrill – I have no idea why because it was always filled with insignificant little bits and pieces. I believed in Santa Clause and the Tooth Mouse until my teenage years. Somewhere in Africa the tooth mouse has a little house built with all my baby teeth.

When it was my birthday, my mum allowed me to choose the dinner menu. This was the privilege of the birthday girl or boy. My mother made a big fuss about birthdays – she made me feel special on this day. She was always there to wake us with a big smile, a present and a carefully selected card.

I grew up with an abundance of fresh fruit – my mother always bought our apples by the box. She would arrive home with half a cardboard box of golden delicious apples, each individually wrapped in purple tissue paper and carefully laid out on trays, three layers deep. They came straight from the tree and they tasted like heaven. Guava, lychee, mango, orange, peach, banana, paw-paw and red-flesh papino – there was no scarcity. In our garden we had a small orchard of yellow peach trees and when the trees were laden with peaches, my mother and father would start a production line to prepare and preserve the peaches in syrup. The process filled an entire day and for months afterwards the jars would line up on the shelves in our pantry, colouring that corner of the larder yellow.

I grew up with the smell of fresh fruit, muesli muffins and banana bread, freshly cut grass, yesterday-today-and-tomorrow blooms, and black-and-white photos taking shape in our own dark room. And I walked with bare feet whenever I could.

Boundaries that shaped

My home was an academic one; my father was a professor and our house was full of books. Time spent in the lounge happened against the backdrop of a wall full of books shrouded in seriousness: complete collections of encyclopaedias, academic literature, highbrow novels, a family Bible and a hefty old medical book. I always handled these books with respect – holding my breath in awe in their presence. Sometimes I would open the big medical book and read about gruesome illnesses. We never needed to go the local library for our projects - our house *was* a library.

My upbringing was conservative, influenced by Calvin: my parents were cautious and strict. In our house the outlines of what was enough were clearly defined. When television was first introduced my father bought a black-and-white one; he wanted to make sure it wasn't some fad and that the TV trend would take off. He was not one to take risks, but instead was committed to providing stability.

My mother sewed, knitted, smocked, baked and took immaculate care of us. Prayers were an important part of growing up and hers were extra special. She would have a list and depending on priority and need, thus we either moved up or down the list. I don't think we ever came off my mother's prayer list. She spent many nights on her knees, praying me through exams and trials and tribulations. My mother was a high school teacher who taught me in my last two years at school. Living in the same house as my schoolteacher meant I never quite got away from the educator.

My mother provided us with a wholesome harbour. She introduced us to books, and once every two weeks she would take us to the library to choose three books to read at home. She made the most delicious macaroni and cheese; moist chocolate cake; oats "crunchies"; lemon meringue; Jewish cake and "Jan Smutsies" – little cupcakes with jam centres. On Sunday's she would produce a cooked lunch with a protein dish, salad and pudding. Sometimes my father would top this with a bottle of sweet white wine.

My father was a physicist, a precise man who liked to know the position of north and south, used a Fibonacci sequence as his password, and his tools were all in neat rows and arranged from tallest to shortest against the wall in our garage. My father's hobby was woodwork, and he would disappear for days on end creating furniture from Cape teak, yellow-wood and Imbuia. During that time he would be grumpy and withdrawn – almost as if in the garage the process of creation produced an intense struggle between the carpenter and the item he crafted. He loved to work with wood; as if the palms of his hands wanted to unravel its secrets. Or was it the other way round – did the wood want to unravel his? The finished product always brought an end to his grumpiness and a glow-of-pride to his face. I don't think he ever thought he would be leaving his mark on pieces of furniture scattered all over the world. It makes me smile to think someday someone will find his signature carved in a discreet corner of an item; a signature that would tie the item back to a garage in Randburg. My father knew how to service a car, design a house, plan a garden, and fix almost everything.

For most of my school years we had a live-in domestic servant (or "maid" as she would have been referred to in those days). Salhpina lived in a tiny, dark room in the courtyard, with no proper shower facilities. Her bed was lifted onto bricks so as to protect her from the "Tikoloshe" (a mythical creature said to be evil). I always wondered why her room had only one small window, why she had to bathe in a stainless steel footbath, and why her toilet was an old-fashioned one with a chain. She had her own cutlery and crockery – and at night she would listen to the radio in her small room. Our neighbourhood banned streetlights so as to deter the domestic workers from socialising on the pavements at night. Salhpina took care of us with pride and dedication until one day she came home with a union letter of demand instigated by the Black Sash woman's league for an increase and my mother let her go. By then we were grown-ups and this was the first time I became aware of activism regarding the rights of servants. When the rumblings of tension and defiance came to the streets of our neighbourhood, the white "madams" responded by invoking their power. Salphina's Black Sash letter happened to arrive at the time when my mother's nest was empty and the need for a full-time servant no longer pressing. But above all my mother was not in the mood for trouble and there was to be no discussion or negotiation with Salphina.

Although we had a domestic servant we had to tidy our own rooms. Every so often on a Sunday - while we were at Sunday school - my father would do a bed and cupboard inspection and when we arrived home would find our beds or shelves stripped because they were untidy. Attending church and Sunday school was not negotiable, and the occasion called for a demure dress, tights and shoes, obligatory hat, and a coin for the collection box. My head was not a good one for hats and I loathed floppy ones. I also dreaded the boring church service, long prayers, and having to sit like statues. The same families always sat in the same rows – there was little room for change. I experienced God as an imposing man on a big chair in heaven - with an index finger ready to point whether you made it to the left or the right. At the end of the school year we would get a coloured stamp for 100 percent Sunday school attendance. We always walked home from church and on the way my brother and I invariably ended up in a scuffle as we tried to make it home first so as to grab the Sunday newspaper's comics section. There was something special about the newspaper on Sunday – as if it was a bonus for making it through the week. Our scuffles about the comics section annoyed my father; he did not like fracases.

After the customary Sunday lunch of meat, rice, vegetables and pudding my parents always went for a nap. And for the entire time of their sleep we weren't allowed to make a peep. I spent Sunday afternoons holding my breath, and I remember how relieved I felt whenever I heard the first stirrings from their room; it meant that my solitary confinement was finally over and that it was time for our four o'clock coffee and cake. Sometimes my father took us on a drive through other neighbourhoods to fill the remainder of the afternoon. During these outings I wondered about wealth and diversity. I imagined myself in other homes, as if their grass was greener than ours. It felt as though others were better off than us; as if their grass was greener than ours.

Television arrived in our house in 1976. At the time I did not know that South Africa was one of only a few countries unable to watch the first man to set foot on the moon; that our leaders at the time compared television with atom bombs and poison gas; and that in homes elsewhere in the world TV was part and parcel of everyday life.

Broadcasting started with an hour or two in the evenings and for the rest of the time there was the constant presence of a test pattern on the screen. The newness of it all fascinated me, and whenever I saw the test pattern, there was the promise of a screen that could come alive at any moment. We talked about the programs at school the next morning, and as the others chattered about the stories, colours, and clothes worn by the characters, I kept mum – my experience was in shades of black and white.

Beyond the edges of our suburb a whole new world was waiting to be discovered. In the absence of television, we would gather in the lounge to listen to our favourite radio dramas. We would sit in complete silence, each of us engrossed in a private viewing of the settings, stories, and characters in our minds. Magazines and newspapers were highlights in our weeks. There was always the excitement of a next instalment.

In my circle of friends I felt inferior. I never felt as beautiful, well-dressed, clever, talented, or as popular as some of the others in my school year. My parents were not fond of parties or sleep-overs and spontaneous gatherings were not encouraged. Our house was not one of those homes where people congregated.

Every Sunday night my father would summon us around an old newspaper on the floor of the laundry room so we could polish our school shoes until they were black and shiny. He would not settle for anything less. We had to take care of our shoes – there was no room for scuffs and holes due to neglect. During the winter my father would administer fish oil followed by a piece of home-made fudge. He didn't want us to get sick.

I had a respectful fear of my parents. There was no reason for this - it simply was. I could not find my voice to tell them about a bicycle accident I had, which left me concussed; or the gaping hole in the soft skin between my thumb and index finger caused by a knife and which I nursed for weeks; or the white mouse I got at school and hid in the bottom of my cupboard; or the nightmares that scared me at night. My parents did not like white mice and they did not like upheaval. One day after a few days away I found the mouse gone, along with the noses of several of my dolls. For some reason I tended my concussion, throbbing wound, nightmares at night, and my deceit about a hidden omnivorous scavenger in silence. I could not find my voice.

My father was a self-contained but intimidating figure; tall and serious. I would fear his wrath - his reaction never explosive, but piercing. But he was also the one who occasionally would lie next to me on our red oriental carpet in the formal lounge. These were moments of tenderness: the two of us, side-by-side like two crayons on an A4 sheet, on the deep colours of royalty and structure – in silence. After all he was the one who would rock our sausage dog to sleep at night.

My world revolved around the confines of our immediate suburb and town centre. Bo Peep – a stationery and gift shop; Stellas Drapers – where I got my first bra; the Greek corner café – where we collected white plastic safari animals in granadilla ice creams, an off-licence bottle store, and a post office were within walking distance from home. Both the post office and the bottle store had two entrances, one for whites and one for blacks. I never felt comfortable seeing the blacks queueing while the whites got preferential service. At no time did I witness any agitation or protest at the injustice of the segregation; instead I sensed calm, freedom perhaps, as if the servants and workers had accepted their lot in life. In our community, taking on the power of the Apartheid laws did not seem to be an option anyway.

At Bo Peep I bought my pens, pencils, and erasers that smelt like new dolls. Stellas Drapers was an Aladdin's cave with shoes, clothes, haberdashery and rolls of fabric. Every now and then my mother would bring home huge out-of-date Simplicity or Butterick pattern books from Stellas for sewing inspiration. These books fascinated me – the drawings of the models and clothes enticed me into an imaginary world. I couldn't wait for the moment when my mother was finished with the books and I was allowed to cut out the models. I spent hours creating families with surnames, scenarios, and different lives. There was so much choice: women of all ages, toddlers, men and boys. I loved to play with these paper dolls; to open the shoebox and bring out the various "families" I'd created. They took me into a place of both possibilities and empathy.

Once in a while, when it was time for my mother's electrolysis appointment, we would go into Johannesburg's city centre. Here there were all the colours and choices in John Orr's department store and the swanky Carlton shopping centre. When I was much older my mom allowed me to go to the flea market in Hillbrow; and for many years I treasured a silver name necklace bought at the market.

During my last year at primary school the netball coach told me I was too fat to make it into the A-team – so I stopped eating and almost became anorexic. We never spoke about this; it was one of those forbidden subjects that settled in the silence as if they did not exist. With this came a constant struggle around food, and weight became my nemesis.

My childhood was secure, reserved and predictable. Our house did not hold hugs and I never saw my parents cry – it was not the "done" thing. In our home the outlines of what was enough were well-defined. Growing up in our family was contained, like the colours and patterns on a roll of fabric enclosed by a selvedge on either side; the colours unable to spill over. My childhood was happy, yet from an early age, without me knowing, a little layer was forming around my heart like a veil over the face of a bride. It was as if somehow something was missing.

Destiny

From an early age I envisaged a future with a husband; two children two years apart; a career; two cars; and a home with a garden, swimming pool, bougainvillea and avocado tree. My vision was one of order, control and success. No major ructions.

I moved through school and university with reasonable ease, started my working career in the corporate world, and when my first relationship blew up, decided to do an MBA. At business school I not only received the golden qualification of the time, but also found myself a husband: a charming Irishman.

The O'Daly grew up on a farm in Ireland. Their home was compact, the family the size of a soccer team, resources were limited and the facilities stretched. According to him, when they ran out of space his mother would put the younger ones to bed in tallboy drawers. Growing up the family shared towels and toothbrushes; in their home there were no boundaries as far as these things were concerned. The smell of fresh soda bread, rock buns and apple pie always filled the kitchen, and the meals were hearty and wholesome. There was always room at the table for a neighbour or a passer-by. At the age of 13 the O'Daly left the farm for a boarding school in Clara, County Offaly. Clara was a long way from home, and on a number of occasions in winter when the bus broke down he had to walk the nine odd miles home in the snow. The O'Daly was studious and after he graduated from university he took a globe, spun it and his finger landed on South Africa. No world was too big for the O'Daly.

The moment the O'Daly landed in Johannesburg he tore up his return ticket – he knew he was home. During his first weekend in his new homeland he took his brand new second-hand Mazda 323 and travelled to the Kalahari Desert. From the word go he packed in loads of doings – as if he had to catch-up on a lifetime in Africa. The O'Daly built himself a career from scratch and in the process embarked on a number of courses. He too had his eye on the golden qualification of the time and five minutes before the closing time for applications he enrolled at Wits Business School.

Towards the end of the course we began to notice each other; listen to music or go to movies where we would end up talking on the pavement for hours afterwards. The O'Daly would wink at me from the other side of the classroom and within two months, before I could announce to anyone that we were dating, he asked me to marry him.

We married under the watchful eye of Cathkin Peak in the Drakensberg. Our wedding was a down-to-earth affair in a tiny chapel with two guitars, georgette and lace, Gypsophila, satin ribbons, and a handful of friends and family. Immediately after the ceremony the skies opened up and dumped enough rain to nearly flood the Champagne Castle Valley.

We settled in our first home and became fellow partakers on the treadmill of life. For us it was about careers, ambition, cars and a serious whirlwind of activity. Things were going according to plan until the first unexpected hitches in our world came in the form of ovulation charts, fertility drugs, laparoscopies, little jars with semen and test tubes. We struggled to have children – it was the one thing we could not control. Every fertility treatment was followed by an excruciating wait to see if I was pregnant. There were the many disappointments and tears, but somehow in between treatments I became pregnant and gave birth to a little girl. From the beginning she was Ruby. When she was six weeks old I handed her to our nanny and returned to work.

The struggle to have Ruby took its toll, and when she was a year old I was diagnosed with postnatal depression. The highs and lows of trying to create a new life – and failing time after time – were too much. Expecting Ruby brought me face-to-face with the challenge of attachment. For the entire duration of the pregnancy I was too scared to get attached to the baby – scared I might lose him or her. When I got to hold Ruby for the first time I was unable to bond with her, too frightened something might happen to her. Maybe the biggest blow for me was the realisation that we are not creators, and that the miracle of a new life belongs entirely to the realm of wonder. I felt overwhelmed in the presence of a new life. I took Prozac for three months and moved on with my life.

Somewhere in my pursuit of motherhood, and when Ruby was barely two, ovarian cancer arrived like an uninvited guest in the night. One night after surgery I was getting ready for the evening visiting hour when the O'Daly and the specialist came in. At the time the visit seemed odd because the doctors did their rounds in the morning. The specialist sat down and started to talk. His words came out like chicks trying to scatter to safety, as if they did not want to stay in the room. Until one slipped out with chemotherapy at its heart, and at that moment I understood – I just knew. The walk from the specialist's office to my room was the O'Daly's longest walk. In one moment my world came to a standstill. One word and in that instant the vision I had for my life changed.

Somewhere in the blur my mother came. I wasn't able to talk. A few others gathered around my bed. My brother brought a flask of coffee. Inside the small room my clan pulled together and encircled the hurt and crippling fear left by the diagnosis.

Outside the hospital window Hillbrow was getting ready for a busy night. That night in Hillbrow was one of my longest nights.

My father arrived the next morning from East London with his navy travel bag and airplane ticket tucked under his arm. He came with the authority of head of our home; and he brought with him resilience and stillness.

On the back of the diagnosis came a desperate battle for life: chemotherapy, visualization, prayers, special diets and a fragile faith. The battle happened around me – I felt excluded. I was merely an object somewhere on the battleground. In the wake of the battle I was left detached from the world, from my heart, and from my breath. I was in a constant grip of fear in varying shades of black.

I was afraid for others: how will the O'Daly and two-year-old Ruby cope with my demise? Will the cancer win, and if not, will the disease return at some later stage? The fear tightened the veil around my heart.

We were advised to fit wigs before the start of chemotherapy. The O'Daly and my mother took me to the Cancer Association in Braamfontein where a bland woman presented a number of second-hand wigs. This was a safe place from where to start, and in any case, whoever tells you how to go about shopping for a wig? As I tried them on Mum would say, "That one is nice," and when I tried on the one in a bob hairstyle both Mum and the sales woman said it was perfect. The wigs were all horrible and I wished someone would acknowledge that they were unsuitable instead of trying to pretend. In the presence of cancer there is a lot of room for pretending.

In the presence of my life-threatening diagnosis I became very aware of the O'Daly's plight as unidentified patient. He was the one who had to witness both my suffering and his own; and be frightened and brave, resourceful and helpless at the same time. He also had to keep everything together, from falling apart at the seams. I realized he too needed care and attention, and I wasn't able to give it to him.

My first chemotherapy session happened as an inpatient at Johannesburg General Hospital. My stay in hospital coincided with a general strike; this meant visiting the hospital after dark was unsafe. There was unrest in the air and I received my first treatment in a general ward where there were not enough staff to mop up the blood spills; where the beds were filled with desperation; and my visitors were unable to spend much time with me. My days in the Jo'burg General were long and lonely.

The picture of my perfect future had blotches on it. I moved through cancer from treatment to treatment and from blood marker test result to result – one of the lucky ones. The periods in between check-ups and scans became longer and longer, and as time passed, the thoughts that linked every twitch and pain with cancer became less and less. Every so often there was a little scare and I dealt with these by holding my breath. I never experienced true joy at big progress milestones; relief and gratitude, yes. My encounter with cancer had numbed a part of my being, and the loss of innocence settled in my sacral centre. Much too soon I forgot about the scare, the wigs, my fresh intentions, and slowly fell back into old patterns. Before we knew it we were back on the treadmill of life.

Faith healers and prophecies

We bought our second house in Fairland on a whim; one Sunday afternoon five minutes before six in the evening. On our way home from a social lunch we decided to investigate a new development at the other end of our road. The salesman was irritated, his briefcase was already packed, and now he had to put it down and show us a house. The one he showed us wasn't the one we liked, but instead we asked to view a bigger one. He was reluctant to show us because he thought we looked a little out of place.

The moment I stepped through the front door and saw the terracotta tiles and open living spaces I knew we had to have this house. We had to scrimp and plan, but we did it. I loved the place. I loved the open flow between the reception rooms; the exotic garden with pergola and swimming pool, the stepping stones, and the view from the front door onto Northcliff Ridge.

We moved in and transformed the walls into a colour palette to complement the terracotta, and the garden into a little paradise. One morning the O'Daly woke up and said, "Oh shit, we now have two homes – we better sell the first one." The realisation didn't keep the O'Daly awake at night – not much did. Instead he kept his focus, sold the house, created a wine cellar and built a tree house for Ruby at our new home. It was such a happy place.

We did not have great success with pets. Ruby's hamster kept on escaping and our neighbours would find him in drainpipes and tight corners and return him to us. Hanging on to him became a full-time occupation. The hamster was followed by a white bunny that could climb fences and chew through barriers. When we could take the bunny's antics no more we bundled him into a gym bag and took him to the Benoni bunny park. The drive to the park was long and once we got there we realised that all the rabbits in the park were brown. There were millions of them. As our bunny popped out of the gym bag a drove of brown rabbits descended on him and attacked the innocent white bunny. We made a quick exit - without looking back, and pretended we were not connected to the frightened spot of white.

Through all the bumps and hiccups of illness, infertility, changing jobs, setting up businesses, and climbing the ladder of success, a five-year plan always guided our household. At the end of each year the O'Daly would take out his list and tick off the goals we had met; his ticks delivered almost always a full-house. He was that kind of a man – a visionary with an incredible source of energy. It was as if our lives were contained in the framework of a business plan, with not much room for listening to the heartbeat.

And then on one of our trips to a summer in Ireland we were coerced into meeting two faith healers. We were reluctant, as faith healing was foreign and did not fit into the framework of our life plan; it wasn't our thing. My mother-in-law was persistent and had already made the appointment, so before we knew it, we found ourselves in a small room at St. Patrick's College in Maynooth with Pascal and Mary, two beautiful unassuming folk. They knew so much about us it gave me goose bumps - intimate details that no one else on earth could possibly know. During our visit they said "Ireland is your destiny." And they asked eight year old Ruby, "Do you have a little brother?" When she said "no," they asked again. "Do you have a little sister?"

"No."

Much of what they said resonated with me, but the part about a little brother or sister for Ruby went straight over my head; back in Jo'burg my gynecologist was waiting to perform a hysterectomy on my return. I left Maynooth a little unnerved, but at the same time secure in the folds of a five-year plan.

Two months later I became pregnant. I did not know how to react to the news, and all I could do was flitter around the edges of it being true. It took me nine weeks to gather enough courage to tell the O'Daly. When we broke the news to Ruby she left the dinner table in a rush for a gulp of fresh air. Nine months later when a little boy was handed to me, my whole body was covered in goose bumps. That night the same specialist who treated my cancer dropped in to see me – it was a little odd as the specialists did their rounds in the morning. He came in and stood next to my bed, a perplexed look on his face. And then he told me that he had contacted all his colleagues all over the world, that with my history a pregnancy was completely impossible, and that he could not explain it.

From the beginning the little boy was simply Ed. I could not stop looking at him – it was OK to give in to the moment. Not even the excitement around the Cricket World Cup could stir our bond-making. I finally had my two children, nine years apart.

I desperately wanted to take Ed to the faith healers in County Offaly – after all they *saw* him before he existed. Or was he perhaps already there from the beginning of time? Destiny and master plans began to intrigue me; there was so much I did not know.

We waited for Christmas and took Ed on a trip to Ireland. This trip also gave us an opportunity to baptize Ed. The ceremony was a private affair in the church in Kinnegad with only the Irish family present. In Ireland babies are generally baptized shortly after birth, and I struggled to find a christening robe to fit our chubby eight-month-old son. We ended up squeezing him into a borrowed newborn sized christening gown, unable to close the buttons. Ed nearly walked to the baptismal font, but the local contingent reacted with joy. The presence of a miracle boy meant it was OK to break the rules.

When the faith healers saw him they were not surprised at all. As a matter of fact they recalled the vision they had seen the summer of the year before in great detail: "We saw the hands of God reaching all the way down from heaven and placing a baby boy in your lap." The vision was so clear that they were convinced he already existed. This episode touched me in a profound way. During this visit they re-confirmed that Ireland was our destiny.

We kept in touch with the faith healers, and every year made a point of coming to the house in County Offaly where they based their healing ministry. I didn't realize at the time that in some small way they became my spiritual mentors. Unbeknown to me I had embarked on a spiritual journey.

New horizons

One night an unsuspecting O'Daly was trying to send data over a telephone line when the phone suddenly rang; at the other end of the line was faith healer Pascal with a message he received earlier in the day – a message that nearly knocked him off the pedestrian bridge in Maynooth. He said: "You are on your way, my boy, you will be leaving Africa." The O'Daly was befuddled and I thought, "Yeah, likely. "

Barely three months later, the O'Daly was approached to head a corporation in Athens and we started the process of packing up. It was a very bizarre situation; an offer completely out of the blue and from a totally different industry and unlikely corner.

We left in stages, and one day during the last few weeks I finally acknowledged the stirring within and asked a wonderful Johannesburg pastor to baptize me. He did so on a crisp spring morning, in a freezing swimming pool. I was dressed in a white robe for the occasion – the ritual witnessed by our nanny and little blond one-year-old. As the pastor and I entered the pool, the water somehow heated up and I was dunked. The pastor told me that it often happened when he performed baptisms – the water heats up. The nanny was dressed in her Sunday best and all through the proceedings her face was alight with a big smile. On that day we connected over the wonder of a water ceremony – this was after all a ritual she was accustomed to in her faith. We were two women – mothers to the same two children, nine years apart.

My last six weeks in Johannesburg were long and empty; caught between eager-to-go and sad-to-leave. The little blond boy and I were left to wrap up our house and tend to the last of the roots. As the hourglass was running out, an annoying estate agent raised an issue about our house. She was unsettled by how our walls were painted in shades of Caribbean green, iris and yellow against the terracotta of the floor tiles – such prominent colours interfered with her sales pitch. I finally closed off the colour dilemma by giving in to magnolia. When we left our house, the walls were back to the same neutral colour as when we'd bought it; a blank canvas. It was as if we had never lived there.

We left on a bright blue spring day. On this occasion the Petrea at our front entrance was dressed in a mass of purple flowers. Next to the white wall the row of pink and white Iceberg roses the O'Daly planted were in full bloom. Somewhere on the ocean a 40-foot container was on a Mediterranean cruise. Inside the dark container our possessions and memories of forty summers were on a journey of a lifetime: my favourite old floppy doll, first swimsuit, recipe books with Ouma's chocolate crunchies and Jan Ellis pudding, two Sheffield cutlery sets, pots and pans, a huge Samsung fridge, two wooden giraffes and a tricycle.

We said goodbye to our nanny of 13 years, and when the taxi left for the airport, I did not look back. South Africa - land of colour, rhythm, music and my heart.

PART 2: INTO THE WIND

Then pray that the road is long.
That the summer mornings are many,
that you will enter ports seen for the first time
with such pleasure, with such joy!
Stop at Phoenician markets,
and purchase fine merchandise,
mother-of-pearl and corals, amber and ebony,
and pleasurable perfumes of all kinds,
buy as many pleasurable perfumes as you can;
visit hosts of Egyptian cities,
to learn and learn from those who have knowledge.

K. P. Kavafis (C. P. Cavafy), translation by Rae Dalven

A new clan

Hellas greeted us with a warm, dry autumn kiss, and as I landed in the country of blue and white, no-one even noticed. I fell into chaos – Athens was a world so foreign and topsy-turvy that there was nothing in my frame of reference to compare with. I had to start from zero.

Within the space of one day I lost my career, full-time nanny, network of family and friends, and became a stay-at-home mom with a toddler. I was transported into another reality, and it was as if the universe was saying: "Let's make sure she doesn't work; let's make sure she spends some time getting to know herself." At the time I had no inkling of this plan – I was more inclined to wrestle with my circumstances. To toil was something I took as normal, and in everything I tackled, my default approach was to wrestle with what was in front of me. I thought I was in charge and that by working hard at it, I could change things left, right and centre.

Our first stop was in a rented apartment in the leafy suburb of Kifissia, and soon after I arrived I was greeted with an overflowing laundry basket, school lunch boxes, demanding toddler, and a never-ending trail of clothes. My days revolved around the pick-up and drop-off times of the school bus; and sometimes bearing the brunt of the grumpy bus driver when I waited on the wrong street corner.

Shopping in a foreign alphabet and in denominations of thousands (Drachmas) was a challenge, and a simple trip to the supermarket became a major, intimidating process. Everything was different; and there was no-one to lead this one. I felt as though I had landed in a huge toy box full of Lego pieces – one of those boxes with many sets all mixed up in one.

We moved into a five-story house in Dionysos, a suburb in the mountains of northern Athens, a mere 20 minutes away from the coastal village of Nea Makri and port of Rafina. The house came with an escalator; enough marble to build a small temple; a basement big enough to hold an engine room and park a fleet of cars; a septic tank buried under the front garden; doors with thick steel bolts to (according to the locals) keep the Albanians out; and a collection of balconies. As the saying goes, a Greek house without balconies is like a woman without breasts. The house was a mirror image of the owner's own house next door, built for the oldest daughter for when she got married. True to Greek villa proportions, the house resembled a small apartment block. From the front of the house the view stretched all the way to Marousi in the distance. The streets in Dionysos were lined with pine trees and big villas. Our landlord, his wife and three daughters received us with both a rental agreement and the desire to adopt us as members of the family. The three girls spoke fluent English, the matriarch could manage a couple of words here and there, and the patriarch spoke no English at all. I had to integrate into a neighbourhood without words.

The patriarch hailed from Kalamata. A successful and eccentric property developer, his wife served him from head to toe. Both their house and their summer house each held two blood pressure machines; one for use with a stethoscope and the other with batteries for those times when his wife was not close by to hold the stethoscope. Panos did blood pressure in a big way. He also had a hearing aid, and wherever he went, a crystal-clear, high-pitched whistling sound followed him. His wife called him the bionic man. I was uneasy in his presence – he couldn't hear me. Panos was an intimidating figure and I was unable to decode his body language. His three daughters had him wrapped around their little fingers; for them he was a harmless bear. The patriarch loved to swim in the sea and whenever he went swimming, he left his wife on the shore holding his Siemens hearing aid.

I struggled to have a smooth conversation with the matriarch – these usually took place around her small kitchen table over two cups of Greek coffee. Somehow I always understood her stories; her burdens did not need full sentences to find their way into the space between us. She loved to feed me, as if that was her way of enfolding me with welcome. Without ceremony, she stepped into the role of both mother and sister. From very early on our landlord and his family made it clear that the mere thought of us leaving Greece would devastate them.

When the ship with our possessions finally arrived in Pireaeus, it took a bribe and a push to get our container delivered to our house. The truck came with a team of removal men, chatty public relations lady and a baklava cake; and when the truck nearly blocked our street for a whole day the neighbours arrived like ants from an ant hole to investigate. In between *freddo* coffees, the men carried the furniture and many cardboard boxes into the house. I became the Fat Controller in Thomas the Tank Engine, directing the workmen to the various floors. The boxes were stacked up everywhere – brown cardboard boxes with the contents of my life. Unpacking them was like opening a lucky dip at Christmas. Familiar things looked out-of-place in the new setting, and the new furniture and appliances we purchased before our departure – that went straight from the shop floor to the container – looked like they belonged somewhere else. I spent many days afterwards emptying the boxes and eating sweet baklava cake. In our new house I came to know the new, unfamiliar sounds: the echoes of breath along the marble and wooden floors; the silence of the mountains; and a heating system in the basement that launched itself at regular intervals with a humongous roar.

I started life in my new homeland in the grips of a deadly paralysis, and all I wanted to do was close my eyes in the hope that everything would go away. Overnight I was engulfed by loss, isolation and boredom. I was unable to think about my purpose or vision, or the next day. If that was not enough, I had a busy toddler who climbed onto tables and readjusted the switches of all our machines and appliances.

No-one besides the neighbours knew my name. When there was nowhere else to turn, I surrendered. Unaware that I had a choice, I simply fell into the force of the wind – into that scary place where only the moment exists.

It's all Greek to me

Overnight I became responsible for all the chores and little tasks around the house: keeping the hungry diesel tank full, the sewage tank empty, and the plumbing and electricity working. Dionysos became the set for a play and I became the observer, able to watch from a distance as the characters stepped in and out of the storyline. It never occurred to me that I could step into the role of director.

In a newly built house, as I discovered, there is always a requirement for a plumber or electrician somewhere along the line. The plumber arrived with a buzz of the doorbell and simply introduced himself as "plumber" through the intercom. He arrived with eyelids so heavy they looked like coin slots. I let him in and watched him find his way up and down the stairs with eyes that could barely see – there was no eye contact. He attempted the installation of our washing machine via a mobile phone and translator, and then as suddenly as he appeared he left on a hunt for a supposed pipe for the appliance. The translator informed me that the pipe was a requirement to save us from the "smelly waters" in our new house. Until then I had never considered the notion of "smelly waters." The plumber was never seen again. A week or so later a jovial silver-bearded chap arrived to complete the job. He arrived with both an assistant and a handyman – all three on one motorcycle, with not a single helmet amongst the three of them. When the North-African handyman took over as both installer and translator, Ed thought he was back home in Africa and joined the team. When the job was finally done, I wrote my first cheque in Greek.

My first couple of weeks was without transport, until one day we stuffed a briefcase full of millions of Drachmas and visited a car sales showroom. The local bank manager was indignant when we asked for a cheque book; he said that cheques were available in ones or twos but not in books. And there was no such thing as a hire purchase or lease agreement; car sales happened in cash. In fact, everything happened in cash, and for this reason I used a Spitz shoebox to hold my monthly stash.

We made a couple of visits to complete the car deal: first the small deposit to proceed with the order, followed by a slightly bigger actual deposit, and finally a visit with a hold-all filled with Drachmas to pay for the car. While the car salesman counted the notes we slipped out for espressos and pastries. We couldn't believe how many small bakeries were scattered within easy reach all over the place – this delighted the O'Daly. He was a big pastry man.

Some weeks later a little silver car arrived at our home and Ed responded with "mommy's turtle." I was so happy I felt as though in this little car I could fly to the moon and back. I began to explore the local neighbourhood and beyond; found myself on the wrong side of the road; learnt when to park on which side of the road, depending on whether the month was an odd or even number; and discovered the cobalt blue sea on the other side of Pendeli Mountain.

Few homes in Dionysos had numbers to identify them, and to find a specific house it meant you had to follow your nose. Our house was number nine, and when Ruby painted a big nine on our front gate she caused a holy commotion in the neighbourhood. A crotchety neighbour further down the road consulted his ordinance map and took exception to our number nine, because with our house a nine his could not be number fifteen. I soon realized that there were no rules and that at any stage someone could wake up and decide to change the number of a house, or build a villa the size of a small apartment block, or change the flow of traffic down a road to suit him.

To park anywhere in Greece was an art. There were no parking metres in shopping streets and no law enforcement – the Greeks parked everywhere. Finding a parking space was near impossible and I was grateful for a car the size of a turtle.

We arrived in time for Halloween and at the international school found a feast, bonfire, and Jack O' Lanterns with scary faces. The O'Daly was a master pumpkin carver – he knew how to create the perfect eerie grin. For some reason he found carving Greek pumpkins difficult. This meant Ruby's entry into the pumpkin dungeon ended up with one huge square eye, no eyebrow, a silly smile, and without a prize.

I felt inadequate and out of place in the school community. The families were from all over the world; an ex-pat community, well-heeled and sporting DKNY, Jimmy Choo and with Filipino nannies in tow. Many families moved through the school en route to other destinations, and some eventually returned home. The whole ex-pat thing didn't do it for me – the community felt inauthentic and distant. In this space I wasn't able to find a soft place to land.

We discovered the Greek *taverna*: both meeting place and extension of the home kitchen. We discovered them in the middle of nowhere; next to the water's edge, perched on the side of a hill, or tucked away in a village. Finding the real gems nearly always required local knowledge. These gems would be the busy ones; packed with locals and buzzing with conversation. They spilled out onto pavements, roads or beaches, and they served lamb, lemon chicken, *souvlaki*, grilled fish, *tsatsiki*, *horiatiki* (Greek salad), fresh bread and *fava* (chickpeas). The food was affordable and delicious, and we always left the *taverna* completely stuffed and happy.

We also discovered the Greek cafés: places to hang out, lounge and be seen. Here dessert was served: chocolate brownies, ice cream, frappes, freddos and cappuccinos. The cafés were always full of locals, and I wondered how they managed to fit in work around the time spent drinking coffee. There was never any stress or urgency, no rush or panic; only time, chatter, cigarette smoke, and the repetitive clicking motion of *koboloi* (worry beads).

Our local village, Rodopoli, was at the other end of a narrow road, a stone's throw away from our house: a mishmash of homes, shops, chickens in dusty backyards, big old pine trees, and *tavernas* clustered on street corners. In the summer the pavements filled with wooden tables and chairs where locals sat and connected over bright gold beers. I always longed to join in.

Seeing through eyes for the first time

When we left South Africa we gave our nanny a ticket to Greece as a going-away present – a small thank you for thirteen years of stepping into the role of mother, housekeeper, nanny, au pair and cook. Johanah took care of our two children; always dedicated and meticulous. She witnessed their first steps, first words – never those of her own children. And she consoled and comforted our children – never her own.

Johanah was born in Bochum, a small settlement in the Limpopo Province of South Africa. In Bochum houses were pieced together with bits of scrap material and leftovers collected and gathered from somewhere else. There were no gardens, running water, electricity, pavements, or tarmac roads. And there were no fruit bowls on tables, comfortable beds or swimming pools.

Johanah was born in the late 1950s. While she was growing up she experienced a life filled with disadvantage. Schools for African kids were few and far between, and she had to walk for miles in both winter's cold and summer's heat to get to school – often without shoes or warm clothes. The facilities at her school were completely inadequate and Johanah left school early to find work in Johannesburg, some five hours away. She barely finished primary school and became a mother at a young age. While she earned a wage in the city, her elderly mother took care of her three boys; she would see her sons only three or four times a year.

Johanah had no passport, had never been on an airplane, could barely understand English, and had never seen the sea. Her concerned big sister wanted to be reassured that once she was on the plane, she would know at which stop to get off. Before we left Johannesburg we did a dry-run at the airport, and I explained about security checkpoints, passport control, terminal gates, seat belts, tray tables, toilets, food trolleys and conveyer belts. These were things we took for granted. And I explained that there were no airplane "stops" between Johannesburg and Athens. This was a huge undertaking for Johanah.

There was big excitement when we collected her from the Ellinikon airport close to Glyfada. For a newcomer, driving from Dionysos in the north to the airport in the south took some audacity and nerves of steel. This drive was my first introduction to full-on road chaos. Nothing could have prepared me for this experience. Johanah was the last passenger to appear through the doors – with her bright red jersey, green pleated skirt, head scarf, brown loafers, jester brooch and a huge white smile. She looked a shade paler for her experience and her first words were: "I did it!" When Ed saw his other mother, he did a double take and found himself in little boy heaven.

Johanah could not believe the many white buildings in Athens, as well as all the cars and the foreign alphabet. She was 8000 miles away from home with her two white children. During the five weeks she stayed with us I took her to the sea, and for the first time in her life she could put her feet in the cold November water. We visited the Acropolis, Ancient Corinth, the island of Hydra, a bonfire and Halloween celebration at the international school, and travelled along the coast of Marathon and Schinias.

In a world of extreme xenophobia people stared at her; as if she was not allowed to belong. But then again they also stared at us; reluctant to approve for us to be in their world. Johanah kept her head high – she was the mother of five children and she knew how to be comfortable in her own skin. Every afternoon she waited for the striped school bus – she did not care about the grumpy bus driver.

Too soon the time came for her to return home. We travelled the long drive to the airport with apprehension. In her suitcase she had dried pumpkin seeds, painted pine cones, a bottle of sea water; a collection of round sea pebbles, Greek biscuits and a little heap of Greek soil. When it was time to say goodbye our little blond boy wouldn't let go of her; he tucked his head in her neck and would not move. He was too small to speak, but somehow he already knew the taste of farewell. A crowd gathered around us – people curious to witness goodbye. She left with her suitcase bulging with memories and a few foreign words in her mouth. There was a new horizon in her heart; a place with a sea, strange alphabet and two children. I was touched by this courageous woman.

For months afterwards I couldn't help but wonder if she had planted the pumpkin seeds in Bochum.

Blue

Some years before we left Africa an old work colleague handed me a couple of Greek holiday brochures. We met by chance and somewhere during our catch-up the subject of Greece came up – totally at random. The brochures fell into my hands as if the gods were sending me them with a little wink. Greece had always intrigued me; as a student I dreamt about a Kontiki tour that would include Greece, but never got round to making the dream come true. There was something about the white buildings and the blue sea – I had an urge to respond to the call of blue without limits. When I showed the O'Daly the brochures he instantly dismissed the whole notion of Greece. He had no interest in the place, not even to look at the brochures and dream. And here we were in Greece; in the land of mythology, history, democracy, Greek gods, churches and blue.

My first introduction to a Greek island was Hydra, the beautiful little island in the Saronic Gulf. We arrived at a Piraeus and stocked up on fresh croissants, warm sesame bread sticks and chocolate pastries. There was a nip in the air. Arriving in Hydra was like stepping into a picture book: a quaint harbour with sleepy *tavernas* at the water's edge; yachts and little fishing boats moored in quiet rows, holding within them dreams of a next summer; and a number of donkeys and mules standing like statues while waiting for something to happen. Not even the irritating flies could elicit the smallest reaction from the animals. The air was filled with a vague smell of donkey pooh, freshly baked bread, and an unbelievable silence. Neither vehicles nor bicycles are allowed on the island. In the narrow cobbled streets heavily burdened mule trains followed locals in worn-out shoes. Cats of all sorts and colours roamed the place: they were on top of statues – draped over some admiral's face; asleep on steep white steps; inside pram baskets; and under dinner tables.

After a lazy brunch we took the narrow road to the beach. We simply followed the sign that said "beach, 12 minutes" and hoped for the best. The sea was like a mirror, and in the distance I saw the dark green hills of the Peloponnese disappear into the water. There were countless shades of blue; the sea was a swimming pool without an end.

Summer cottages were placed precariously against the sides of cliffs: cornflower blue trimmings and stone walls mixed with weathered colour washed paints. I did not want to leave – I wanted to remain in this beautiful place.

We left before the sun disappeared on the horizon. The hydrofoil boat was packed with many heads. From the back all I could see were heads bobbing up and down, left and right; blond heads, red heads, bald heads and grey heads.

Anything but humdrum

My first months in Dionysos took me back to my childhood – I had to learn how to walk and talk as if from scratch. However, this time the boundaries of a secure net to hold me and guide me were missing. Some days the challenge was too huge. But there were the little achievements, such as making an appointment, or returning from a successful grocery shop visit, or finding a new route, or reaching out to someone new.

One-by-one I began to put the Lego pieces together and I became co-creator of my new life. One by one I found a hairdresser, pharmacist, general practitioner, paediatrician and gynaecologist. I decided not to travel to South Africa for these (as so many of the ex-pats did) – but instead do as the Romans do when in Rome. I took out my Athens street map and I sniffed out the addresses: I found them in obscure locations, in white coats and with fashionable spectacles.

Getting directions from a Greek was no different than getting directions from a Paddy. Such directions generally do not include the bare basics of pinpointing the point from which to proceed; the direction to take; correct number of crossroads to pass; or the real distance between milestone points. A mile could be anything between one and five kilometres. The directions usually involve a detailed description of the route *not* to take, or may point out some obscure pub or bad bend in the road as landmarks. In Greece I was told: "You go, you see the Weber on the pavement, you look, and you find." When I went searching for the optometrist opposite the Weber barbeque it took me two weeks to find the place. The reason for the difficulty was that by now it was November and the Weber barbeques were packed away for the duration of the winter months.

Shopping for clothes was intimidating – the boutiques in Kifissia were small and trendy and their clothes were geared towards very thin people. There was never enough room to simply blend in to the poky shops for inconspicuous browsing. A sales assistant always followed me up close, and whenever I touched the fabrics or colours, the assistant would respond with disapproval. I soon learnt that the unfolding and draping of items to see/feel how they flowed was not appropriate.

When I could postpone attending to my hair no longer I braved a very hip hair salon in Kifissia for a hair colour; a combination of copper and gold with not too much copper, and certainly not permanent. My head was the biggest in the entire salon and my hair the finest by far. Finding a workable solution took a mobile phone, conference call and lots of gestures. I missed my hairdresser in Johannesburg. Every six weeks for eight years I had visited the house in Norwood with its beautiful pressed ceilings, wooden floors and walls painted in muted colours. Daphne and I spent many hours chatting over cups of tea, Sun glitz hair colours, scissors and hair brushes. She had an extraordinary hairbrush, one with very few bristles left after years and years of blow-drying, and one that understood my fine hair. I always thought the brush needed to be patented as it produced such amazing results. Daphne was able to read me and my hair like a book: she knew when there was a need for a touch of red, or a little more blond, a touch of hazelnut brown, and when short or long. She owned my hair. I always left the house in Norwood with a big hug and a hairdo that moved in the sun.

Festive days

When I was convinced the skies over Attica could only hold blue, soft grey clouds appeared, and smothered the sun and the blue sky until there was no life left in them. Blue disappeared and left Athens with icy cold, grey, wet weather – something I had not associated with Greece. Winter had arrived, and with it came a house filled with red, runny noses and dreadful coughs. Some days Attica was covered by a big, black, ominous sky with roaring thunder and surreal strips of bright lightening. On those days the skies would open up and flood the dry land, leaving the landscape green and wet. Most of the roads became rivers and the potholes flourished in the muddy water.

Our first Christmas arrived accompanied with joy in the air: a Christmas Bazaar at the international school with tombola tables and a menagerie of stalls selling books, candles, jewellery, pashminas, preserves, cookery books and Christmas tree decorations; a Santa Claus in one corner; Boddington beer, *gluwein*, large round waffles and mince pies; and Christmas carols. At night the neighbourhoods of Kifissia, Ekali, Drossia and Rodopoli became alight with fairy lights everywhere – they spiralled up tree trunks, bushes and lamp posts. Nativity scenes decorated many a patio, and the matriarch next door made sure their patio would not disappoint with a plastic Joseph, Mary and baby Jesus. For more than a month Mary and Joseph glowed on two steel garden chairs while baby Jesus rested on a flowerpot. The whole Christmas thing in Athens is very beautiful, but very intense.

In our lounge I decorated the Christmas tree given to us when a friend's marriage broke down – a deluxe tree bought from the Garlicks department store in Johannesburg. Each decoration took me back to a specific time and place. Over the years I collected Christmas tree decorations to mark occasions and places; and now they were on display in a window in Athens.

December is the month of my parents' wedding anniversary. To celebrate their golden anniversary, we travelled south to the salty waves of the Cape coast. This was my first visit back to my heartland; back to family and familiar things; and back to a nation with the colours of a rainbow.

We arrived in the most beautiful Cape with my heart stuck in my throat. This was going to be a beach holiday, and we made sure to cover both the west coast and Hermanus and Gordon's Bay on the south coast. We resembled four white marshmallows on the endless beaches. We travelled up the west coast from Jacobsbaai past Moerie Se Baai to Saldanha Bay; and north to St Helena Bay, Shelley Point and Paternoster, where we watched a dozen whales in the calm sea. In Jacobsbaai we stayed in a stone house at the edge of the blue water – a place lined with special memories. At night we went for long walks under a striking Ramadan sky, surrounded by silence. The only witnesses were a number of small colourful fishing boats in the silver bay. They paused in the safety of the bay – on the other side of the dunes were the vast Atlantic Ocean and the white foam of the waves where they make their living.

My parents retired to Durbanville, a municipality north of Cape Town. This was not a familiar place and I didn't know what to expect during our first visit to their new home. The house was no longer the family home, but the moment I stepped inside I experienced all the joy of being reunited with a trusted old friend. The new home and neighbourhood didn't matter – my parents were the harbour.

A stone's throw from their home we discovered the wine cellars of Nitida, Altydgedacht, Bloemendal and Meerendal. My mother spoilt us with homemade apple crumble, moist chocolate cake, bran muffins, Jan Smutsies, buttermilk pudding and custard. On our last evening in the Cape we dined at a restaurant on top of a hill. The sunset and the view were breath-taking: Table Mountain, Robben Island, the Atlantic Ocean, and the beautiful Boland mountains. I saw my heartland as if for the first time.

Much too soon it was time for the big plane to take us home; and in an instant I could've sworn the beaches, my mother's treats, and the reunion with family never happened. Within the blink of an eye we were back in Athens. The taxi driver was there to meet us with his taxi and a big, white smile. Vangelis and his taxi service came as part of the O'Daly's job and we glided home through the traffic – no need for sighs, or hooting, or sweating, or swearing.

Our home in Dionysos waited for us with a nasty smell in the air; the kind of smell you want to try and ignore and pretend it does not exist. Vangelis kept his cool as he carried our luggage out of the cab and into the pong. I was back in my homeland.

During our absence the lower floor of our house had been invaded by the dreaded smelly waters. The sewage was oozing out of the wall, determined to fill the room. There was a pong on the outside and smelly waters on the inside – the New Year started on a depressing note. After a tense couple of days the septic tank truck arrived and sucked away the smelliness. I learnt the valuable lesson that a septic tank needs to be emptied on a regular basis, and that the contents do not simply flush away.

As if smelly water was not enough to deal with, during a wild stormy night our staircase became flooded and poured water like Niagara Falls from the attic all the way down four floors to the garage in the basement. When I thought my head was finally above water, our heating system collapsed. The heating disappeared on the same day the big freeze arrived in Athens. For a couple of days we had no hot water and no heating. I learnt another lesson, that a diesel tank needed to be filled on a regular basis.

For two whole weeks I left our two green suitcases unopened in the corner. Packed away inside were my holiday memories, and my voice. And I turned forty without the bells of a celebration.

From this point on two countries were going to weave my journey: heartland and homeland. One place has the colours of a rainbow, and the other the colour blue.

Mountains, monasteries and ancient places

Both the O'Daly and I were determined to make the most of our time in Greece – we were eager to explore and from the word go were restless to make new tracks. We had an insatiable thirst to discover. Our exploration began with places within easy driving distance from Dionysos. Our first journey took us to Ancient Corinth in the Achaia province of Greece. Tucked away on the western side of the Isthmus of Corinth, the city was founded in the 10th Century BCE and became both the largest city and richest port in ancient Greece. Rome destroyed the city in 146 BCE and a century or so later Julius Caesar re-founded the place as a Roman colony. Corinth had the reputation of a wild city and it became the base for St Paul's missionary activities in Hellas. Being in the presence of so much history blew my mind.

The drive there took us along the beautiful Saronic Gulf where many ships lined up in the bay, patiently waiting for the green light to enter the port of Piraeus. First we stopped at the Corinth canal, an impressive slit in the rocks of six kilometres long and 24 odd metres wide. From the bridge above, the water was a tempting turquois. I imagined the struggle of ancient people crossing the isthmus by hauling their vessels over the rocky ridge before the canal was made.

On the hillside behind ancient Corinth we discovered the Acrocorinth, an impressive castle built against the steep rock-side of a mountain. During the middle ages the Acrocorinth served as citadel protecting against invasions of the Peloponnese. The view from the entrance to the castle held the blue of the Gulf of Corinth; tidy small patches of agricultural land; autumn coloured vines; restful villas; olive and orange orchards; the dark green mountains of the Peloponnese; and the road leading south. The outlines of the castle on top of the mountain became our anchor point in that part of the world.

Ancient Corinth became one of our favourite places. We returned there again and again; like we did the Acropolis in Athens, Nafplio, and the other treasures on the Peloponnese. The Peloponnese became a staple feature on the itinerary for any of our visitors; and with every visit the imprints of these places became more familiar.

Living in a Mediterranean country meant that we were on the tourist trail, and with our first batch of visitors we ventured further afield and took the road north to Meteora, the land of monasteries. The four-hour drive took us through Lamia, Karditsa, and Trikala to reach Kalambaka, a village nestled against the impressive rock formations of Meteora.

After Lamia the road winds over a mountain onto the Thessalian plain; a fertile plain surrounded by Mounts Pindus, Olympus, Pelion, Othrys, Ossa and Agrapha. Although on the surface the valley looked fertile, the villages along the way were very poor, complete with small squatter settlements and smallholdings with peculiar collections of junk. Passing through these villages transported me into another time and place.

We found Meteora at the cradle of the Pindus mountain range on the western edge of the plain of Thessaly: 24 gigantic, perpendicular rocks in a variety of shapes and shades of grey. Six of the rock pillars each had a monastery positioned on top as if suspended in the air. The buildings melted with the rocks, and crowned them like tables decorated and ready for communion.

The beauty took my breath away. The rocks looked so unreal – they could equally have been part of a Hollywood film set. About 600 years ago Byzantine monks chose these rocks to worship God; and they crowned the summits of the rocks with buildings, complete with wooden galleries and corniced rooftops. The biggest of the gathering of monasteries – Grand Meteoron – was built in 1344 by sixteen mountain-climbing monks. We took the many steps to get to the top of Grand Meteoron – a scary climb with a busy toddler. The steps were carved in 1922, and until then visitors to the monastery arrived by means of extremely long rope ladders. When the ladders were pulled up, the summit became totally inaccessible. For those who were too weak or nervous to climb the rope ladders, free-swinging rope nets were used to hoist them up.

As I stood on the top of Grand Meteoron I felt as though I was in heaven. I could see the snow-capped Pindos Mountains in the distance, and Kalambaka and the vast Thessaly plain below. For the first time in my life I experienced a monastic silence. From this vantage point the peace was palpable and through this high window life looked very different – my vision was transported way into the distance. At the same time this moment of pure bliss could not last as I had to get our busy toddler back down the steps.

We followed the narrow road down past Varlaam, Roussanou, Agia Triada, and Agios Stephanos to our accommodation for the night. Kalambaka village was cold, grey and without its peak season colours. We had decided to do Meteora in a 'monkly' way – we chose basic and budget accommodation, and headed for the *Koka Roka.* Although the name conjured up images of cockroaches we felt adventurous enough to book into the friendly inn. The place was not much pension or boarding house as advertised, but rather like camping under a roof. The walls had gaping holes – inside the temperature was below freezing. After unpacking we settled in front of a warm fire in the little *taverna* downstairs. The place was straight from a movie set with the main actors a Greek mama, her son and another hanger-on. Mama fussed around us in her black dress and filled us with beers, ouzo, homemade wine and whiskey. Supper was cooked almost entirely on a worn out grid over coals in the fireplace: *souvlaki*, lamb and chicken served with chips, Greek salad and bread. We had to share side plates, cutlery and glasses. The hanger-on spent the entire evening on his chair against the wall, watching our group play Balderdash. He never moved.

Breakfast was served in the same *taverna* in front of a big fire. It consisted of bread toasted on the grid in the fireplace, Greek coffee, strawberry jam and Feta cheese. Outside the clouds were low and touching the rooftop of the *Koka Roka*. We took a slow drive up the hill for one last look at the monasteries and to deliver the special Greek bread made by our Dionysos matriarch for the monks. The matriarch took great pride in baking for holy men. Soon enough we were above the low cloud and in the softest snow, and against the snow-white flakes the "rocks of the air" looked stark and mysterious. The veil of snow added an air of calm and beauty. There was no doubt that these places, once home to bold hermits and monks seeking refuge, were significant spiritual homes.

There is something special about visiting a new place for the first time: it widens the frame of reference, and it deepens the spectrum of colour in the heart.

The next stops in our "Travel Greece" guide were Delphi and Arachova. The two hour drive north-west took us through green hilly countryside, past cotton fields and empty cotton picking trailers, and orchards lined with silver olive trees. The mountains were imposing and somewhere along the way we found a lonesome shepherd tending his woolly sheep on the edge of the road – lost in his own world while listening to his Walkman.

Against the steep slopes of Mt Parnassus and perched on an angle of 50 degrees is bustling Arachova. The place has three schools, two churches, two banks and a small post office and its narrow streets are lined with quaint houses, colourful *tavernas* and small hotels. On this winter's day the shop fronts were bursting with animal skins, carpets, preserves, sausages and trendy skiers with sunglasses and warm jackets. Arachova was built by King Philip II of Macedonia in 334 BCE, and according to legend Saint George killed a dragon in order to leave the water running free for the people of Arachova. A little further up the mountain we found the snow slopes of Mount Parnassus. The short drive onto a plateau was both breath-taking and nerve-wracking. The Greeks are not keen on putting up barriers, and they manage to build roads where many others would simply turn away. Here a white world greeted us. Until that moment I had not associated Greece with snow and skiing – the white took me by surprise.

The snow peaks were invisible behind the big grey clouds but the terrain was thick and heavy with snow. Only cars fitted with chains were allowed to continue to the ski centre, and as this was a recce mission, we were without chains. Very little could stop the O'Daly – he had a lot of nerve. Born an eternal optimist, the O'Daly was fazed by little, and driving up a snow-covered mountain without chains would not be a problem. On this day however he had to accept defeat when the police forced him to turn around. Instead we stopped for a roadside picnic with Rooibos tea, *biltong* sticks, samosas all the way from Jo'burg, and Lindt hazelnut chocolate. The green pine trees were covered by a heavy blanket of snow, and around us children were rolling around in it. As I stood in this winter wonderland little snowflakes brushed my cheeks. The mere sight of the ski slopes made us jittery and eager to ski – at that moment I could imagine the speed of the downhill run. I could feel the cold air brush against my face.

New routines

It is said that the smallest fraction of time the human mind can register is the time it takes between the moments when a traffic light turns green, and when the Greek behind you beeps his horn at you. They love their car horns. After four months on the chaotic roads I graduated to the category of "reasonably accomplished Greek driver", and no longer needed a tranquiliser before and after a trip. I had learnt the tricks of the trade, and had a better understanding of the Greeks' interpretation of the Highway Code which includes jumping stop signs, overtaking on double solid lines, parking anywhere and everywhere, driving against one-way traffic, and a million other things. I had joined the horn brigade and became capable of using mine at the slightest provocation.

This told me that I had moved into stage three of getting to terms with culture shock. Stage three is where - if you haven't packed your bags and returned home - you start to embrace some of the local customs, appreciate what is good and come to terms with what is not so good.

Right from the start the expat thing bothered me. The habit of reminiscing in my mother tongue (Afrikaans) about things back home did not appeal to me. I didn't want to fall into the trap of "when we…" Instead I had a strong desire to integrate into my new world; almost as if there was no past. Soon enough someone dragged me along to a Newcomers wine, olive and Feta tasting event; and into a large group of English-speaking women in our area. Although I didn't want to admit it, I found comfort in their midst – we were all faced with the same challenges. I wasn't sure why I was resisting the easier way to integration, or why I was so bent on tackling my Greek journey without the support of sisters in arms.

The O'Daly had a fair commute to get to his workplace. He had to drive over Pendeli Mountain on a dangerous, winding road where shrines were dotted along the roadside like punctuation marks in an essay – marking the places where lives were lost. Sometimes the mountain was covered by a thick coat of fog and mist, and then the O'Daly had to crawl his way over the mountain, inch by inch. The fact that he could be driving home only to discover that a crucial piece of road was suddenly missing intrigued him. As if someone had rolled up the road and removed it from the scene. Or that a detour could lead him on a wild goose chase around the outskirts of a suburb, or that a road could simply end in an olive grove. For the O'Daly it was incomprehensible that a road could end without notice.

As if the usual chaos on the roads was not enough, extensive road works to prepare for the 2004 Olympics appeared all over Attica. When the Germans built the new airport Eleftherios Venizelos in Spata, the Greeks forgot to build a road to connect the airport with the city of Athens. The new airport elicited a lot of debate and controversy – the Greeks made it sound as though the new airport was in a different country; somewhere they had no clue where to find it.

Twice a week I went to a class in Kiffisia to learn Greek. Alongside women from all over the world I struggled with the new alphabet, gender, which parts of the word to accentuate, and how to unscramble the words in my mouth. We took our notes in English, Afrikaans, German and Arabic. Of course every classroom has its studious pupil, and our teacher's pet was from Australia. She was a teacher of classical English, an Olympic gymnastics coach, and she carried nuts and dried fruits in her lunchbox. Whenever I asked the teacher a question, Tammy would answer me.

Our house became busy with all things Greek; Ruby joined a Greek dancing class, our toddler acquired a new vocabulary, and the O'Daly talked about his wish to learn Zorba's dance. The Greeks love dancing – their dance is one that touches, and its rhythm one that stirs. According to Nikos Kazantzakis' *Zorba the Greek,* a devil inside him tells him to dance every time his heart is at the point of bursting. As he dances, his anguish disappears. This was my first introduction to dance that stirred.

I came to know the Greek temperament – one that could flare up anytime and at any place. I found the Greeks expressive in their joy, and with little moderation in their disapproval. Their conversations were loud, and both significant and insignificant things could elicit a rant and rave. I began to see another way of expression, and at times the different way of communicating nearly drove me mad.

As we settled into our Greek life we became familiar with the various intricacies, customs, and festivals. February is carnival month, and this meant that the numerous Christmas decoration shops were now packed with the colours and charm of everything carnival. Bright decorations, puppets and vibrant masks were on display everywhere; even the blossoms arrived as if on cue in time for the celebrations.

Life in Greece with two children nine years apart brought interesting challenges. At one end the British Embassy School's Personal and Social Health Education programme informed the children about body parts and puberty and Ruby came home with questions about ovaries and "tentacles". At the other end I started Ed's potty training course and for the first few days he carried the lime green potty around with him everywhere he went. At night the potty went to bed with him, which meant the O'Daly had to remove the potty from Ed's face before he too could retire to his bed.

Green

They say there are forty two shades of green in Ireland. My first introduction to the little green island happened during a solo trip before we were married. I arrived at Dublin airport with big permed hair, a yellow jumper, loafers, suitcase and a fuzzy photograph of the O'Daly clan. Beforehand the O'Daly took me through the long line-up of siblings, and for each of the faces he gave me a name and a story. Travelling to Ireland to meet the in-laws was a big step for an Afrikaans *meisie* (girl); especially when an outdated photograph was the only companion to guide the introduction. The few days on the farm involved heaps of food, lots of "I beg-your-pardons?", and a constant stream of locals coming to inspect the white African that landed in their midst. I felt like an alien and I struggled to understand the Irish accent. On Sunday I joined as many as could fit into the car for Sunday mass; the priest mumbled from beginning to end – his words like a flock of frightened sheep scrambling around a pen with no way to get out. During the mass the only thing I could say was "and also with you."

With our move to Athens Ruby missed her first communion and during the mid-term break we travelled to Ireland to attend to this unfinished business. At the same time we had to attend to the O'Daly's father, who was extremely ill. On a number of previous occasions Boss Daly tried to check-out from this world. He gave the O'Daly instructions regarding his funeral; he did not want any flowers, wanted to be dressed in a habit and not a suit, and he wanted to be laid to rest in the graveyard facing west. For 40 years the man known as "Boss" tried to die, and when this did not happen he was convinced there was a conspiracy to keep him alive. He was obsessed with crossing the Jordan.

Each day we made the hour-long journey to Navan to visit the Boss. Nothing could have prepared us for the shock of seeing such a frail old man in a grey county hospital. A bleak reception area pointed to the various sections: male surgery, female surgery and mortuary. The bare steps lead us to a general ward where grey men in striped gowns were staring at the door. Here we found the Boss. He looked tired of holding on – he was ready to move on.

As if the sky knew about the depressing hospital room it responded with a generous supply of snowflakes big as goose feathers. As the white flakes were about to touch the ground the wind would scoop and toss them against the bleak landscape. The days were unbelievably cold; in the fields a sprinkling of new lambs were snuggling up close to their mothers.

Ruby's first Communion was held in the privacy of the chapel at St Catherine's in Maynooth. When she had to repeat "I will give you everything I have and all I am" she responded with the promise "I will give you everything I have and everything I have not."

While in Ireland we dropped in to see the faith healers in County Offaly. At this meeting they asked Ruby "You have not finished unpacking yet?" to which she replied "Yes, we still have a few boxes to unpack." They responded: "That is not what we mean, there is no need to complete the unpacking; you will be moving again." We had barely arrived in Greece and I thought, "yeah, likely!" Was there a plan unfolding at some other level? What was this thing called destiny, after all?

Living far from family meant that there was always the possibility of receiving the dreaded phone call with news of illness or death. The call came and early one morning the O'Daly left for a cold grey Ireland to attend his first ever wake – the wake of his father. Boss Daly was a great storyteller. During our visits he always settled in next to the warmth of the Aga, and from this vantage point he would launch into storytelling. Here he became narrator and creator, and he was able to weave suspense, fantasy, history and devilment into the words with such ease. The Boss was a humble man, hard worker and faithful provider for his family. Towards the end he indicated that he would be happy if three people turned up to attend his wake. This was not to be; when he finally crossed the Jordan the funeral turned into a distinguished affair with a large crowd of people and two cabinet ministers. The demise of the Boss marked the end of an era.

When it came time to say goodbye in Ireland, spring arrived in Hellas and the landscape exploded with stretches of white daisies, red poppies, and purple, pink and yellow flowers. The bright colours looked delicate in the dust and rubble of winter's aftermath. There were blooms in the trees and shrubs, and in gardens the roses were waiting with baited breath for their turn to appear in April. The air was filled with a new energy.

Spring also brought a thick coating of pale yellow pine tree dust, and it covered every balcony, car, bicycle seat, and surface. The dust slipped into every fold and nook and cranny, and became impossible to contain. I was never keen on dust but in Athens I had no choice but to go with the flow of dust - dust in a variety of colours. The playgrounds were particular traps for the dust, and at the feet of Pendeli Mountain the marble dust turned everything white. During the "big dust cloud" Ed got covered in white and left the playground with a "goodbye swing, goodbye slide, goodbye graffiti and goodbye saw-see."

The O'Daly brought Hob-nobs, Kimberley biscuits, Coconut creams and Mikados from Ireland. He called the Jacobs Coconut creams "*spring-sprongs*", and he rationed us to one "*spring sprong*" a day. Whereas he was able to hang onto a packet of sweets or biscuits for days on end, I was unable to resist the urge to finish them in one go. Not even resorting to the threat of a best before date could ever help my cause – for the O'Daly a ration was a ration.

Mapping through a maze

In our new homeland bureaucracy was an art form, and life in Greece would not be the same without an introduction to the social insurance institute IKA. With our new Sri Lankan housekeeper came the need for a monthly visit to the local IKA offices – a process designed to rob anyone of his or her self-esteem and make them feel like nobody. Every time the long queue led me to the same faceless person who would draw a pink file from a steel filing cabinet, and record my payment manually. There was always someone in the queue ranting and raving at a bland IKA official. The officials were skilled at barricading themselves behind the counter; they knew how to be dictatorial, and they knew how to torture. There was no roadmap of how to navigate through this foreign maze – I had no choice but to step way out of my comfort zone to make things happen.

Three workmen took more than a week to install our elevator. They arrived at the crack of dawn when our house was still dealing with bed heads, dirty nappies and milk moustaches. With a fair amount of drilling, banging and smoking they completed the installation and put an end to the dangerous lift shaft we had contended with.

Independence Day arrived with blue-and-white flags, costumes, themes and parades. It marked the Greek War of Independence from the Ottoman Empire in 1821. Ruby joined her Greek dance class in a local parade – an African Irish posing as a native from the island of Naxos. The music was soulful and the show of patriotism heart-warming. I wondered what it must feel like to be part of such unity – of sharing one thing, that of being Greek. Witnessing such patriotism made me question where I belonged. I did not see myself as an Afrikaner; South African yes, but that meant being part of a rainbow and not part of one clear unity. To add to this, I had become a traveller: I was neither here nor there. I wondered what it must feel like to live in the security of belonging to a tribe. Being surrounded by this show of patriotism stirred a longing deep within my heart.

With the arrival of spring we began to explore the beaches at Nea Makri and Skinias. Nea Makri is at the bottom of Penteli Mountain, where the winding road meets the coast, and Skinias is a little further away on the other side of Marathonas, the birthplace of the marathon. In 490 BCE the Athenians defeated the Persians at the bloody battle of Marathon. After their victory the messenger Pheidippides ran the 42 km from Marathonas to Athens to announce the victory. Then he collapsed and died from exhaustion.

During the summer months Skinias changed into a beach resort with loungers, music, *frappes* and beautiful brown bodies. This part of the coast became our local hangout; close enough to load up the children after school and pack in a couple of hours of beach time.

The moment I thought I had escaped my first European winter unscathed, dense grey clouds brushed past our windows and balconies and left the mountain tops white with snow. When March brought record temperatures and the newspapers reported that Greece was heading for a Saharan drought, we had packed away our winter gear and swapped our coats for bathing suits. Now out came our thick sweaters and warm duvets, and we fired up the beast in the belly of the house to, once again, dip deep into the diesel tank. This was my first experience of fresh snow softening the edges at home. The snow continued all night long, and the next day my car was like a little cotton wool ball in a carpet of white. I was excited to experience snow as part of a normal day.

A bold blue sky appeared and as suddenly as the snow had appeared, it vanished. With our wanderlust never too far away we returned to the Peloponnese, and the little gem of Nafplio in the Argolid province. When the town was built in the 15th Century it consisted entirely of two impressive hilltop fortresses. In 1821 Nafplio served as the headquarters for the Greek revolutionary government and later became the first capital of Greece. We explored the old town with its Venetian architecture, *plateias*, hillside stairways, pebble beaches and the most beautiful sea. In one of the narrow streets lined with *tavernas* our car brushed the red and white tablecloths, and we held our breath as the O'Daly dodged the tables so as to avoid knocking over the little vases with fresh flowers. The O'Daly's nerve was able to take him down the narrowest of lanes; even if it meant knocking over a table display or two. Little did we know at the time that Nafplio would become like a second home to us.

Pascha (Greek Easter)

Greece is an orange paradise. We bought a juicer and throughout winter the most delicious oranges formed part of our daily diet. They were sweet, juicy and plentiful. By the end of the season I had to dig deep into the orange heap at the supermarket to find the ones that were still alive with colour. The arrival of Easter meant that the colour orange was fast running out.

In Greece Easter is bigger than Christmas: the festival starts with Clean Monday, the first day of the seven-week period of fasting before *Pascha*, the Greek Orthodox Easter. Clean Monday is a national holiday and traditionally a day reserved for picnics and kite flying. On this day men become boys and relive their kite-flying youth. They compare knots and string and plots to enhance the tail of the kite in order to get the highest, smoothest flight of all. We spent the day with friends at their villa in the foothills of Mount Parnitha. On clean Monday no meat is consumed, and the main meal that day consisted of all things fishy and cheesy, special flat bread, lots of Ouzo with ice and water, and halva for dessert. The special flat bread is made on this day alone and we waited in a long queue for ours.

We spent most of the day flying our kites; and we struggled to hold on to the strings with painful hands turned red with cold while attending to annoying runny noses. Not even my ski-jacket could keep out the cold and my hands and nose were frostbitten. At some point our kite decided to fly away, on to the port of Pireaus. I tried to follow its path, but all I could see was a sea of other kites, each one a tiny little sperm swimming against the gloomy grey sky.

During Holy Week fasting becomes an obsession, there is a mad scramble to get to church for the special Masses, and the tone becomes solemn. Radio stations play serious music, television channels show religious films, and the demeanour of the locals becomes subdued.

On Great Friday we celebrated our own Pascha with a barbeque, many gin and tonics, *Pascha* bread, red hard-boiled eggs, and a fully matured L'Omarins red wine. Elsewhere flags were at half-mast and funeral services were held for the crucified Christ. We could not let out our plans of an early Easter celebration – such deviation would have caused a complete commotion. And we spent many hours on a mellow walk down a musical memory lane: Four Jacks and a Jill, Joe Dolan, The Tremeloes, Queen and so many others. Outside the house the dark green pine trees stood in silence in the soft drizzle.

On this day I became aware of an intense pain in my left leg; something I could not explain, but thought would settle down and disappear. On Easter Saturday we took our kids, overnight bags and my painful leg to Ellinohori, a small village high up against the hills with a full view of the Gulf of Corinth. In this place time ticks away slowly and the people are hearty and laid-back. We followed the narrow winding road past a patchwork of olive groves and vineyards. A kaleidoscope of colours were etched against the dark grey sky: the brown of the fertile soil, silver green of the olive trees, purple of flowers, bright green of new vine leaves, and the scarlet of the many poppies.

Our hosts could not speak any English, so we smiled and ate a lot during the lunch. We stuffed ourselves with home-grown olives, roast peppers, feta cheese, fresh bread, olive-oil and "*krasie aspro*" (white wine). When we could eat no more we went for a walk up the hillside to ease our full bellies and get to the view from the top. I never got to see the view from the top, but instead was forced to wait on the side of the foot path when the throbbing pain in my leg became unbearable.

On Saturday evening of *Pascha* everyone goes to church: a minute or so before midnight the lights are dimmed, and the candle light from the altar is passed from white candle to white candle symbolising the passing on of the light from person to person. The priest proclaims "*Christos Anestei*" ("Christ is Risen") followed by the ringing of bells, hand-shakes and greetings, firecrackers, and general pandemonium. Outside colourful flags decorated the church and in case we did not notice the happy Easter, the arches of fairy lights displayed "Kalo Pascha" in giant letters.

We tried to guard the light of our collection of candles so they would stay warm. Ed was fascinated by the wooden carved Pinnochio attached to the side of his candle. We were supposed to carry our candles home, make the sign of the cross with the candle on the door lintel, and carry the new light into each of the rooms. As we were in Ellininohori, far from home, our candles were not able to carry the light into our home spaces and instead went quiet.

After the church service we sat down to entrails soup. This was time to crack the shells of our red-dyed hard-boiled eggs with the next person, knowing that whoever's egg cracked last would receive good fortune in the coming year. None of our eggs cracked last. This was our first Easter without chocolate eggs.

On Easter Sunday we didn't join in the festivities but instead took a sedated drive back to Athens. We were spared peeling and slicing all the cracked eggs for an egg salad at lunchtime. In every second backyard there was a lamb on a spit; and in a circle around each lamb a small group of people who took turns to turn the lamb and guard the fire. The aroma of roast lamb followed us all the way home. We were on our way to the Eleftheros Venezelos Airport to meet my parents, and start our vacation with a trip to Paros. Or so we thought.

The north wind interfered with our ferry plans and because the pain in my leg persisted, the O'Daly checked me in at the Iatriko Kentro – a private medical centre not too far from home. An ultrasound confirmed the diagnosis of a deep vein thrombosis in my leg, and with my English magazines, overnight bag, and Lufthansa Velcro slippers I took occupation of a room on the ninth floor. The room overlooked the bland rooftop of an unsightly old building – complete with washing line full of flapping clothes, a couple of satellite dishes and the neck of a big yellow crane. During the first two days I shared the room with a portly Greek lady with a big, bright yellow IV drip, and humungous snores. True to the Greek tradition her visitors stayed all day, and our room was filled with a constant noise.

When a very famous old Greek singer vacated his room to the full view of TV crews, I moved into his room. Peace at last – but very alone. I was not allowed to leave my bed and quickly learnt the crucial word *papia* – the Greek word for "duck", because in hospital lingua the bedpan resembles a duck. Three times a day my leg was wrapped in aluminium soaked bandages, and there were the many tablets, injections and blood samples. Twice a day my two physicians visited me; they resembled Walter Matthau and Jack Lemmon, or Oscar and Felix. They were always together as they moved around the hospital corridors, as if they were attached at the seams of their white coats.

Oscar and Felix never discussed anything whatsoever in front of me. They asked one or two superficial questions and gave one or two superficial answers, and if the O'Daly was in the room, they lured him outside for a private discussion. In their world I did not exist. On my first night in prison I was whisked off to the cold basement of the building for an invasive CT scan. Between the four radiologists no-one could explain what was about to happen, or why. The room was freezing cold and I felt overwhelmed by fear and isolation. I was unable to communicate with anyone – I was in a medical horror movie and for a moment I imagined I was about to disappear into a black hole, never to return.

Television was my main source of entertainment and I passed the time by staring at women's club volleyball and "Who Wants to be a Millionaire" in Greek. My days revolved around the rhythm of the food trolley – I was in solitary confinement, and my parents were on holiday at our home in Dionysos. While I was in hospital the brown African rain arrived in Athens. This annual phenomenon happens when dust storms over the Sahara turn liquid and find its way to Athens. Watching the world outside my hospital window getting covered in brown mud did nothing for my mood.

I desperately wanted to go home but Oscar and Felix ducked and dived around departure dates. They kept on changing the goalposts, as if they were fundraising for the hospital. There was no room for negotiation. Leaving became an obsession – my parents were visiting and the measured time with them was slowly ticking away. When I was finally discharged, we went from the hospital straight to the ferry port for our ferry to Paros; and we never told Oscar and Felix.

We arrived in the peaceful, out of season port of Paroikia, where many houses were still awaiting the return of the holiday season. A short drive further is Naoussa, with its houses even whiter than white amidst the surrounding blue – an irresistible union of two colours. During our stay on the island Naoussa was our home. Two beautiful days gave us access to the turquoise water of Kolymbithres beach. There were quite a few nude bathers and I had to keep Ed at bay when he wanted a closer inspection of one man in particular who was stretched out with a fine display of what looked like two rather large aubergines.

To drive around the island takes an hour. Spring was in the air and the meadows were full of red poppies and yellow daisies. Golden fields of barley stretched all the way to the edge of the blue sea and the landscape was dotted with many little white and blue churches. The Greeks are generous with their churches - one was even perched on top of a large rock in the bay. In the port at Naoussa colourful boats were daydreaming of waves and sea-foam. We dined at *taverna* tables at the edge of the water while the rest of the world felt a lifetime away. In the narrow alleyways in Paroikia, weather-beaten locals on donkeys moved past the colours of bougainvillaea, geraniums and roses as if they didn't exist.

I could see why visitors to Paros often decided to settle on the island and not return home. For us it was different, we had no choice but to return to blood tests and the O'Daly's business meetings which were lined up like markers on the mainland. It became as difficult to leave Paros as it was to get to Paros; for three days strong winds meant no ferries could leave the island. In Athens Oscar and Felix were unaware that I was not recuperating at home and they were anxiously waiting for the results of my blood test. When we finally left Paros on a huge, jam-packed high speed Catamaran for Piraeus, we were completely worn out from all the waiting around.

Back in Athens the last week-and-a-half with my parents passed in a blur. We visited Nafplio and Ancient Corinth, and much too soon my parents were gone. For a couple of days afterwards the taste of goodbye filled my mouth and I felt completely numb. When the first day of May arrived I had no inkling of joining the other families as they gathered flowers in the countryside to make wreaths for their front doors. In sympathy with the empty spare room our front door remained wreathless. All around us the many roses all burst into colour: it was May - the flower month in Greece.

The patriarch invited us to their summer house in Kiato, on the edge of the Gulf of Corinth. Getting an invitation from the patriarch was considered an honour. This was our first introduction to this particular coastal spot and one that would become a regular one. Kiato was not the place for tourists, but rather somewhere Athenians flocked in summer. The sea was like a lake – the water clear and salty. The high salt content of the water made it easy to float on the water for hours. On the pebble beach there were lots of pebbles in all shapes and sizes; they mesmerised me. Ed and I spent hours hunting the beach for pebbles to create as many themes possible according to colour, shape, or how they felt in the hand. Whenever we found one with a white marble ring somewhere all around its shape – as if someone painted the line with precision - we were delighted. We loved the simplicity of the place, and we loved being at the edge of the sea.

Back in Dionysos, on one particularly hot night I struggled to sleep and retreated to the spare room where I wrapped myself in a fitted sheet to escape the mosquito onslaught. We were out of mosquito pads and the little devils were driving me crazy. I wasn't long gone when tremors woke me from my sleep. Suddenly the bed moved, picture frames rattled and the walls vibrated. I sprinted down the passage to find the O'Daly completely incoherent; he mumbled something about a truck passing by our house and turned over to continue his sleep. Back in the spare room I waited for the aftershock, and sure enough, it came. Around me the quake played out as if in slow motion – every second felt like a couple of minutes. Houses in Athens are built to withstand earthquakes, and yet when the tremors happened I felt frightened and helpless. We learnt the next morning the quake registered a modest 5.7 on the Richter scale, with its epicentre somewhere over Skyros. At the time of the quake I never thought of joining the locals on the pavement, where they gathered to share the trembles and the fear. The matriarch was eager to talk about the "quick earth" in Dionysos – for her living under the shadow of earthquakes was one of those things.

Being in Athens meant we had access to some unusual cultural experiences. There is something out-of-this-world about witnessing a ballet performance in the shadows of the Acropolis. On a hot summer evening we squeezed into the Odean of Herodes Atticus theatre for a Kurov Ballet Company's performance of *Swan Lake*. The theatre dates back to the Roman Period 160 AD. During the first half of the performance a broken moon watched from the sky above. The stage setting was perfect: immaculate dance against the backdrop of ancient arches. When applause filled the night and the prima ballerina took her bow, I felt I was dreaming. My eyes were focussed on the bunch of long-stemmed red roses in her hands; the red petals sharply contrasted against her snow-white tutu.

Solitude

On a quiet blue weekend we headed to the Monasteries of Meteora for the second time. The last time we were there was in the white magic of winter and we wanted to see the majestic "rocks of the air" dressed in their summer cloaks. So we pottered along the road north and whenever the road came within spitting distance of the sea I battled to resist the call of the blue water. Once over the mountains at Lamia the vastness of the Thessaly planes greeted us – a patchwork land in shades of green, brown and yellow stretching all the way to the horizon; the road a straight black line as far as the eye can see. Under the ruthless sun each little patch was a hive of activity: migrant workers with leather skins and rugged faces hoeing in between neat green rows in the dark soil, or bailing hay in yellow fields. In some of the fields water sprinklers were spraying small rainbows in their mist. And on the narrow road worn-out tractors crawled along at a snail's pace. On the Thessaly plain we were a lifetime away from the blue coast where people were browning themselves in the sun for pleasure, and where a generous sprinkling of rather large bodies were parading about squeezed into tiny bikinis.

In the summer sun the huge rocks at Kalambaka looked even more surreal – the monasteries mysterious and solemn on top of their world. Late Saturday afternoon we followed the road alongside the Notia Pindos mountain range to little forgotten places such as Kastania, Orthovouni and Trygona; a world far removed from e-mail, text, Google and Athens. But the storks knew how to find the location – they built a huge nest on the top of a village church tower, and they settled in for the night with their heads etched against the evening sky. Back in Kalambaka a man was walking his cow on a leash.

On our previous visit Kalambaka was nothing more than a sleepy hollow, but in the heat we found the evening air filled with expectation. At night the main road became a pedestrian road and chairs appeared on the pavements in front of the tiny *tavernas* and bars on both sides of the road. The road was transformed into a theatre with chairs two deep, one behind the other: blue chairs, yellow chairs, director's chairs, cane chairs and any other possible chair you can think of. At about nine the people crawled out of their homes and holes, dressed to the hilt, and walked up and down the street in what is referred to as the "bridal parade". There were lads dressed in black with gel in their hair; old ladies in their Sunday-best dresses; families with boisterous children; and young girls in tight, skimpy outfits. Within the wink of an eye all the chairs were filled by onlookers; mostly men – two deep. This was the highlight of the week – an event anticipated all week long. We joined the parade, and walked the 200 metres up and down the main street.

We left this fascinating place at the crack-of dawn: in the fields a mom-and-pop act were picking melons and watermelons; at the local *kafeneio* in small villages men sat waiting with their elbows on tables and chins resting in rough hands; and in a backyard a cow was drinking her own milk from a white bucket.

During the unique summer show of Meteora we received news that the sale of our home in Johannesburg was completed. Without fanfare or final goodbye our lovely home left us – we now had one homeland only.

Blue summer

The summer heat in Athens was unbearable – most days reached Kalahari Desert summer temperatures. There was no need to check the weather forecast as every day was red-hot with blue skies. There were no Highveld thunderstorms to bring relief, clear the air and cool down the earth. An endless heat surrounded me all day. At night it filled my nose, covered my pillow, brushed my legs, and lined the bed sheets. The heat waited for me in the morning when I left the house and filled my day – wrapped tight around my body. We went through litres and litres of water every day. The sun beetle chorus switched on around eight in the morning and carried on well into the evening; until the last one finally ran out of steam. All day long the words of their chorus would echo in my ears.

We headed back to the beautiful Peloponnese; followed the route through Corinth, Argolida and Arcadia regions to Laconia. There was always the anticipation of getting through the mountainous terrain and tunnel into Arcadia, over the flower-filled fields around Tripoli, and down a steep mountain pass until Mount Taygetus becomes visible for the first time. Homer dubbed Tayetetus "Perimiketon" or "the long one". Nestled against her base is Sparta, the capital of Laconia and pit-stop on our route.

In ancient times Sparta dominated the Peloponnese with its legendary disciplined and invincible armies. The Spartans produced almost no memorable literature, art, or architecture, but are remembered almost exclusively for their martial skill. Ending with the capture of Athens in 404 BC, the 28-year Peloponnesian War was Sparta's greatest victory. Although this domination of Athens was brief, it was testimony to Sparta's unparalleled military skill. In the end, rocked by earthquakes, the empire was unable to sustain itself and facing revolting slaves and a depleted male population, Sparta finally collapsed.

The training for a life of war began early – even before conception. The legendary law giver of Sparta – Lycurgus – believed two fit parents produced stronger offspring, so he ordered all Spartan women to undergo the same rigorous training as the men. Newlyweds were only permitted the occasional get-together with the hope that the heightened desire of the parents would produce more robust children. Strong and healthy boys followed a severe regimen of training under an adult Spartan. They were forced to walk barefoot to toughen their feet and wore a simple piece of clothing in both summer and winter to expose them to drastic weather changes. Food was basic and no temptation of any kind was allowed. They had no fear of death.

Our home for five days was Cavo Grosso in Mavrouvouni, a stone's throw away from Gythio. Here little rustic "shaki"-coloured cottages exist in a garden with pink bougainvillea, bright hibiscus, yellow lemon trees, roses, the sweet smell of jasmine, and big fat palms. Mavrouvouni is situated at the edge of a lush green valley – a peculiar little village with a collection of ancient stone buildings and other houses all placed higgledy-piggledy on either side of the narrow little roads.

The nights were balmy and beautiful. In the evening the mountains on the Mani peninsula became layers of pinks, blues and purples against the setting sun – a symphony of pastels on the horizon. There were little or no tourists and a small number of Greek holiday-makers. This was a slice of paradise. We spent our evenings with a picnic basket on the beach, or at a *taverna* at the water's edge in Gythio. At the bottom of the clear water there was a small collection of cutlery, dropped there by accident. In the dark night the cry of a single bird was like an exclamation mark in the air.

During one of our days in Laconia we took a drive to the province of Mani: through a fertile valley that looked like a bouclé weave of dark green (orange trees) and silver (olive trees); past many ruined castle towers on hilltops; quaint villages tucked against the mountainside; rows of beehives; and through the harsh and remote landscape of Areopolis to the caves at Pirgos Dirou. With its subterranean river, the Glyfada Cave is one of Greece's most magnificent natural attractions. The caves were discovered at the end of the 19th Century and opened to the public in the early seventies. We were all bundled into a small blue flat-cut punt for the 30 minute boat ride into a colourful, magical underground world. The caves were dark and eerie; we were surrounded by stalagmites and stalactites in all the colours of the rainbow. Inside the echo of dripping water stirred the silence. As we ventured further into the enclosed space, the water felt deep and the passageways endless. I imagined the passages reaching all the way to Sparta and on to the centre of the earth.

On our last day in Laconia we decided to investigate the islet of Elafonisos, situated at the bottom end of the eastern most finger of the Peloponnese. With the winding roads, regular stops due to car sickness, and drooping spirits, we worked hard to get there. As we crossed over the last mountain pass we spotted Elafonisos: a small brown mound surrounded by gorgeous turquoise water. A five minute ferry ride took us across the water and onto the island. In contrast with the coolness of the caves this little brown landscape was barren and hot. We headed for Simos, nothing more than a *taverna* in the final throes of completion, two toilets and some shaded parking places. We parked our cars and took our bones, drooping spirits, umbrellas and beach bags in search of the beach. As we passed through the scorching red sand dunes we spotted the water – an oasis in the barrenness. The beautiful beach and water in several shades of turquoise stunned me. There were two beaches on either side of a tiny peninsula at Simos, back-to-back – both picture-perfect. At this moment I was bowled over by sheer beauty. The locals made us promise not to tell anyone about Elafonisos, so that the island could remain a little gem. After a wonderful meal at a *taverna* in the harbour we took the road home to Mavrouvouni.

We returned to Athens with a gem in our hearts and a seal on our lips. The Peloponnese became our extended home – by now we were beginning to feel at ease in our homeland. We were mobile, the summer exciting and the newness of the place no longer intimidating. In the shops the mountains of red and black cherries made way for mountains of peaches, nectarines, apricots, melons and watermelons. There was always a feast of fruit.

Rainbow heartland

August was the perfect month to leave Greece. For the whole month everything comes to a standstill; the heat becomes unbearable and Athens empties out as everyone scatters to their summer houses. It was a good time to re-connect with my heartland.

The southern hemisphere was under a winter blanket and the obvious thing was to head for the Northern Cape and a spectacle I had not seen before. August is the time of year when Namaqualand, the Bokkeveld and West Coast respond to the first rains with a colourful display of wild flowers. We travelled from Malmesbury past the Koue Bokkeveld Mountains (which is directly translated as "Cold Buck Shrubland") to Citrusdal, were we stopped for Milo and dried pears. All along the road the many orchards were showing off the last of their winter oranges. From Citrusdal we followed the spine of the Cederberg Mountain to Clanwilliam and over the steep Vanrhynspass onto the Bokkeveld Plateau on the edge of the Knersvlakte. The landscape was wide and open, with rugged mountains and hills dotted as far as the eye can see. There is no pollution in this weathered land.

Our base was a bed-and-breakfast in sleepy Nieuwoudtville. The town is lined with historical sandstone buildings and is rumoured to be the bulb capital of the world. In spring, depending on rainfall, geophytes (plants with underground organs) of every description bloom in the area. Here we found space, silence and stars.

This world was so far removed from the chaos and raw beauty of Greece, and the many shades of green in Ireland. In the Northern Cape I was nothing more than a mere speck in the vast landscape. I was an anchor point for three different storylines; three places that share the same sky, and whose diverse threads connected in the chambers of my heart.

Around Vanrhynsdorp and the Knersvlakte people make their living from sheep, wheat and rooibos tea farming. We came across green wheat fields and as far as they eye could see luscious green shrubs formed a velvet blanket over the countryside. Every here and there a hillock made a small bulge under the green blanket.

The days were wet and cold and as a result the blooms were shy. During the first two days we could only see a hint of the various shades of pastel through the closed eyelids of the flowers. Under the endless grey skies the Knersvlakte looked particularly desolate.

On our last day Niewoudtville delivered a spectacular display of Namakwa daisies in orange, yellow and white. We were saved by one patch of sunlight – the bright colours took my breath away. A short distance from Nieuwoudtville, on the road to Loeriesfontein, we discovered a forest of quiver trees. The branches reflected the sun in striking gold. The name "quiver tree" comes from the custom of the San people to use the branches of this tree to make quivers or arrow cases to hold their poison arrows. The quiver trees stood like a troop of brave soldiers in this barren world.

Much too soon it was time to return to our home in Greece. While in my heartland I delighted in my favourite things: visiting Woolworths, the Marks and Spencer of South Africa that demanded a cult following; Mugg and Bean muffins; Steers take-away *slap chips*; *biltong*; speckled eggs; Liquorice All Sorts, De Wetshof Bataleur wine, and my mom's treats. For three whole weeks I felt the mother country's heart beat in my chest and its breath in my lungs. Whenever it was time to say goodbye, sadness gathered like a thick curtain behind my eyes.

As we flew over Greece on our way home I saw how the rainless summer had taken its toll on the land. But the brown land had waited for me, and Athens greeted me with a warm autumn kiss on the cheek. All I wanted to do was rest my weary head on her brown chest for a little while.

The to-ing and fro-ing between places was exhausting; there was this endless cycle of rainbow, green and blue. My life consisted of a sequence of here, there and everywhere. Each time I returned to Hellas I experienced a period of numbness. I reacted by retreating into my own world – sealed inside a Croxley Cambridge envelope without an address or a stamp. In this place of limbo I struggled to breathe – all I could manage was very small movements. In this quiet place I swallowed the many emotions of life in a foreign world.

I arrived back in Dionysos ahead of the next batch of visitors and found myself with a mop, Hoover vacuum, and iron in one hand and "Let's Go Greece" in the other. To make matters worse three Greeks arrived one morning out of the blue to install a new kitchen in our family room. They came with their toolboxes and not a single word of English between them; and for a whole day transformed our basement into a noisy, dusty workshop. At the end of the day they left more grime and dust than we had before the big clean-up after the brown rain. They carefully rolled up the cable and pipes of our Speedqueen washing machine and placed the appliance in a corner, as if it was a piece of surplus furniture. When we asked the patriarch about the surprise kitchen he explained that a villa needs two kitchens, one for the family and one for entertaining.

To mark my homecoming the municipality of Rodopoli decided to add two waterless days into an already chaotic situation. Like the glitterati we bathed in mineral water, washed our hair in mineral water, and flushed our toilets with mineral water. I was so fed up I came close to leaving Dionysos with my tail between my legs.

Blue autumn

Our first anniversary in Greece came and went without fanfare. Even in a foreign existence, life had a way of rolling on: one day into another, season into season, and one year into the next. I enrolled Ed at the local Greek nursery school and on his first day he rushed down the steps to meet his yellow school bus – his old soul tucked in safely under his bright baseball cap. He always left with his Thomas the Tank Engine school bag, lunchbox, change of clothes, big smile, and favourite Lufthansa aeroplane playing cards clutched close to his heart. He was two years old. When the yellow bus dropped him home later in the afternoon he simply announced: "Good day, Momp."

The Hellas autumn days were beautiful: warm during the day, with some days even as high as 31 degrees in the late afternoon, and cooler at night which made going to sleep a lot easier. Some of the roses came back to life with spots of brilliant colours, and the vegetable stores were filled with all sorts of grapes, peaches, plums and heaps of red apples. At night Pendeli Mountian would watch over Dionysos – its outline in the shape of a quiet giant stretched out on the hillside. When the moon was full every curve of his body was etched in detail against the sky.

I was privileged to be in such a beautiful place. On one of our journeys home from the Peloponnese, as we were making our way across the Argolid peninsula towards the coastline of the Saronic Gulf, we discovered Ancient Epidavros and its nearby Sanctuary of Asklepios. Greece is like that – wherever you go, you literally trip over ancient sites.

Epidavros is a small, tranquil village on a thin strip of earth between the sea and the pine covered mountain slopes. Large numbers of brilliant green orange trees are squeezed into small orchards on this ribbon of earth. The nearby Sanctuary of Asklepios is situated in a sheltered, fertile setting. In the centre of the enclosure we found the temple dedicated to the healer god Asklepios. Surrounding the temple were places of worship and colonnades where the sick could rest and receive their cures. Outside the enclosure were the dwellings of the priests, doctors, a gymnasium and some baths. The sanctuary also housed a stadium in which athletic and musical contests were held every four years. In its heyday it must have been a magical place to visit for healing – the energy was palpable.

Under the patronage of Asklepios – known by his followers as "Deliverer" – Epidavros became famous across the ancient world as healing centre. The centre reached its greatest fame in the early 4th Century BC, when the sick would travel miles for both medical and mystical cures. At the sanctuary diagnoses were made during dream visitations; here surgeries and direct godly intervention took place side-by-side. This resonated with me – after all, we had first-hand experience of the mystical alongside the medical.

Over the centuries, the complex became increasingly grand with the donations of former patients, growing to include temples to Themis, Aphrodite and Artemis. In 426 AD Byzantine emperor Theodos closed all pagan sanctuaries, and the healing centre at Epidavros became silent. I wondered about the politics at play for such a decision to have been made; and I felt shame at the loss of such a valuable tradition at the hand of presumption.

As I stood in the open-air theatre with the 55 tiers in front of me, I wondered whether the beautiful surroundings ever distracted the audience from the acting that was happening on the stage. We dropped a coin on the centre stage, and the sound reached every corner of the theatre; from anywhere in the theatre it was possible to hear the penny drop. The theatre was initially constructed to accommodate 6,000 people, but later expanded to house 14,000. Miraculously the theatre survived a number of severe earthquakes reasonably intact. This corner of the world is covered by grace.

Back in Dionysos I was reluctant to pack away the last of the summer spirits – it was a happy time. Slowly life returned to normal and we settled into a gentle and familiar routine. The slurry truck driver became a member of our payroll, and every so often his truck could be heard chugging away in the background. And we were in the middle of the preparations for the 2004 Olympics; there was a large amount of hullabaloo in the press and the construction took over every conversation. The time leading up to the Olympics was an exciting time to be in Greece.

After three successful visits to a local hairdresser named Vasilis, I felt ready to raise the subject of colour once again. I had given up on words such as "copper" and "gold" and instead decided to have an open mind. Vasilis took me to a huge colour chart and introduced me to "closed" and "opening" colours; he tried to convince me that an "opening" colour (blonde) would be much better than a "closed" colour (red). We debated the issue and I decided to leave the issue of colour for another time.

On the way to our local village, Rodopoli, I was often stopped by someone or something in the road. I became used to finding the frail old shepherd in the middle of the road herding his brown goats; his toothless smile bouncing off his translucent skin. Or the old man who shuffled with a walking stick – his bottom lip protruding from a gummy mouth, as if his lip was trying to touch the tip of his big nose. In this neighbourhood anything was possible.

Tower houses

During a mid-term break we returned to the Peloponnese and the magnificent land of Laconia. Our first stop was Mavrouvouni, on the coastline of the Laconian Gulf. The owner adopted us on a previous visit and promoted us from the "customer" category to the "family" category. With this promotion came an open invitation to arrive at any time, even during the winter months when the place was closed, and a bungalow would be unlocked especially for us.

We ventured further on up the Peloponnese to Areapoli and then headed south down the Mani Peninsula towards the tip of Cape Tenaro. Mani, the middle peninsula of the Peloponnese is divided into three areas: Out or "Exo" Mani, Deep or "Mesa" Mani and Lower or "Kato" Mani. Our focus for the afternoon was the middle section, Mesa Mani.

Exo Mani stretches from Kalamata to Platsa – a landscape covered with gentle fields, olive groves, beehives and goats for Africa. When we reached Mesa Mani we were struck by the barren, unforgiving countryside; the place was as bare as the moon. In fact the landscape was so desolate that only rocks and the odd prickly pear and twisted olive tree were brave enough to grow there.

Little rain falls in Mani and over many, many years the salt winds that swept from the Mediterranean across the peninsula had eroded the topsoil and twisted the trees into huddled shapes. I imagined living in such a naked world; a world without shelter. Mesa Mani was also known as "The Land of Evil Counsel" – which referred to its inhabitants, notorious for their dangerous and war-like nature. The Maniotes used small metal pots for boiling water (*kakavia*) as makeshift helmets during attacks and feuds.

All along the road south were stone Tower Houses clustered together in ranks in small forgotten villages. Some of the villages hung on to cliff tops for dear life – as if they could slip off and disappear into the sea at a moment's notice. Others were safely tucked into the folds of the Sangias Mountains – an extension of Mount Taygetus. Many of the stone towers and houses were in a state of collapse and this made the place appear even more eerie.

During the Ottoman Empire and after the fall of Mystras in 1460 many refugees fled to the Mani. The peninsula became crowded and the naked land was unable to support the many new inhabitants. Man responded with bloody feuds for control of the inadequate resources, and the ferocity of these feuds resulted in dwellings becoming fortified in the form of tower houses. Neighbours blew up neighbours, and the Maniotes thought absolutely nothing about stealing from one another.

We cruised along the Mani peninsula in glorious sunshine. At the little village of Alika we took the left fork in the road, and travelled up a steep, scary mountain pass. Here, we were greeted by a mountainside covered from top to bottom by row upon row of stone terraces. In my head I could hear the Pilgrim's chorus from *Tannhauser*; I closed my eyes and imagined the music washing over the stones and bringing them alive with colour and people. The place needed music.

For the entire journey we never saw another vehicle. Nothing moved. We stopped for cookies and cream ice cream in the charming *plateia* of Lagia - real people in a world of stone. To the one side of the *plateia* stood the façade of an ancient building, with a forgotten blue door. In this world of stone the colour palette consisted of the yellow light bulbs decorating the *taverna* roofs, a terracotta church dome, the cobalt sea, and a small white marble cross against the blue sky. A bus arrived, dropped off and picked up no-one, made an awkward three-point turn, and left. At a small table two other travellers had *frappes* and their maps to keep them company.

With a big jar of local *meli* (honey) in our car we proceeded on the narrow cliff-side road all along the coastline. Around every outlet another tower house village appeared nestled within the mountainside. Here bougainvillea, terracotta tiles and blue and turquoise window shutters coloured the landscape.

The Maniotes acquired a reputation for ferocity and courage that was second to none and every man was always armed with as many weapons as he could manage. They were referred to as mountain dwellers so laden with weapons they looked like hedgehogs. As if a huge sword was not enough the Maniote would also carry a gun on the shoulder, an axe, club and short spear in the hands, and sometimes even keep two or three primed pistols in a waist sash. In the Manie an eerie silence followed the last family feud.

A rock

We left the middle finger of the Peloponnese for the Cape Malea peninsula. The road from Githio to Monemvasia coiled through a landscape laden with olive and orange groves; one or two small non-descript villages; and a full view of two of the three bottom fingers of the Peloponnese as they marked a border in the Mediterranean; their mountains like vertebrae on a spine. Once over the mountain ridge, the Mirtoan Sea reached wide into the distance. The full stretch of the peninsula all the way down to its southern-most tip was visible – framed by the winding line where land meets water. Around one last bend the Greeks' own rock of Gibraltar waited for us – like a capsized ship in the water.

From the coastal town of Gefyra The Rock looked completely uninhabited – there was no clues as to what was at the other side of the narrow causeway; not even the slightest hint of the Byzantine city hidden behind a high buttressed wall. We parked our car on the side of the narrow road and realised access into the ancient city is by foot through a single entrance in the western wall. Entering by foot meant that we had to re-pack our sprawling belongings into fewer, more manageable suitcases. Not even bicycles are allowed inside the walls of Monemvasia. We entered the city coughing, and carrying our bags like we were packhorses.

On the other side of the wall an amazing world awaited: narrow alleyways with higgledy-piggledy paving stones, many arches, oleander blooms in pink and white in odd corners, geraniums potted in big olive oil tins, unusual stairwells and steps, miniature courtyards, child-sized doorways, and buildings crammed together in a cheek-by-jowl way. Outside a tiny shop an old lady sat on a chair crocheting with frail fingers – the cotton thread white against her black dress. Her wrinkles were translucent; they covered a lifetime.

Monemvasia was first established in the spring of 583, and in the next century-and-a-half became the most important city on the east coast of the Peloponnese. The city's geographic location was advantageous in two ways: its proximity to the unassailable cliffs afforded its inhabitants ready protection, while the two wide bays provided a harbour for numerous ships, and led to the rapid growth of a maritime population.

Within a few years the city flourished and became one of the main intermediate stations and reshipment centres on the busy trade route between the western Mediterranean and the Levant. Monemvasia's people were able to notice every ship that sailed from Asia Minor on its way around the Peloponnese. The settlement of Monemvassia began on the tableland above the rocky cliffs, and continued with the construction of houses at the base of the cliffs, in front of the ascent to the plateau. In this manner an upper town and a lower town came into being.

Our little two-storey cottage – one alley back from the main pathway and with a stamp sized patio on the roof – looked out over the square and its 13th Century church. From the small windows I could see the pastel rooftops of the lower town and the endless sea. Most of the houses towards the western side of the town are owned and carefully restored by Athenians. The process of restoration on a rock fascinated me: all building material had to be carted in by wheelbarrow, and all rubble removed by wheelbarrow. Behind the carefully supported façades of the original houses the builders created the new homes in limited space. The detail of the houses all jam-packed into the lower city was magnificent.

Our house contained a hodgepodge of cutlery, crockery, glasses, pots, pans, old refrigerator and a hot plate. There were no microwaves, TV sets or radios. The doorframes were low and the bathroom so compact the visitor could sit on the loo and have a shower at the same time, if that was what was required. The medieval city held the bare necessities; as if the walls were enough to hold the space.

Within the city walls there was no noise – complete silence. The locals spoke with lowered tones and the only sounds of life could be heard in the main pathway around the small souvenir shops and restaurants.

The O'Daly took the kids up the zigzag pathway to the top of the rock and one of the most beautiful worship spots in Greece – the 12th Century Church of Aghia Sophia. I sat on our postage size patio in the glorious sun and followed their three hats exploring the place where once an upper class used to live. I closed my eyes and imagined a bustling city from many years before.

At night the village became magical; the impressive rock on the one side and a sleepy sea on the other. As the sun said goodbye, the white feathery clouds in the sky turned pink. I looked at the rooftops in all the different shades of pastel; each one was a beautiful work of art. And we were in this painting – four tiny brushstrokes against the backdrop of a rock.

When it was time to cart our belongings back down the main pathway to the entrance in the western wall, I was sad to leave. On the way we had to dodge a number of workmen carting heaps of rubble in wheelbarrows in the blistering sun - their torsos wet with perspiration. As we left the remoteness of Mesa Mani and the womb of Monemvassia, I felt privileged with the experience of such beauty.

An imperfect world

One Tuesday, as we were lounging in the basement, news broke of the 9/11 terrorist attacks in New York. We sat in disbelief as the disaster unfolded. The attack scared me – not the kind of news I wanted to receive in a place where my roots were still very tentative.

September was meant to be the start of a new school year, and here in a single day the world had changed irrevocably. The O'Daly was deeply bothered by the events in America – he was sure that another event of calamitous proportions was about to happen. This strong sense of foreboding unsettled me. At the time I was in the final stages of becoming an impresario for one night by hosting a performance of an Afrikaans singer in Athens. So strong was his sense of foreboding that the O'Daly urged me to call off the event.

The O'Daly had a very strong sixth sense. While still in the business of insurance he had a vivid dream of a tsunami one night. He woke up the next day and bought a whole bundle of reinsurance. The brokers at Lloyds of London laughed, thought the man had finally lost it, until a week or so later the South African east coast was hit by a major storm which left a trail of devastation and the other insurance companies licking their wounds. I always took note of the O'Daly's notions. However, this time I thought, the flight tickets were bought and invitations sent out – let the show go on.

From this day on the sense of calamity stayed just under the surface. Around us the seams of our world began to look a little more fragile than before. The O'Daly remained adamant that something catastrophic was to happen in our lifetime.

When our second winter arrived, we knew to brace ourselves for the accompanying rain. Roofs started leaking, potholes got bigger, and many roads got smaller as parts of the tarmac were washed away by the rivers of brown water. The thirsty land responded with patches of bright green everywhere, and on the outskirts of Dionysos, the vineyards at Stammata and Drossia took on the depth of autumn colours.

By now my meet-up sessions with the matriarch next door became all the more personal as she shared some of the things in her life the patriarch and their three daughters could not be bothered with. When she tried to talk to them her words simply bounced off the marble surfaces and scattered on the floor like pins. She would move between matters of the heart to other things with such ease, and the conversations always ended up with diets, "ball cheese" and the "downstairs." I struggled to understand her: "ball cheese" referred to cottage cheese - not ricotta or mozzarella, and "downstairs" could mean anything from the bottom half of a set of clothing, the bottom of a page, overleaf of a page, a building storey or two down, or any other thing remotely related to "bottom." Amidst her welcome I always struggled to find the right "bottom."

With both children at school and the housekeeper in most mornings, I joined an ex-pat Bible Study group and came to know Saint Paul. I loved following in his footsteps while in the folds of the country with the blue and white flag. At the time Paul visited Athens, the city was full of philosophers and freethinkers. The Athenians didn't lift a hand to persecute him as their motto was one of "if it works for you, go for it!" After all, Athens was the birthplace of democracy. Every new idea gave the Athenians the chance to have a good, healthy debate. I too discovered the Greek's thirst for challenge that comes with debate. The Athenians left Paul traumatized; many times they left me traumatized as well. I discovered Athenians are seldom – if ever – wrong.

After years of challenges my gynaecological problems were beginning to catch up with me and I needed a little operation. I booked into a private Greek women's hospital where they deal with everything from hearts to babies to bunions. I disregarded the option of travelling to South Africa and the known, and instead opted for an operation in Athens. Once again I became voiceless as the enthusiastic cleaners, nursing staff, secretaries and food ladies tried to make conversation with me in a foreign language.

On the morning of surgery a cold trolley took me down to the operating theatre – my legs dressed in white stockings, blue paper slippers on my feet, and a blue hat on my head. The German lady gynaecologist met me in the theatre; her Greek gynaecologist husband was there as well. The trolley driver delivered me onto a very short bed – I had never been on one of those during a waking moment. My two white legs were attached to the stirrups which left my posterior to the full view of the bright eyes of the operating lights. This was an operating theatre, but all around me people were milling around. There was banging and clanging; people talking in loud tones; mobile phones ringing; and passers by shouting remarks through the open door. There was an endless shuffling and fidgeting around me – I was sure I had landed at a bazaar. The German doctor shook her head and said she could not get used to the chaos.

Out of the blue, and without an introduction, an olive-skinned man with small beady eyes in green theatre gear appeared at my side. There was no space on the half bed for my arms and when he tried to insert the needle, my arm kept flopping off the small bed. They said not to worry about the flopping arm, that they would sort out the arm in due course. Around me in the theatre the noise was gaining momentum, as if building up to a crescendo. At one point the olive-skinned chap broke into song; the German doctor looked at me and all she could manage was a chuckle. In this theatre there was no Schubert playing; no silence; no dignity; no counting to ten until gone; and no gentle departure into no-man's land. All I could do was look at the chaos through heavy eyelids that would not close.

During the operation I became conscious and felt the most excruciating pain I have ever felt in my life. There was a significant amount of pulling and tugging. I tried to lift one of my hands, to move an eyelid, my mouth, anything to get someone's attention, but every part of my body was weighted down. I was trapped inside. This episode frightened the bejeebers out of me, and I wondered if this was what no man's land was like – that moment immediately before you cross the Jordan?

Back in my room a camera was monitoring my every move – there was no room for a quick dash. The cries of new born babies surrounded my room, and sounded like the Dionysos cats at night-time. I loved the fact that I could turn over and block out those sounds; they belonged somewhere else.

Back at home a pensive snowman was waiting on the lawn; he had two black beady eyes and sticks for arms. I could not help but think, was he perhaps thinking of Africa?

Christmas adventures

Before our second Christmas could settle into Dionysos we left for Cape Town on the back of ferocious Siberian winds. We left behind a frozen world and spent ten precious days in the Western Cape. Another Christmas with parents; reunions with friends; visits to Jakkalsfontein on the west coast and Gordon's Bay on the Rooi Els road; an English breakfast cooked on a Weber; wine tasting at cellars in and around Durbanville, close to Hermanus, Franschoek and in Stellenbosch; South African Rand shopping-till-we-dropped; and New Year in the folds of family. Being back in my heartland with time to stock up on sights, smells, tastes and sounds was a big treat. The vineyards at Durbanville were neat and green, the days soft and comfortable like a pair of worn-in Caterpillar boots.

The time to leave came with the inevitable pain of goodbyes – saying farewell never became any easier. Our pilot took us on a final circle over Table Mountain, Hout Bay, Leeukop, Robben Island and the magnificent long white beach at Jakkalsfontein in the distance. We left Cape Town on the 3rd of January with a few items of light clothing to keep us warm on the drive home from Athens Airport to Dionysos. Unbeknown to us, that same night the skies opened up over Greece and dumped the biggest mountain of snow in more than a decade. The snow even covered central Athens, the Acropolis and the beach at Voula. Airports were closed and at our stop-over we had to brave the sub-zero streets of Frankfurt in skimpy summer clothes. When we finally arrived in Athens, the landscape was unrecognizable and snow-white. The familiar olive tree groves were barely visible under the blanket of snow. We arrived minutes before they closed the airport again.

At the airport we were met by a complete melt-down: crowds milling around huge stacks of bags and suitcases. We soon found out that our luggage was missing in action. Inch by inch, amid a blizzard we struggled our way to our car in the deserted car park. We were met by arctic Athens. At the airport both the escalator and lift leading to the car park had long stopped working – the lift door was wide open and the inside filled with snow. We were near frozen by the time we reached our car.

It took a gruelling four hour drive to get home. At one point we got stuck in a heap of snow and as a line of cars built up behind us, a mysterious shepherd appeared from nowhere: a huge bulk of a man with a long black bushy beard, dressed in a black cloak, with a walking stick in his hand. He looked like he had descended straight from the mountains, and with two rough, stained hands he helped us with the big dig. And when the job of freeing our car was done he disappeared into the white afternoon as mysteriously as he had arrived.

The northern suburbs of Athens looked like quaint Alpine ski villages, and the main south-north road - Kifissia Avenue - became a narrow snow track. I could not recognise any of the usual landmarks; all along the road cars were left on either side of the road – abandoned and completely buried under the snow like white marshmallow bumps. None of the roads leading off Kifissias Avenue existed anymore, but instead had become beautiful pristine ski slopes. The place was dead quiet – as if not a single soul had ever moved or lived in these streets.

By the time we had run out of both road and grip, our car came to a dead halt in Rodopoli – a little village two-and-a-half kilometres from our home in Dionysos. Suddenly there was a commotion in sleepy Rodopoli with our car blocking the narrow road. Two local lads looked at us in our light gear, looked up at the sky, looked at the car without snow chains, sniggered, and then helped to move the car somewhat out of the way. From our final landing point the O'Daly and Ruby walked home to collect warm clothing while Ed and I waited in the car. As the darkness came the snow started again – I had no idea what would happen next. The O'Daly always had a plan and on the way to our house he hijacked a sleigh from a stunned Dutchman who was out playing in the snow with his children. Not only did the O'Daly get the sleigh to help with the recovery process, he got the Dutchman thrown into the deal as well. Two hours later they returned to collect me and Ed, and as much of our hand luggage as possible, for the final leg of our long journey home.

Getting to our house was uphill all the way. We struggled through knee-deep snow in the dark like an Afghan refugee family trekking over a mountain. Every so often Ed would fall off the sleigh and disappear into the snow. We would dig him out from under the snow, dust him off, put him back on the sleigh and press on: a little gingerbread man with arms straight-out in his yellow ski jacket about three sizes too big. He had no idea what was going on.

To get into our home we had to wade through a ton of snow – shoulder high. Our house was like a fridge. The matriarch arrived from next door with a cooked meal and the warm food saved our lives; little did we know that it would be our last warm meal for a while. Nothing was moving and it became clear that nothing was going to move for some time.

We commenced a week of solitary confinement. In order to manage our expectations the O'Daly stacked all our supplies on the kitchen counter: a tin of Heinz baked beans, tin of artichoke hearts, some six boxes of cheese fondue mix (donated by friends who had left Greece for good), and a few other bits and pieces. Early Sunday morning the O'Daly and Ruby – dressed in full ski attire – walked for three hours to get more supplies in Drossia. By the time they returned with bread, milk, carrot yogurt and a slab of chocolate, they were covered by snow from top to bottom. On their way home they could have sold the bread for the price of gold. For the most part of a week the snow never stopped.

When the time came for the bold and the brave to start moving, a security company collected the O'Daly in a 4x4 vehicle and took him to work. They spent hours travelling to and from the office. Throughout our imprisonment we also experienced several electricity and water cuts. Our home became like a house on "Big Brother" and we were trapped in an unfriendly, cold home – not even able to manipulate our way to get voted out.

The first sign of life in our street came on Tuesday when Panos – his face unshaven and wearing a tracksuit, dressing gown, Russian hat, and two plastic shopping bags peering out of his shoes to protect his feet from the snow – started shovelling. However, it took two more days, a small excavator and four Albanians to make some sense of our section of street and the entrance to our houses. Our suitcases arrived three days later; the Woolworths dried peaches and nectarines were like manna from heaven.

We arrived back in Greece with a new currency. Our wallets, purses and shoe boxes filled with brand new crisp notes and shiny coins. For a whole week I was unable to spend my Euros.

The snow left Athens ugly and messy. It looked as though a tornado had moved through our homeland – unsightly heaps of brown snow and broken trees were everywhere. The Greeks became very animated; they moaned and groaned and blamed the government for the snow chaos.

Somewhere between the old year and the new one we lost a week in a mountain of snow. We were hardly out from under our snow blanket when I received a complementary facial from a local Beauty & Diet company. The timing was perfect: I could do with a treat. So I did the traffic thing and the parking thing and the brave thing of entering the world of perfect people. Upon my arrival at the swanky premises I was moved into a tiny office the size of a cupboard, with no ventilation. In this confined space a too-perfect Greek chap with gelled hair and wearing a biscuit coloured suit introduced his company. A fake smile never left his face and he couldn't care less where I came from, or where I was going to after our meeting.

The next moment the Aesthetics Manager arrived to take over from the biscuit suit man. She was perfect too, skinny and gorgeous, and without any notice she dropped deep into my physical history through her small fashionable rectangular spectacles. When she asked me to take off my clothes for closer scrutiny, I realised there was something wrong with this picture – we were now into areas very far removed from my face.

She inspected my body through her specs from a distance of 10 centimetres and announced that the real problem was the "belly", and that my stomach needed some serious attention. According to her my posterior and legs were fine – but the belly, this was the culprit. Before I could open my mouth she picked up the telephone and rambled to someone in Greek, and seconds later a doctor arrived. Now it was his turn to dig and delve into my medical history. I had to repeat every detail twice, and after every answer he would bring his head real close to mine, eyes screwed up, and ask "Whaaat?"

The two slapped a contract in front of me; from their demeanour it was clear they meant business. Everything about them signalled "sign now or die in this room". The Greek content of the contract gave me my escape from the torture room, and I took my belly home. I never had the facial after all, but the episode was a wake-up call: I realised how out of shape I had become, and that it was time to re-connect with my body.

View from the top

Kaimaktsalan (aka Voras) is a mountain range in the prefecture of Pella, in the heart of Greek Macedonia. Voras forms the border between Greece and the Former Yugoslav Republic of Macedonia (aka FYROM). I very soon discovered never-ever to refer to 'Skopje' as in 'the Republic of Macedonia' as that annoys the Greeks to no end. The Greeks have claimed the name 'Macedonia' as theirs and theirs alone, and according to them there will only always be a FYROM and no Republic of Macedonia.

In Turkish, Kaimaktsalan means the "view from the top." And we discovered the most magnificent world on top of Mount Voras – a place where the winter colours are blue and white.

I never thought of Greece as a ski-destination, but we heard about a few resorts and left for a mini ski-break on top of Mount Voras. We had little knowledge of our destination and it took us nine hours of hard work to reach our spot on top of the world. For most of our journey we travelled either in the dark or below a dense blanket of smog that covered most of the road north. We even bypassed Mount Olympus without noticing it. Every now and then an impressive snow covered mountain peak would appear through the smog and delight us.

Our expedition coincided with a major threat by thousands of farmers to protest against slashed subsidies. At the entrance and/or exit to every town on the national road a fleet of tractors were waiting to form a roadblock at a moment's notice. Hundreds, if not thousands, of all species of tractors were lined up, leaving the smallest of gaps for vehicles to pass through. On the roadside the farmers waited, some guarding *souvlaki* on small fires. We were lucky to escape a total blockage on our way to Voras.

A short distance before Salonica (Thessaloniki) we turned westwards and headed for Edessa. The town is perched on top of a steep hillside and is known for its waterfalls, many little streams and bridges, cherries, and soft velvety blankets. The agriculture in the region is intensive with acres and acres of beautiful cherry, peach and apple tree orchards. Once through Edessa we saw very little evidence of snow on the South face of the barren mountain range ahead of us. In the snow-less landscape, I was beginning to think our ski-dream was not going to be. The fact that our expedition fell right in the middle of the Halcyon days did not help our cause for snow - these are two weeks in the middle of winter when Greece experiences summer.

Unlike the ski resorts we have been to where you hang out at the bottom of the mountain, take a gondola or ski lift to go up the mountain, and then ski down the mountain, the Voras resort is on top of the mountain. To get to our final destination we had to make our way up a steep narrow winding road (with no barriers) and hairpin turns too numerous to count. During the last 25 kilometres we must have climbed a nail-biting 1,5km in altitude. And then we went around one last steep bend and were almost on top of the mountain when we got our first glimpse of the snow.

The resort consisted of a stone building with restaurant and cafe bars, a ski equipment shop, doctor's rooms, small tuck shop, and about nine *domatia* (rooms) on the second floor. There are two further mountain huts in the ski area for "refuelling" purposes. Our room for the two nights was a boarding school dormitory crammed full with bunk beds. We all filed into the awkward space and with the night came a struggle with my duvet; a battle to keep the inside from jumping out and coiling itself around my body.

Given that we arrived late on a normal school day, the resort was empty; we were alone on the mountain. Early Saturday morning the Thessalonians descended upon the place – car and busloads full of people, and the resort became a hive of activity and music. At about five in the afternoon the droves took their leave and the mountain became ours. Lunch was hearty and unpretentious, and tended to end two hours later with a glass of *Tsipouro* (ouzo). A great solitude covered the mountain early in the morning and late in the afternoon; for as far as my eyes could see the other highest peaks stood like white islands in the sea.

Sometime during our first lunch both the waiter and bar-lady disappeared, and left the entire dining facility open to us. I had never experienced not paying for a meal at a restaurant – the next day when we enquired about the bill the waiter responded in Greek, "Relax, what is the rush?" At nightfall a huge chill crept up the mountain and left our evenings bleak and cold. The half-a-dozen of us, including the chef and his helper, stayed snug in the warmth of the stone building while a lonesome Husky guarded the door. Outside the droning of a single snow machine groomed the slopes for the next day – the only sound in the endless night.

All the ski runs were around the main Voras peak. There were no trees or mountain paths – the terrain consisted of wide, white slopes. The snow was good, but we tried not to make comparisons with the snow powder in the Rockies. At night Ed refused to part with his ski boots.

We spent our last night in Macedonia in the traditional mountain village, Agios Athanasios, some 30 minutes down the mountain road. The village is built entirely out of stone and wood. Small, narrow cobble roads; charming stone buildings, carefully restored; a lonely horse tied to a front door; and in one corner a miniscule wooden stall that sold preserves. I wanted to know more about the place, but there were no postcards, and no knowledge other than the "village was abandoned at some stage for a bit."

However, the locals knew about this magical village and that is all that mattered. It was the perfect venue for après-ski. There were no shops in Agios Athanasios except for one ski shop. The narrow street was lined with *tavernas*; we picked the one with pomegranates placed around the stone fireplace for good luck; white embroidered cotton curtains in the windows; Greek music; wholesome people; and the most delicious food.

On our way home to Dionysos we were treated with the beautiful Thermaic Gulf on the one side, and on the other side majestic Mount Olympus – uncovered and proud. Until this point our view of Mt Olympus was from our Voras vantage point, and suddenly here she was right in front of us. The drive home felt endless. Somewhere towards the end of our journey the tractors finally caught up with us; they blocked the national highway and sent us inching our way through a busy little town, resulting in monstrous traffic jams.

Kaimaktsalan was a wonderful treasure that waited to be discovered well off the beaten track.

An Easter marker

One peaceful Sunday the Matriarch called me to collect a special gift. The gift came all the way from a monastery close to Kiato and turned out to be the neck of a freshly slaughtered goat. While she handed me the heavy supermarket bag she mumbled something about a lamb, chickens, and the vegetarian monks at a monastery a kilometre or so above the town of Kiato. Halfway through the conversation I realised she was not handing me an Easter lamb, but rather the neck of a goat – a final bleat still locked in its red throat. She took the gruesome contents, removed a couple of stray long black goat's hairs from the flesh, and launched into a discussion about goat's neck recipes with such passion it was as if she was talking about a new Jamie Oliver dish. The goat's head took me straight back to the farm in Haenertsburg, the freshly slaughtered sheep, and the feeling of horror in the pit of my stomach.

The parcel found its way into our fridge – a less than appropriate gift for an almost entirely vegetarian household. I was unable to open the parcel and separate the neck from the matriarch's plate, and it became my challenge to dispose of the offensive parcel – plate and all. I had visions of the entire stray cat and dog population of Dionysos storming our dustbin – the one we shared with our neighbours – in search of the goat. I visualised a dog running through the neighbourhood with a goat's neck in his mouth. In the end the goat left with our cleaning lady for the depths of Athens – and freedom.

Shortly after the episode with the goat the O'Daly arrived home one day a little rattled. I was surprised to see him rattled as very little unnerved the O'Daly. On this day he announced that during an argument he told his chairperson she was a bitch. He gave no explanation or justification – that was all he said. My first thought was that it was a career-limiting move, but then I realised the significance of the moment as the O'Daly had never used the word "bitch" before. We were in Greece on a two-year contract with the possibility of an extension of another two years – either way Greece was always going to be a temporary stop on our way. I felt a sense of disappointment – I was hoping for another two years in the land of blue and white. From that moment on the O'Daly kept mum about the matter, as if the incident never happened.

Things became icy at the O'Daly's workplace – they wanted to throw us out of Greece immediately. The O'Daly responded with resolve – we would leave for Ireland after the summer. Our time was up, and as the Offaly healers Pascal and Mary foretold, Ireland was ready to receive us.

The prospect saddened me; although the two years in Greece came with frustration, they were carefree and happy. From this point on there would be three places that weaved my journey – a heartland with the colours of a rainbow, one homeland with the colour blue, and another with the colour green.

A month of silence followed the O'Daly's announcement. Mute not because of the full impact of the news, but because the O'Daly started writing a book, and when the O'Daly wrote he had no excess words to share with anyone. He managed to finish the first three chapters of the book. Mute also because the weather was simply too cold to talk. Along with the mass of brand new poppies and daisies came a series of vicious cold fronts that left us exposed and cold to the bone. My soul wanted warmth, but our homeland responded with an arctic chill.

Pelion

When I thought the Hellas chamber of my heart had been filled to capacity with special treasures, we discovered Pelion. The Pelion peninsula stretches down from Volos (on the east coast of mainland Greece) almost all the way down to the northernmost tip of Evia Island – snub in between the Aegean on the east and the Pagasetic Gulf on the west. On the Gulf side of the peninsula the landscape slopes gently into the quiet sea. Many tiny beaches – half-hidden between trees – are scattered along the coastline, every so often accompanied by a charming little village on the shore. In contrast the landscape on the Aegean side is rough and wild with steep, rocky slopes that plunge straight into the deep sea. On this side of the peninsula the roads are daunting – narrow and winding, barely hanging on to the side of the mountain; sometimes even crumbling at the edge, with no barrier whatsoever between you and a huge vertical drop down to the sea. Getting to the few secluded beaches from this road literally meant a sudden drop of about a kilometre, straight down the mountainside.

The northern end of the peninsula is dominated by the main bulk of Mt. Pelion. Forests of oak and chestnut trees covered the upper slopes of the mountain, giving Pelion's contours a rounded, smooth appearance. On the lower slopes we found every conceivable shade of green: from the silver-green of the olive trees, to the bright shades of the poplar and plane trees, to the bottle green of the pine needles.

Although our three days in Pelion were incredibly cold and wet, we still fell in love with this beautiful, magical mountain. After the barren beauty of most other parts of Greece I was surprised to find a landscape so incredibly lush.

We left at the crack of dawn and arrived in mundane, Mullingar-like Volos at the foot of Mt. Pelion a little more than three hours later. After inching our way through the crazy Volos traffic we could finally head for the mountains. Our first stop was at one of Pelion's most beautiful villages (designated by the EU as a protected architectural site), Makrynitsa. Makrynitsa is built like an amphitheatre along the mountainside and is sometimes referred to as the "eagle's nest" or "balcony of Pelion." The village was founded between 1204 and 1215 and its trade around the Balkans was based on silkworm production and tanneries. No vehicles are allowed inside the village and all I could hear were the sounds from the many clear streams and splash fountains.

Makrynitsa on a weekday morning in early spring was very much still asleep. In the main *plateia* under a huge ancient plane tree we found the one-aisle basilica of Saint John the Baptist and a *taverna*, with chairs and tables still deserted after the last summer. Along a narrow cobbled pathway through pomegranate and plane trees only one tiny *taverna* was open for business. From its small wooden patio we could see all the way to the Pagasetic Gulf. Outside a solitary donkey waited with no words. Lunch in front of the open fire consisted of *Fasolada* (traditional bean soup), *patates*, *tzatziki*, *psomi* (bread) and delicious mountain water.

The typical Pelion house is a fortress-like three-storey building – both imposing and simple. The first and second floors have very few small window openings, while the third floor juts out and consists of a light construction with large windows. The stained glass and painted windows alongside the transparent ones give an unusual look to the overall house. Strolling through Makrinitsa we marvelled at the beautiful slate roofs, well-preserved castle houses, crumbling churches, stained glass lanterns, many fountains and small stone bridges.

From Makrynitsa we travelled further up the mountain to the Xania ski-resort. The slopes were freshly groomed with beautiful snow. From Xania our base for our short stay was a short hop down to the Aegean side of the mountain.

Many of Pelion's 24 villages are tucked away safely in the folds of the mountain amongst lush woods of beech, chestnut and oak. I can see why myths are abundant in this Garden of Eden. According to legend Pelion was both summer resort to the gods of Olympus and home to the Centaur (half man, half horse). Pelion was also the remote home of Cheiron, the wisest of the centaurs, known for his knowledge of healing. His scholars included Asklepios, Jason the Argonaut and the heroes Theseus and Achilleas. When Asklepios, the god of medicine, was born from the womb of his dead mother, Cheiron responded to God's command and took care of the orphan and taught him the art of healing and curing disease. Asklepios soon surpassed his teacher and in Pelion bred the snake that became the symbol of the medical profession. The healing herbs of the peninsula – still in abundance – became the base for his invaluable pharmacology.

We arrived in Pelion at a time when spring was living side-by-side with winter: blossoms against stone, and green against bare. A small detour took us to the little village of Kissos, barely visible from under a mass of dazzling azaleas; a place so private we felt like intruders. From Kissos we headed for Mouressi: round every bend an arched stone bridge with grace captured in its lines. Stone fountains and water streams were everywhere; and houses that took their colours from nature.

When we arrived in Tsagarada the sky and Aegean were one: grey. In the misty evening Aleka's charming inn greeted us with rooms as warm as toast and a cerise pink flokati rug bright against the tile floor. Before dinner we went for a long walk along the mountain road; the smell of the evening and the shades of green filled the air. In the square of Saint Paraskevi in Tsagarada we paused under a huge, wise perennial plane tree; the tree was one thousand years old. Our charming hostess served a magnificent meal. We ended the meal with yoghurt, honey and nuts, and hazelnut and vanilla flavoured coffee.

The next morning we braced ourselves and took the scary road to explore the rest of the peninsula. For most of the day we travelled in bitterly cold rain – at times sleet. We dipped down from the main road to investigate the beaches at Damouhari, Ag Ioannis and Mylopotamos, and continued on to precious Melies.

During the dark ages of the Ottoman occupation, Melies became Pelion's cultural centre and provided refuge to many scholars and artists. Melies derived its name from the abundance of apple trees. At the entrance to Melies, a tiny snow white Byzantine church with bright red tile roof and little cross on the top welcomed us. We stopped for refreshments at a delightful coffee shop: a place with yellow walls covered by framed pictures of antique photos and advertisements, and the smell of cinnamon, pancakes, coffee and friendship. Melies was the perfect place to pause.

Beautiful Melies charmed us with wisteria, azaleas, narcissus, junipers, white blossoms and even a few pink tulips which looked like precious gems in a terracotta pot. The land was laden with apple, pear, cherry, peach, apricot, quince, fig, pomegranate, prune, and walnut trees. And the surrounding areas were overgrown with chestnuts, sycamores, poplars, oaks and beeches.

From Melies we travelled down the coast as far as Milina. We travelled carefully through the coastal villages of Koropi, Afyssos, Kalamos and Horto – careful not to wake them from their deep winter sleep.

In one day we moved through a fascinating world: chairs on empty squares – hurt by the harsh winter and desperately waiting for summer and company; old cottages that keep their memories and secrets behind weather-beaten, closed-up doors and windows; silent ruins and citrus trees undeterred by the wear and tear of time on the surrounding buildings; beehives; coloured flowerpots on steps, balconies and windowsills; flowers blooming in disused feta tins; lush carpets of white daisies; and stone buildings aching with decay. At small *tavernas,* tablecloths were accompanied by empty chairs. And the olive groves stretched all the way to the edge of the sea – lined with soft green grass and scattered with daisies and red poppies.

We returned to Melies in order to meet Jason, the *trenaki,* or little train – a must for our two train enthusiasts. The little train used to be steam driven but was converted to diesel after it set the world alight and burnt down much of the countryside. During spring and summer it chugs along a beautiful track from Lechonia to Melies and back; whistle blowing. The little engine is also called "*moutsouris*" (dirty one) and "*therio*" (wild-one). At the end of the road is the station, ridiculously cute and straight out of the Thomas the Tank Engine series, complete with black engine, four shiny wooden coaches, platform, shed and turntable. Ed was obsessed with Thomas the Tank Engine; he had all the trains, and the figures were on his pyjamas, lunch box, flip-flops and underpants.

The stationmaster was a Canadian Greek and he greeted us in perfect English. His job was to mop the toilets, tidy the platform, and spruce up the *trenaki.* Travelling on the train were the train driver and his assistant, a ticket salesman and the conductor, who spent the entire hour-long journey bonding with Ed. Once the train had left Melies I drove to Ano Lechonia to meet my passengers. On the way there I passed the stationmaster on his scooter – mop and bucket perched on the back of his bike; his face buried in a warm scarf. He was on his way to the other end of the circuit, in time to welcome Jason; and repeat the grooming process with dedication.

On our last day the Aegean revealed its cobalt blue and turquoise edges. We returned home the same way we arrived – leaving behind a snow-world on top of Pelion. The bare branches of the winter trees were dusted with fresh snowflakes: they looked dream-like.

Pelion's beauty is gentle and easy to wear. The peninsula is a spiritual place, and the mountain greeted me with gentleness and a strange familiarity. In the words of Thanassis Costavaras, "Thus I was going, light and unexpectedly calm, if not happy, anyway suffused with all those things that make the world inexhaustibly beautiful."

Moving through Pelion I wasn't aware of how much the healing powers of the place resonated with my soul.

A new homeland

When summer arrived in all its wonderful glory the blue skies, heat and big bursts of colour returned to the land. People congregated on pavements and the sea became a mirror. We had waited a long time for this last indulgence; the end of summer meant a move to Ireland.

We bought a postage stamp-sized house in Kells, Ireland. Although we'd always dreamt about a house in Ireland, neither the O'Daly nor I ever envisaged Kells. I cannot explain how Kells arrived on our landscape. The

O'Daly travelled to Ireland on a recce mission, and in the *Aer Lingus Cara* magazine found a period home somewhere in the Meath countryside "in need of restoration and tender loving care." The auctioneer took him to see this property. However, while they were there she decided that the O'Daly did not look like the renovation type and instead suggested a house in a beautiful demesne outside Kells. The demesne used to be home to Lord Headfort, and when the last lord left, the main house became a preparatory school and the main courtyard where farm animals once lived were converted into houses. A further lower courtyard was built to complement the development. The moment the O'Daly drove into the lower courtyard at Headfort he lost his heart and bought the house on a whim.

Kells is a small market town fifty kilometres northwest of Dublin, on the banks of the river Blackwater. The town first appeared in the historic records as early as 1207 BC followed by a long and chequered history. Kells came into prominence with the construction of a Columba monastery in the early 6th Century. The monastery flourished until the 12th Century – withstanding various attacks from both local and Norse raiding parties. During this period the Great Book of Kells – a decorated manuscript of four Gospels and reputed to be the most beautiful book in the world – was completed. After the coming of the Anglo-Normans in the 12th Century the monastery closed down. A castle was built and over the centuries Kells became a walled town. The town was attacked and burned on numerous occasions, either by the natives or the English until it was completely ruined in the 17th Century.

With major change on the horizon I became focussed on packing in as many memories as I could.

During our last trip from Greece to Cape Town Ed discovered feather picking. The fetish started with a shiny blue Lufthansa pillowcase – decorated with bright yellow suns and moons. The moment he saw the case he became mesmerized; he opened up the cover and found the down pillow inside where one tiny little feather was peeking out. This boy left the womb with his small motor skills highly developed, and with the utmost precision he proceeded to pull out the little down feathers, one-by-one. For the entire flight he did not make a squeak. At one stage they brought him a second pillow to cover an earlier water spill, and he immediately removed the pillowcase and continued his feather picking. Nothing on earth could make him stop, and after 11 hours on the plane we were covered in feathers – for weeks afterwards I picked them from seams and elbows and collars.

The little blue pillow reminded me of my own life: a casing full of remembrance. Ed's feather picking prompted me to take this pillow and follow the casing with my fingers until I found the first little tip. I begin to pull out one little feather after another – each one a thought, an experience, an image or a feeling. The white down felt delicate and soft between my fingertips. As I pulled out more and more fluffs, the memories were dancing in the air. They twirled on their way to the ground – as light as feathers.

The thought of leaving Greece without a permanent base in the country was inconceivable to us. We were sure that securing a little bolthole in the blue was required to free us to leave Dionysos in a yellow taxi when it was time to go. So we bought an apartment in Diminio at the edge of the Gulf of Corinth. Diminio is in easy reach of Athens airport and our beloved Peloponnese. Unpretentious Diminio is tucked in between Kiato and Melissi, on the way to trendy Xilokastro.

At the height of summer hundreds of white cardboard boxes arrived at our house in Dionysos and engulfed me. As usual the plan was to move in stages and phase in one house with another. My attention was focussed on inventories, values and a number of different heaps: one for now, one for Ireland, one for here, and one for Diminio.

The salmon pink leather couch and Oregon pine server from a bygone era were destined to retire at the coast of Corinth. The various heaps threatened to swallow me, sweat was oozing out of every pore of my body, and my mouth felt gagged by the packing tape. In the heat my wings were melting.

In the midst of packing I was challenged with my final Greek test: reporting a break-in into my little silver car. Someone had stolen my radio/CD player and first-aid kit, and for this misdemeanour an entire forensic squad arrived with flashing blue lights. The O'Daly was abroad, already stuck into his new career – somewhere in the midst of all this activity I felt lost.

I had to make three visits to the police station in Ekali to register the petty crime incident. My first attempt ended abruptly with a stone faced lady giving me the rolled-eye and customary "tsk" sound which means something like "whatever." After the first attempt the squad car came to inspect the scene of the crime with flashing blue lights. Needless to say, the two coppers were uninterested in the silver car's tiny broken window and empty space where a radio once used to be. Their police boots, holsters and cop-car were ready for much greater things. My second visit to Ekali also ended with something like, "don't bother me now, come back tonight between eight and ten."

As police stations go, the Ekali police station was a dire building in a neglected garden of a posh suburb. Inside the entrance gate a plastic table, blue checked tablecloth and four plastic chairs were ready and waiting to receive a smoke and a frappe. On this night the building was empty and the brown desks void of any files, papers or writing utensils.

A handsome young sergeant signalled me in. I asked: "Can you speak English?" and he responded with "*oxi*" ("no"). He pointed to a chair next to the desk and then proceeded to help three other persons who were in the queue behind me. This officer was going to make me wait – I could feel the tears burning behind my tired eyelids. And I remembered the matriarch's instruction once that a woman must be like steel, and that she should never cry.

There was no eye contact during the process, and when we got to the "Name" section I knew from experience the form-filling was going to be tricky. My name has several consonants that do not exist in the Greek language. To add to the challenge, the policemen wanted not only my name, but also the names of my mother and father. The officer took ages and a couple of Tip-ex brush strokes to complete all the foreign names. While I was trying to sound out the consonants that did not exist in the Greek language, the two officers were talking and laughing away in Greek. "Are you Catholic?" No, I am a Protestant. "Were fingerprints taken?" No, the squad car came and went. "What was stolen?" The CD player was ripped out. "Really – did they only take the CD/radio player?" No, they also took the first-aid kit, and with this information they opened a case between someone's Protestant daughter, born in South Africa, with an address in Ireland, residing in Dionysos – against an unknown individual – some idiot who left behind a trail of frustration and now owned a radio and first-aid kit. The case ended up somewhere in the archives of Greek police records.

We had a few weeks left to absorb and enjoy every last crumb of sun and sea. I wanted to make sure that we left Hellas with our suitcases bursting with blue; enough to last me for a good while.

The removal company sent gorgeous Dimitris to give a quote for the removal of our house contents to Ireland. In ex-pat circles he was a topic of discussion, and his reputation of tall, dark and handsome preceded him. He was the removal company's trump card and he got our business.

The arrival of the impersonal brown container at our front door signalled the reality of another significant move. Once again the impending change challenged my sense of belonging. How could I extract my roots without leaving them exposed?

A handful of men in company T-shirts arrived in a tiny black car to pack our lives into the many white boxes. They always started with a smoke break and a frappe; Nescafe, sugar, straws, glasses, teaspoons and ice were always on standby. Large quantities of sugar and coffee were consumed to make the frappes.

Every morning less and less of my life would be left as more and more boxes appeared. The smell of stale smoke would greet me, and after they had left the toilets needed to be unclogged. They came with their cigarettes, coffee breaks and runny tummies, and filled the sewage tank under the front garden to the brim. This meant one more visit from the slurry man.

Ed bonded with the men, and in between building tunnels and hiding places with the boxes, he served them refreshments in Greek.

Much too soon our walls became empty and our home changed into a warehouse. Outside on the pavement a container stood waiting. While the sweat-laden guys carried the boxes down the many stairs, the driver of the truck sat waiting, his feet on the dashboard, hair perfectly blow-dried, flicking his worry beads.

In the garden our two tortoises Whisky and Africa were about to become orphans.

Nikaria

It took a daunting drive of about two hours to get to the port of Piraeus on a Friday afternoon. Traffic was heavy, queues endless, and six of us were bundled into our black car with bone-dry lips. We started this journey exhausted: the O'Daly had been travelling non-stop for about 16 hours and I was drained after a three-day packing experience. We had a mad dash to find the right ship, and the frenetic activity at the port left us completely breathless: people lugging suitcases and backpacks to ferries and islands; cars coming at you from all directions; and port officials with whistles and waving arms. Piraeus on a Friday afternoon was best left to those with stomachs of steel. We fell into our seats in the "distinguished" class and finally headed for the Eastern Aegean Sea and Ikaria.

Ikaria got its name from the fallen Ikarus. According to legend, Ikarus and his father Daedalus escaped from the Labyrinth on Crete with wings crafted from feathers and wax. Daedalus was a respected architect and the first king of Athens, and after he had thrown his nephew off the Acropolis he was exiled to Crete. The young Ikarus was so overwhelmed by the thrill of flying that he flew too close to the sun. As a result the wax in his wings melted and he plunged to his death into the sea that now bears his name.

Over the centuries the island became a place of exile for many. In 1912 the island enjoyed a four-month stint as an independent state with its own constitution, currency and stamps. During World War II the island suffered huge losses in property and lives. After the war the majority of the islanders were sympathetic to communism, and in the late 1940s the Greek government used the island to exile about 13,000 communists.

The trip on the fast ferry took six and a half hours, with short stops in Paros and Naxos. For most part of the journey Ed was spinning around the "distinguished" class like a Duracell bunny on steroids. We arrived in the port of Evdilos shortly before midnight and a treacherous drive of more than an hour over a mountain took us to our final destination, Agios Kirykos. At more or less the same time the police arrived on the island to arrest the ringleader of the notorious terror group 17th November – he lived and worked on Ikaria as an icon painter.

By the time we reached our destination we were shattered. Here the General – our other Greek patriarch – greeted us with a spread of stuffed peppers, tomatoes and zucchini flowers. We were near death and opted for our beds instead. The last thing I saw before closing my eyes were the lights of the Monastery of Saint John (Patmos) which looked like tiny little candles in the distance.

Getting to the General's summer home was a marathon, but the next morning we were greeted by a spectacular view from our balcony door - a life-size painting in pastels so gentle they melted in my mouth. The house was situated halfway up the mountain, in the small village of Christos, with a beautiful view of the sea; Fourni island across the water; Samos' nose barely visible from the north-east; and Patmos ahead in the distance. From the first moment I felt the difference in this remote place: this island had kept its soul.

Ikaria is a peculiar place. The locals adhere to a daily schedule by which shops and *tavernas* are closed by day and open much of the night. In Agios Kirykos everything was jumbled: the houses were a mixture of island style (white with blue doors and shutters) and plain (with Ikarian slate or red tiled roofs). Most of the roofs had stones stacked along the edges to keep them from blowing away during the fierce August winds. The roads were narrow and awkward. Rusted skeletons and remnants of old cars, vans, excavators, tractors – and even a cement truck – were strewn on the roadside. At one place an old road sign still stood as no one could be bothered to remove it; on the sign were two arrows and no words. Fresh spring water was available for collection free from several taps scattered around the village. This island definitely does not wear a tourist masque.

In Christos we discovered an old car parked on the pavement with a cardigan wrapped around each of its tyres to keep the tyres warm. The O'Daly did not find the cardigan thing strange at all: in the days before legwarmers his aunt Biddy in Ireland would cut off the sleeves of her cardigans and wear them as leg warmers in winter. Also in Christos we found a surly brown donkey; surly because the locals used him as a lawnmower. Each job took him a couple of months or so to complete, so if you wanted your lawn cut, you had to schedule the donkey long in advance.

No sooner had we arrived, our clocks were reset to local time. Something like: sleep till midday; wake up with a frappe; laze on the beach until five in the evening; siesta until about eight pm; wake-up; ouzo or orangeade at the *Kafeneio*; dinner around midnight and back to bed at around two in the morning. At night the centre of the village came alive.

Our favourite place on the island was Faros: a protected, turquoise bay with fabulous clear water and a small pebble beach a few kilometres long.

Every day we followed the wobbly white line for ten kilometres along the coastal road to Faros. Faros catered to everyone: the little ones could swim and play in the safety of the shallow water between some rocks; swimmers could swim or snorkel the entire breadth of the bay; and the lazy ones could chill out under the big trees on the beach. There were two *tavernas* on the beach – all of ten steps away – and many afternoons we ate *karpousi* (watermelon) and *patates* on our beach towels.

There were always three small boats bobbing on the water and enough people pottering around for the place to remain quiet. Most of the people were Greeks who left the sleepy shores of Ikaria for a better life in the States. Hours passed at Faros without any of us noticing. They simply slipped away effortlessly.

The Ikarians do not like too much activity and therefore they concentrate on activities that do not require much energy, like beekeeping (the bees do most of the work), minding mountain goats (they mind themselves), growing olives and fishing. Getting any business done is a huge challenge. The O'Daly tried three times to get a flight ticket to Athens from the local travel agent, and on every occasion the printer was out of paper. And that was that. All he got was the slight lifting of the eyebrows, which meant "can't do", not now, maybe never.

On our third evening we had dinner with the General on our patio overlooking the Aegean. A full moon joined us as guest of honour for the evening. The General arrived mid-morning to start the cooking process. Around 10pm, and many pots and pans later, we sat down for an early meal. This particular General was a cook of note: stuffed zucchini and chilli peppers; spicy potatoes and oven baked pork; and Durban spices and Bombay saffron. We drank homemade wine out of red-labelled Ouzo bottles, and all along the translations were flying backwards and forwards. Our feast was in Greek. And under the silver moon we somehow managed to make deep conversation.

Around midnight the General – still dressed in his white vest from the morning – broke into soulful song about countrymen leaving, loving and dying. His big voice filled the Ikarian night sky, and saddened the moon. Somewhere during the meal the General's brother-in-law arrived – his moustache a hearty one. While the General sang the brother-in-law would stroke his belly. The brother-in-law was lamenting about his daughter's forthcoming wedding. He talked about the 500 litres of his own wine and 50 kid goats that were ready and waiting for the occasion.

Within two days I had fallen hopelessly in love with the island. A place so authentic and so remote it could as well be at the end of the world. We did not do too much sightseeing, there was no need to. There was no space on the ferry to Patmos and we never mustered enough energy to visit

Fourni for fresh seafood. We did however visit Therma (with its geothermal springs) for the local speciality, *kantaifi* (a type of baklava) with ice cream.

We also spent a day on the other side of the island. En-route to Evdilos along the tiny mountain road we found the most beautiful scenery with high mountains, lush forests of pine and cypress, dramatic gorges, steep barren cliffs, rivers, vineyards and olive groves. Evdilos is a pretty little village with red-tiled roofs all nestled tightly against a steeply sloping hill. In Evdilos the roads were so narrow that trucks had removed chunks of walls as they tried to squeeze through. From Evdilos we travelled through Kampos to the large "Baywatch"-type beach at Mesakti. This day we did the tourist thing and lazed in style on beach beds under grass umbrellas. The beach was followed by lunch at a garden tavern in Armenistis, perched on a rock and overlooking another golden beach. Homemade *moussaka*, *spanakopita* and zucchini balls were served in a place so small you would miss it if you did not know about its existence.

Our last stop was at Christos Raches, a traditional village high in the green mountains, a strange place so sleepy during the day, the shops couldn't be bothered to take in their merchandise when they were closed all day long. In the late afternoon and evening the place changed into party mode with all the shops and *tavernas* open with singing, dancing and music well into the night. The village square looked like a giant stone balcony, overlooking the deep sea.

But for us life at Faros was perfect. At Faros there was no space for time or thought – life on the beach was pure bliss. Each day was stitched together by a cicada chorus, radiating from the trees. The place is unspoilt and we found it easy to surrender to the local rhythm. We camped under the same big tree every day. In fact life under the tree was so blissful that during siesta time, an old *pappou* (grandfather) would settle on a beach bed a few metres away and launch into dreamland with a huge fart. And when he wasn't farting, his big raucous snoring escaped from under his red cap.

One day we stayed until after sunset. The sky and the water and the beach became one. A beautiful picture: the sea was a peaceful dream, few little boats dead-still on the water, and gentle bouzouki music in the background. This particular night we fell in for dinner with the General in our sticky swimsuits and flat hair: spaghetti, tomato salsa with fresh mint, feta and a whole *karpousi* (watermelon). Six of us finished a whole kilogram of Kalathaki Limnou feta cheese. We rolled out of there and followed the dark road home – careful to avoid the grouse family and the fearless mountain goats.

Our days always ended on the patio under the moon: Baileys on ice; tired sun drenched skins; books-in-many-languages on laps; and the littlest white church with blue dome looking serene in a splash of light on the dark hilltop. The moon greeted us with a different face every night: red and round; yellow cheese; bright white; or smoky and mysterious.

On our last night we had supper on the beach – our table placed right at the edge of the water. There is something special about Ouzo on ice next to a calm sea. The evening was silver – Fourni island a soft pink gemstone in the water. A full moon appeared from behind Samos' back and painted the sea with glitter. Our time was fast running out.

Ikaria is a place the Ikarians like to keep to themselves. To visit Ikaria you really need some family connection. We got in as 'adopted family': we had been adopted into the General's clan and with this privilege came the freedom of Ikaria. The General did not approve of our honorary membership in the Patriarch's clan. Panos hailed from Kalamata and the General from Sparti – this was not good as there is an on-going competition between the folk in Kalamata and Sparti as to whose olives and olive oil are the best. When the General heard that we were in the process of buying an apartment in the Patriarch's summer domain, somewhere between Kiato and Xylokastro, he became so incensed that he could not sleep for two nights. On the third day he made one phone call and produced a house for sale in Monemvassia. For us this would have been utopia, but not practical.

It is impossible to spend time in the folds of Ikaria and not be touched by its simplicity, its laziness, and even its scruffiness. It is impossible to move through the place and remain untouched by its people.

There was a farewell committee at the port the morning we left: *tiropitas* (cheese pies), the General, the General's wife and Tzerry, their wire-haired fox terrier. The farewell was emotional: memories stuffed in pockets and bags, tears in our throats and at least half a kilogram of feta in my belly.

When the ship was a few metres away, I could feel this precious world slip through my fingers - my hands and arms unable to hold on. The time had arrived to trade blue for grey; brown for green; bone dry for wet; one alphabet for another; left-hand-drive for right-hand-drive; mainland for island; vast for more confined; and fictional for authentic.

I felt as though our time in Greece was a tad too short; I wanted to stay longer. We were always going to leave South Africa with Ireland as our destination, and here we had the privilege of a detour with Hellas thrown into the mix. The land of blue was the perfect place for the process of de-programming; for thoughts to be challenged and beliefs and values to be tried and tested. Hellas provided the space for inside-out and upside-down.

As far as my own journey was concerned, the phase of living in physical chaos was drawing to a close. It was time to move to somewhere soft – a whole new chapter was waiting to begin in Ireland.

PART 3: SURRENDER

Always keep Ithaca fixed in your mind.
To arrive there is your ultimate goal.
But do not hurry the voyage at all.
It is better to let it last for long years;
and even to anchor at the isle when you are old,
rich with all that you have gained on the way,
not expecting that Ithaca will offer you riches.

K. P. Kavafis (C. P. Cavafy), translation by Rae Dalven

A little green island

The O'Daly grew up thinking Ireland was a continent. To me the island felt really small – as if it could float away at a moment's notice.

Our relocation process was long and drawn-out. In typical O'Daly style we moved in stages, and we took three months to complete the move. Our last days in Dionysos were occupied by a second batch of removal guys and their rolls of tape, packaging material, boxes, frappes and smoke breaks. In-between all the activity we squeezed in last minute haircuts with Vasilis; said goodbye to special friends and Greek "family"; and enjoyed a final supper with Michaelis – the "chicken man" in Drossia. Both Vasilis and the "chicken man" had become institutions in our home. Vasilis knew the ins-and-outs of all our hairdressing needs and Michaelis had the best chicken souvlaki for miles. We adored them. Whenever we dropped in at Michaelis' taverna, he killed the fatted calf for us; he would roll out all the secret dishes that were not on the menu, as if we were royalty, or very close family.

The removal guys packed the last of our possessions into a soulless brown container, and left. We arrived in Ireland at a home already set up; and somehow we fell into the Meath countryside as if we had lived there all our lives. The Emerald Isle gave us her most charming welcome – she was desperate to try and charm us with glimpses of her glory. Most of our days in late summer and early autumn were blue, soft and easy. There were flower boxes and hanging baskets filled with all the colours of Impatiens, Begonia, Lobelia, Petunia, Geranium, Alyssum, Fuschia and Narcissus everywhere; golden bales of hay dotted on tidy wheat fields; cows, horses and black-faced sheep relaxed in green fields; and dewy mornings that left the countryside unbelievably bright and beautiful. In some places Watsonias lined the country roads like small orange flames against the green edges. There was a familiarity about the place.

Settling in

We arrived on a Sunday and the O'Daly collected us at the airport, introduced us to our new home, turned around and left for the airport to begin a life of commuting. For a second time in two years I was dropped at a house in a foreign world with two children and a container or two to unpack. We arrived in Ireland one step removed from refugee status – no-one cared who I was or where I had come from. Here I was, nearly 42 summers tall without a bank account, utility bill, or record of address. I was a nobody.

The kids hit the jackpot with the late Lord Headfort's 22,000 acre domain. Headfort School is located in the 240 year old manor house – a Harry Potter-esque building a stone's throw from our house. The O'Daly was keen on boarding schools, and the school on the estate provided the perfect opportunity to prep the kids for their high school years. For me the whole boarding school thing was as foreign as could be. I had no frame of reference and could not connect with the concept. The moment the grey building swallowed Ruby, she thought she had arrived in heaven.

The school overlooks a golf course and rolling green countryside – the Kells church tower and tips of houses barely visible in the distance. Inside the school building the walls held the ghosts of many stories. On the school grounds kids share their play with bunnies, squirrels and black crows. Outside the windows of our house a fairy forest, moss-covered trees, and a herd of brown Limousine cattle held the space.

We began our new life in Ireland as a weekend family. I assumed the role of taxi driver; every Friday evening and crack of dawn Monday morning I would wrap Ed in a blanket, pop him on the back seat, and head for the airport. I loathed these drives – in winter they meant darkness, cold and more often than not rain. In my vocabulary "no" did not exist. I had spent most of my life doing things that I often did not really want to do. Driving to Dublin airport twice a week on appalling roads was one of those things. Until one day I found my voice and said to the O'Daly "thereto and no further"; from this day on taxi driver Paddy Maguire became his trusted airport transport.

Whenever the O'Daly rang home, our son would ask his father to hold on so he could fetch the thing he made at school and show his father over the telephone. In his world there was no distance, and telephones could see. While he was doing the "show and tell" over the phone, his eyes would smile with happiness.

We landed in our new environment four characters on an oil-on-canvas piece of art – the green paint still wet. At the bottom of the painting a squirrel left its tiny black footprints on the canvas. And in this picture I found an immense peace; a deep, deep sense of personal satisfaction. When the oil-canvas became awash with autumn colours, I started a new journey with a fresh pair of Wellington boots.

The rain in Ireland is very different than the rainstorms in Africa. The Highveld rainstorms rain from a height and they rain colour. These storms always leave the world with the fresh smell of dust softened by water. There is satisfaction in smelling the land after the rain; in the wake of the rain everything is left bright and clean. But when the rain clouds move in over this little green island, they invade every available space; the rain lines my being with the colour grey. On such days the supermarket checkout lady would say "sure, it is another raw old day today," as if her words would excuse the invasiveness of grey.

But the clouds do lift and when this happens, the place lights up and becomes utterly beautiful. When the grey lifts, the landscape responds with such clarity, it still takes me by surprise. Every time it happens it is as if I see the colours for the first time. The presence of grace is somehow more noticeable in the changeover between grey and bright. I realised how in my heartland and in Greece I took the colours for granted. Whenever the night sky opened over Headfort, Ed would tell me he loved the moon and the stars.

If some years ago anyone mentioned that one day I would exchange a busy city career for a life in the country, I would have laughed. And yet, here I was in godforsaken, down-to-earth Kells. The village consists of a supermarket, post office, three churches, a garage or two, newsagent, pharmacy, hairdresser, couple of general dealers, fish and chipper, bottle store and a couple of pubs.

The little green island is home to a Toiseach; Pat the Baker and Johnston Mooney & O' Brien's soft butter crust batch; Hobnobs and Kimberley biscuits; Barry's tea; Ratface Rafferty; and Pat Scully with his thinning Santa's beard and bushy eyebrows. There is inevitably always a

Finbar or a Declan as a neighbour, and black-and-white cows are just one field away.

The narrow winding roads are shared with tractors and trailers, combine harvesters, forklift trucks (often with a full load perched on the fork), excavators and trucks and you name it. Often a huge truck full of livestock will try to manoeuvre its way through the narrow roads, leaving behind its trail of fear.

The faith healers in Offaly always said Ireland was our destiny – and for the first time I could sense the place in my being. I wondered if my travels through Hellas served as preparation for this new challenge. At some unconscious level I sensed the time was ripe to begin the process of working through the sediment left by 40 odd years; to peel away the many layers and find myself. There was no better place to do this than in a world with oodles of water and so much green. There is often a rainbow over the landscape – underneath the colourful bow, the day can be none other than soft.

Our first Christmas in Ireland meant four heads under one roof. There were lights in all the little villages and the streets were filled with a festive atmosphere. We explored the grounds around the school: the seven sisters – a huge monkey puzzler tree with its trunks arranged in a bizarre formation; two guard dog graves; the moat where on some nights the 'claw' (a character invented to scare the children out of exploring late at night) would appear outside the dormitory window; the ice cave used by the IRA in days gone by; the two huts where the 'granny' hangs out; and in the silence of the woods a Robin, maybe two.

At Christmas the caretaker of the school took on the role of Santa Claus. A gentle giant, his job was to take care of the buildings and the grounds, paint the white lines on the water logged sports field, fill the potholes with his tiny antique tractor, drive the school bus, and feed the chickens. As Santa he had to wear a fake white beard on his forehead as well as on his chin – a curtain to hide him from the younger children who knew him so well.

We dressed our green shed in a halo of light for the big day. This time the neon Joseph, Mary, baby Jesus and the little lambs were celebrating without us on their balcony in Dionysos. We had the animals in the frosty green fields. Most days the brown cows were like clay statues in the chill – they didn't move. They were totally unperturbed by the bunny chase close by. Or the important day that was about to happen.

New Year

A brand new year rolled over the stone walls at Headfort and landed in a frozen courtyard. We celebrated at a house across the courtyard from ours:

at the party an assortment of horsy people, a TV soap star, two estate agents and a local bookie. The bookie was accompanied by his girlfriend from Durban who draped herself over everyone like a chenille throw over a sofa. She was a thief of personal space. She smothered me until I had no choice but to escape into the crisp night, and into the New Year.

We spent the morning in an old forest close to Mullingar, on the edge of Lough Ennell. In the stillness of the forest the earth was soft and spongy. All along we had to dodge the many holes in the green moss carpet – they looked like access doors to another world in middle earth. The four of us were tempted to enter through one of the holes and disappear to a place where we could be together; a place where there was no separation between week and weekend. In the silence of the forest a few birds chirped along with our conversation. Much too soon our hungry bellies began to rumble for food. At the edge of the forest the year waited for us with cheeks full of air. We drifted home via the Monastery Inn pub for a hot meal of salmon, soup and brown soda bread. Then onto Granny's farm to inspect the two new wrinkly lambs and a lonesome "foxy gentleman" caught in a snare, his eyes wild with fear.

For ten days over the Christmas period a group of strangers invaded the school at Headfort – eating dry toast and meditating around the clock. We had to tip-toe around the grounds so as to not disturb their meditation. They came from all over the world to taste the calm of Headfort.

On the first weekend of the New Year we left for the UK on a mission to inspect the O'Daly's valley. A brave pre-dawn drive on shocking roads brought us to the port at Rosslare for our ferry crossing to Fishguard in Southern Wales. After three-and-a-half hours on the boat we arrived in the beautiful green hills of Wales: a place carefully manicured and a life that appeared very ordered. The O'Daly was directing from under his Indiana Jones hat; Ed had one-and-a-half eyebrow and a holy fringe after an experience with the O'Daly's Philishave; Ruby' Diskman was attached to her ears; and in our car the lingering pong of someone's smelly shoes.

The drive through the Welsh countryside was magnificent. The names on signposts looked funny and foreign: names full of consonants and impossible to pronounce. The O'Daly was of the opinion that after the pillage spree of the Vikings in AD 800 to the late 1st Century, the Vikings took almost everything, including most of the vowels of the Irish language and left the Irish with an oversupply of consonants.

Our base for the four days was a lovely Tudor style B&B in Burchett's Green. During our time in Berkshire the temperature never raised above two or three degrees Celsius and the days were spectacular. Our pace was gentle and our mood blissful.

We decided to give the centre of London a miss this time but rather concentrate on the countryside around our base. One of the highlights was a visit to Oxford – home place to Inspector Morse and Sergeant Lewis. We browsed the many wonderful bookstores, drank hot chocolate and cappuccino in a little cafe, walked through the narrow pathways, admired the spectacular old colleges and generally breathed in the very intellectual air. From Oxford we drove to Henley-on Thames for fish, chips and Speckled Hen ale in a local pub. The Thames was heavily flooded and ducks and swans were swimming on what was meant to be the road. We passed so many inviting pubs: The Magpie, Boot and Slipper, Six Roses, The Olde Fighting Cock and the Old Devil.

In St Albans we found a cathedral with carvings from different centuries, the longest nave in England, beautiful stonework, Norman pillars with a sequence of 13th and 14th Century paintings, the oldest cathedral tower build of Roman bricks, the shrine of St Alban, an impressive organ and a spectacular rose window with Victorian stonework. But the sacred atmosphere touched me most – I wanted to stay and reflect.

St Albans (aka Verulamium) was a wealthy provincial town in Roman Britain. The town was named after Alban, a pagan who sheltered a Christian fugitive from persecution in his home. He then helped the fugitive to escape by disguising him in his own distinctive clothes. For this crime Alban was executed on the hillside where a magnificent cathedral now stands.

During our last day we surveyed the immediate environment around the O'Daly's workplace in Hare Hatch, taking in all the details: the farm stall some 100 metres away, and the Green Olive – a poky Greek Restaurant in Henley – where we were at home with the menu of aubergines, *tzatziki*, *patates*, *horiatiki*, *souvlaki* and *ouzo*.

I felt sad to leave the O'Daly's world – it was strange to leave him behind. We shared four special days. Every morning started with white snow dust on the ground and a clear blue sky. In the O'Daly's valley every day had the soft and luxurious feeling of cashmere. Ed was quick to point out: "This England is lovely."

The kids and I left early for the ferry at Holyhead on the Isle of Anglesey; the boat trip to Dublin took a mere hour-and-a-half on a super-fast ferry. We returned to the sleepy hollow of Kells to find that the beautiful brown Limousine cattle had been shipped out and in their place much younger bullocks had appeared in the fields around our house. The Limousines lost their lives in a cold factory somewhere. But in the Lower Courtyard mine was beginning.

A blue bolt hole

Some months before we left Greece a teller at Alpha Bank in Greece handed the O'Daly a mortgage in cash notes into his hands, and with the loan the little home in Diminio became ours. From this point on Diminio became our place for sun, recharge and rest. The bank teller could not care less what happened to the money but the O'Daly passed the wad of cash on to the patriarch in return for the key to the apartment.

The closest place for shopping is the metropolis of Kiato. Here locals go shopping on mopeds or bicycles; old and derelict live comfortably next to new and modern; graffiti survives next to clean; visual pollution is rife; and the dated local green busses leave small clouds of diesel fumes at bus stops. Diminio is on the edge of the Gulf of Corinth and across the sea from the beautiful mountains on the mainland.

The night was bitterly cold when we touched down on the familiar runway in Spata – the moment crammed with excitement. We still had a two-hour drive ahead of us but we were back in our other homeland and it felt good. Deep in the dark night Athens had still not closed her sleepy eyes completely. A section of the new Attiki Odos motorway was opened during our absence and the new road shaved thirty minutes off our travelling time to Corinth.

The purpose of our short trip was twofold: to get our new home furnished and to try out one of the handful of Greek ski spots. We also needed family time and the opportunity to get re-acquainted.

We had Saturday to get our house liveable. First we unpacked the furniture and boxes we had shipped to Kiato four months earlier. Then we had approximately two hours left in which to locate furniture stores in Corinth, and make our purchases. When the O'Daly was completing the purchase of our bolthole he stumbled across a branch of Coco-Mat in Corinth. Here he found an eco-friendly store with a range of furniture made from horsehair, seaweed, wool, cotton, natural latex, coconut fibre and solid wood. He also found the store manager Kris and his family. Kris left Kenya on an athletic scholarship (with a damn fine 100 metre time) and settled in Greece. The O'Daly was born with a gift of the gab – he had a way of meeting someone for the first time, and then leaving as an honorary member of the family. He was like a pastor, converting people in shops, in offices, or at events.

With barely minutes to spare we headed to Coco-mat and fell into a welcome of hugs and kisses. The universe had given us a new family in Corinth, of all places. We left with two mattresses in our car and for the rest of the weekend our balcony was our fridge and a local *taverna* our cooker. At least we now had a place to rest our weary bones.

In between the chaos of unpacking and making our pad liveable, Giannis and Nikos arrived to complete the installation of hot water and electricity – the usual just-in-time delivery so famous in Greece. The patriarch was at hand to inspect. We were brave to finalize things without an interpreter.

At the very first opportunity we took our ski itch and left for the snow slopes of Kalavrita. It is an easy drive along the national road to the turnoff at Diakofto, a lazy place at the edge of the blue sea where the houses are planted in between orange and lemon trees. Diakofto is also known for its cog-wheeled train that chugs over waterfalls and steep cliffs through the mountains to Kalavrita.

From Diakofto the road follows a 48 kilometre line up breath-taking mountains to the ski-resort on the slopes of Mount Helmos. The road is perched high up against the mountainside and follows the valley of the Vouriakos River. I was unable to look down at the deep valley – overwhelmed by my fear of heights. In a few places one lane of the narrow road had simply slid off the mountainside and disappeared into the blackness below. The drive was difficult and poor visibility did not help our cause.

A few kilometres before Kalavrita, the Monastery of Mega Spileon (Big Cave) is tucked in a fold in the rocky mountainside. The Monastery is an eight-storey building built into the cliff-face at an altitude of 1,000 m. Founded in the 4th Century the monastery was first destroyed by the iconoclasts in 840, twice by the Turks and finally burned down by the German occupation troops in 1943.

Kalavrita was jam-packed with day trippers; every second shop was a ski-shop. We stocked up on snow chains and moved on. From Kalavrita the ski resort is 15 kilometres further up Mount Helmos. As you leave the town you cannot help but notice the huge white cross, mute against the mountainside above Kalavrita. On this spot 1400 men and boys lost their lives in December of 1943. In retaliation for the murder of one of their troopers, the occupying Nazis gathered all of the town's men and boys under the pretext of a stern reprimand about the murder. But instead, from the trees above the hill, lurking troopers opened fire. When the shooting stopped, the Germans walked around and shot anyone still alive. The women and children were locked in the schoolhouse – a German soldier disobeyed orders, unlocked the door and set them free. For this deed the soldier never returned home. The women went searching for their men, only to find the many bodies on the hillside.

The road to the ski resort was lined with day trippers throwing snow balls and building snow men. The countryside was picture perfect. Halfway to the resort the police turned us back; a bus had tumbled over the mountainside and the road was closed. By the time we finally admitted defeat, a snow storm had started and our drive down the mountain was a daunting marathon. We still had one day left for skiing.

On our second and last attempt to ski we found the road closed at the Diakofto turn-off. We stopped at the barrier in disbelief and a racing-green road patrol car came towards us from the direction of Kalavrita. We rolled down windows and began an English conversation with two very Greek officials. The answer we got to our question whether or not the road was open was "maybe." This response was all the O'Daly needed to proceed and we took "maybe" and tackled the mountain.

We very soon learned what "maybe" meant, that already on the foothills large sections of road were wiped out by massive landslides. Enormous boulders had crashed through retaining cement walls and ended up on the road. After a few kilometres we were in the snow line. From that moment on the journey became a harrowing challenge: added to our experience from the day before were icy road surfaces and one lane open to travel on. The other lane was covered under a mountain of snow – it was the heaviest snow fall in Greece in 80 years. I was happy for the wall of snow to block the view to the severe black drop down the mountain. The sky was blue, the world white, and through a gap in the mountains I could see the blue-green water of the Gulf of Corinth.

Our second attempt to Kalavrita took three hours: all along the way chains on, chains off; chains on, chains off. At Ski Bill ski shop, Vasilis, alias Bill, informed us that the ski resort was closed: too much snow! "Five metres of snow - we don't know what we must do." I had never heard of a ski resort closing due to too much snow. On this trip skiing was not meant to be so we settled for a fine lunch in the tavern *To Spitiko* where we dined with local men in long black coats, beards and woollen caps.

From there we visited the monastery Agia Lavra a few kilometres outside Kalavrita. The monastery was founded in the 10th Century and has also been burnt down several times by the Turks. Here Bishop Germanos of Patras raised the banner of freedom on 18 March 1821. At one time the monastery accommodated 1000 monks. In 1943 the Germans executed four monks and the caretaker who were too old to escape into the mountains along with the younger monks. The execution took place beneath the big Platanos tree where the flag of independence first flew.

We spent one day in Athens and in this limited time we squeezed in medical check-ups, haircuts, rounding up our wine collection and other bits of lost property, and a meeting with our old housekeeper. We had dinner with our favourite "Chicken-man" in Drossia and stayed over with a friend who had our wine collection under his wing. Our hectic day started with homemade Pretzels, coffee and a moment of calm. In Dionysos patriarch Panos was most upset that we did not sleep over at his house; he was ready and waiting to give up his bed for the night.

Breakfast was followed by another breakfast of *tost* and tea with the matriarch and a tour of our old house. The house was empty, except for the gaudy chicken lamp our Sri Lankan housekeeper gave us as a farewell present, the two tortoises Whiskey and Africa, and my little silver car which now belonged to the matriarch's daughter.

We dropped in for breadsticks and tea in Ekali; coffee at a tiny writer's table in a little coffee shop where I shared so many thoughts in the past; and pizzas in Kifissia. We left Athens like proper travellers: a stove on the back seat, duvets bundled in green refuse bags and a boot full of shopping and wine. Somewhere under all the stuff our two children were buried. The moment we left dreadful Elefsina behind us, I could feel my chest open up. I struggled to cope with the chaos on the Athens roads, and I realised I was no longer Attiki fit.

We were delighted to arrive back in our cosy little nest in the still of a winter Diminio. Our house was warm as toast, and I loved the freedom of our own space. The view from the balcony was beautiful: for the most part the sea-green sea melted with the lilac hues of the mountains and sky on the horizon.

Our last day in Corinth was most memorable. The sun appeared, the snow covered mountains looked spectacular, and close friends drove all the way from Athens to be with us. We shared a bottle of Vergelegen Chardonnay; brave to entertain with only tumbler glasses, a few plates and a leaky Chinese bathroom.

Setting up home went well. But our ski dream never materialised. We left Kiato in the early morning hours and boarded the plane with smiles on our lips and turquoise in our eyes. Both kids were ready to return to the snowdrops at Headfort.

The Peloponnese had become deeply rooted in our hearts; I felt so happy and privileged to move through its familiar smells, tastes and sounds. There was still a vast world waiting to be discovered. Blowing through Hellas left me fulfilled. We moved through the place without any constraints or baggage, with the bittersweet knowledge that we could return whenever we wanted to.

Alone

The Irish are very comfortable to talk about superficial things – I am not sure they like to venture into things too personal, too painful, or too ecstatic. In this part of the world experiences aren't shared, but instead words travel through rooms and empty spaces. No-one really lingers long enough for the words to find a home; to penetrate the skin, let alone the heart. In Ireland they draw a veil over the heart and soul because of what other people might think or say.

I resorted to generalisation in order to deal with the insecurity of my place in this new world – I was not ready to own my space, and see the beauty in difference. On the little green island I felt alone. And when I entered the outside world I left both my pain and joy at home, safely tucked away behind the old stone wall at Headfort.

At the beginning I felt intimidated to share my words with the gentry; it was as if a conversation required a straight back, carefully folded legs, and all the best manners in the world. Well-heeled words were about horses and heirs; personal trainers and high society functions; Eton and stiff upper lips; and real castles. I had to choose my words carefully. I remembered precious dialogues with friends in other places; times when words paused on small coffee tables and the taste of cappuccino and dreams remained on my tongue long afterwards.

In this part of the world you do not make medical appointments; they make you. The appointment is always for some arbitrary future date that may or may not fit in with existing schedules. Ed's appointment arrived through the mailbox in a brown envelope addressed to The Guardians of so-and-so. Inside the envelope there was no contact number, but only a date and a time. When the allocated day finally arrived we made the trip to the red-brick hospital in Mullingar.

I took Ed because the consultant wanted to be sure the pneumonia he had several months before had cleared up. At the hospital a note on the doors warned us about the dreaded Winter Vomiting Bug. We arrived at the Outpatient reception desk, clocked in and moved on to the waiting room. The place was busy. Everywhere people were sitting staring – speechless.

When it was our turn, Ed completely lost it and delivered an unholy tantrum that nearly brought the walls down. A tantrum so huge I thought it did not belong in the world of almost-four-year-olds. He did not want to get undressed, and then he did not want to get dressed; he did not want to be measured or weighed, and when we made up a number, he wanted to be measured and weighed. Two brave nurses tried to console him with an "I was good at the doctor" sticker but all they got was a snarl. Dressed in my elegant coat and black pointed boots I struggled to compose myself. This was not a friendly place. The corridors smelt of stale air and disinfectant mixed with the smell of pain. In the cafeteria people were eating muffins, raisin buns and mash potatoes – coloured by the stale air.

We met the consultant, a "blow-in" from the East. He scratched around in the file and mumbled a few words that disappeared into his stethoscope - my small talk echoed on his desk. We left with an instruction to come back in another three months' time to see if the pneumonia had really, really cleared up. I took the boy and the tantrum, and left the place. At the reception desk there was no-one to make a follow-up appointment because between one and two the place is empty. I escaped from the system into the grey drizzle, never to return.

Back at the school the new matron awaited me; a portly person with a clipboard. She wrote her words on the clipboard. The matron did not appear fond of the older girls – she did not like their frivolity and awkwardness, so she tried to shape the particularly unconventional ones with snubs and insults. Under her regime there was no place for the soul. I discovered the combination of this matron and our untidy Ruby was not a good one.

One afternoon I found Ed staring out of his bedroom window at the chimney pots on the roofs across the courtyard. He wanted to know and understand how it was possible for Santa Claus to fit through the narrow chimney pots on the roofs at Headfort. He caught me off guard and I said nothing. The next day he wanted to know again, so that he could put an end to his "midnight-mares' about Santa and the chimney pot, monsters, witches, goats and foxes.

During the week I tended to the hormones and tantrums; the clipboards and nightmares; and the anticipation of a reunion with the O'Daly on weekends. It was not ideal.

Our weekends with the O'Daly became predictable: some time to decompress from the stresses of his work, some time to do mundane things, some time to fit in a few special things, and then some time on a Sunday to get into the right mode for the week ahead. On one occasion the O'Daly and Ed took their coats, *wellies* and proper spears, and like two African warriors disappeared into the raw afternoon to hunt the foxes that bugged Ed in his nightmares. Ed knew from an early age that proof of a successful mission was a fluffy red tail in the hand. When the O'Daly was a young lad himself, foxes were a real problem, so the Department of Agriculture paid a bounty for every fox killed. They paid half a crown per fox tail presented – what they did not know was that the O'Daly was an environmentalist and that he never killed the foxes but instead chopped off their tails. At the time of his childhood there was a whole community of tail-less foxes around their farm.

The trips to the airport became equally predictable. The Monday morning drop-offs happened long before it was time for the morning to wake up. Part of the routine was espresso on the stove top to kick-start the day. Sometimes when we poured the coffee we realised the O'Daly forgot to add the coffee. Then he would start all over again, and the night would smile as it knew the day could not begin without that cup of coffee. It was always dark when I collected the O'Daly at the airport, and on rainy nights the rain formed silver lines in the headlights. I got to know the road so well I could drive it with my eyes closed.

We planted a row of daffodils and they lined our fence like tiny soldiers in camouflage. In winter they would disappear and leave us wondering when their yellow flowers would reveal their whereabouts once again. Around the courtyard glorious displays of daffodils added colour to the green window boxes. But when our line of yellow soldiers marched in, they always took first prize.

At Ed's nursery school in the woods they were learning about the countries of the world. It so happened that the first country was Greece. I loaded all my memories in a box and took them to school for display in the classroom: an old "home" flag, beautiful icons, a piece of marble, olive tin, *koboloi*, and Greek party songs. The next week they covered South Africa. Once again I packed my car full of memories for display in the classroom: spears, Knysna birds, giraffes and little *rondavels* (round houses). There were so many things I could not take because they were buried in my heart. For two whole weeks my memories were on display: homeland one week and heartland the next.

The third week they learnt about Ireland. On this occasion my car was empty because I was still too new to this peculiar little island. In this place the words are neutral; the world revolves around the GP; hedges are not perfectly groomed; in spring the motorways are lined with daffodils; and the aeroplanes are green.

A touch eccentric

When we returned from a trip to South Africa, Paddy Maguire was there to meet us at Dublin airport with his red Corolla taxi car. He was dressed in a white short-sleeve shirt, big smile and familiar Meath accent. After the heat of Africa the Sunday morning felt especially chilly. We meandered home through the Irish countryside, on little country roads and lane ways, determined to avoid anything resembling a motorway. Paddy had never driven on a motorway – he was far too scared to venture there. He also avoided ATMs, terrified that they may not give out the correct amount of money, or none at all.

From the back of the car all I could see was his hair – a bunch of silver steel wool. His eyes talked to me from the rear view mirror. I was exhausted after our 20 hour journey but it felt so good to hear Paddy nattering away in that delicious Irish accent. I was delighted to be home. I could not believe how much the countryside had changed during our absence. A spectacular show of fresh new leaves, tulips, blossoms, bluebells, London's pride and other spring flowers welcomed us. There were dandelions and daisies in the grass.

Our drive took us past a cabbage and broccoli field, at which point Paddy announced nonchalantly that he did not let out a fart but that the smell belonged to the rotten vegetables in the field. All I could think of was our crazy schedule in Johannesburg – a schedule with too many rows and columns. From the moment we arrived it was a race against time, and I felt as though I was involved in a game of Pictionary, trying to draw memories against a timer.

In the fields were dense furze bushes, intense and yellow against the green. The mere mention of furze bushes got Paddy all worked up. He believed it was criminal to leave furze alone: he thought these bushes swallowed hedges, consumed grass, and if not destroyed would eventually gobble up the whole of Ireland.

As the various shades of green flew past the car window, Paddy announced that the problem with Africa was that the place was completely scorched and that it had no green at all. What did he know about the beautiful vegetation of the Cape and the well-kept lawns and gardens of homes in the suburbs? Or the magnificent white beaches and lagoons; the blue of the sky; evenings framed by pink mountains; or the energy in the colours of the rainbow. He did not even know Simon van der Stel is asleep on top of Stellenbosch Mountain.

We got separated from the O'Daly at Heathrow. His normal luggage, a guitar, and a weapon of mass destruction – a six-foot bow with quiver and arrows – slowed him down. The O'Daly always helped in making conversation with Paddy, but this time there was no-one to step in as shield against the non-stop blather. Paddy told me the problem with a particular manufacturer of "fierce fast cars" was that at a certain point in time the water pump bursts and the engine falls out. I was thinking about the warmth of long standing friendships; a nanny with a headscarf and bare feet; and the wonderful pulse of adult nephews and nieces. And I was thinking about well-known smells and tastes and smiles; the excitement of filling in gaps; the awkwardness of hearing voices from the past; and the soft outlines of parents.

Paddy carried on about the rhododendrons at Headfort - he told me how many years ago masses of them arrived in boats, imported by wealthy landlords. A great number of them did not survive but some of the most beautiful ones can be found in the grounds of Headfort. Meanwhile I was thinking about a reunion with a friend I met soon after our arrival in Greece. She was my first proper girlfriend – a friend with whom I could share women things. I wondered why it took 40 years for a close friend to arrive in my life. Seeing her in her new driveway in Jo'burg made me realise how many memories we shared, and how many of those I had simply filed away. Thinking about the bittersweet times we spent in Greece nearly broke my heart.

Visits to South Africa are special, and I always look forward to making the trip. But I found it exhausting to move between here and there; between home-place and heart-place; and between green and rainbow. Two sides of a coin – separated by a long flight, and a buffer of grey space. There was always the moment in between; when I was neither in the warmth of my heartland, nor in the gentleness of my green homeland. Here I was left with a feeling of nowhere. I was a split person with one half of me in Africa and the other half in Ireland. And it was draining to be split in two.

On top of that the African half of me is further split into many little pieces. Pleasure is always mixed with regret: on the one hand the immense joy of sharing time with loved ones, and on the other hand the regret of too little time.

Once back in green my words and thoughts about Africa did not come easily – as if they were too tender to be let out and be committed to paper. And when they did fall out I was too scared to breathe around them – scared that my breath would lift the letters before they have had time to dry. Scared that they may become scrambled and disappear like dust into the green.

Paddy thinks Latin is not a real language; he reckons it was merely a mumbling thing that was made up way back when the Catholic thing began so as to confuse the Protestants. He is adamant it was never a language. Paddy thinks he knows everything about countries and languages and religions, but he only knows everything about almost everyone in Kells.

As we unloaded the car Paddy told me about his size 12 feet and that he buys his shoes at the Dunnes sales for Euro 5 a pair. He usually bought six pairs at a time. He felt sorry for men with small feet because they couldn't buy six pairs of shoes at Euro 5 a pair. I did not care about his feet because I was home – I had fallen into the soft arms of our house at Headfort.

We arrived back amidst first communions and just in time for the summer term at school.

A sense of permanence

On the other side of Kells is the metropolis of Navan. Pierce Brosnan may well have lived in Navan as a child, but for the most part Navan is not the world's most exciting place. Before the M3 motorway was built I spent months trying different ways of avoiding Navan; until I realised, with Kells comes Navan – they're a package deal. Navan is one of those annoying places to drive through and on top of that, the shopping is uninspiring. When Ed needed shoes I couldn't find any as the spate of First Communions had consumed all the footwear in Navan. In every shop I was told that black shoes would be back in stock in three months' time. While Ed was trying on shoes at Jack Kiernan & Sons in the main street, we found more than what we had bargained for. The O'Daly disappeared for a minute and re-appeared from the back of the shop strutting a chic travelling coat. I was impressed to see such a beautiful coat in Navan, and it suited the O'Daly perfectly. One thing bothered me though, we were in a shoe shop and shoe shops do not normally sell coats. As the O'Daly was trying out the pockets for comfort, he discovered a few Euros in one of the pockets. He also discovered that the jacket belonged to the owner of the shop and in the nick of time slipped it back on the hanger before the mistake could be discovered.

With our first spring in Ireland I became filled with an indescribable feeling of joy that woke me early in the mornings and kept me awake until late in the evenings. I loved the thrill of the long evenings; a courtyard alive with children on bicycles and rollerblades; bird chatter in the trees; a playful feeling in the air; and being able to witness the tiny steps of a new bunny.

Spring is the time of year for delicate daisy chains, rhododendrons in colours of watermelon, cerise, white and red; and poppies sprinkled like drops of blood against the green. Spring is also the time for buttercups to cover fields and lawns with their yellow. There is something about a solitary white horse surrounded by a field of buttercups; the beauty of white and yellow – of grace in action. In flower boxes Iceland poppies were waiting in patience for the Busy Lizzies to join them in a burst of summer colour. I didn't like it when the gardeners at Headfort had to mow over the buttercups.

Our home in Ireland became a port for friends on pilgrimage, and from time to time our house turned into a monastery for a day or two. When three friends we met in Greece arrived, we travelled to the Hill of Down and hired a barge for a return trip down the Royal canal to Furey's Pub a couple of miles further east. Our trip started at a small B&B and coffee shop close to the O'Daly's home place. The sky was mixed-up and as we took off in the "Lily Pad" the jovial owner, Irish tricolour and flittered Japanese flag were there to wave us goodbye. The speed limit on the canal is four miles per hour, and our skipper for the day was the O'Daly. For this occasion he was dressed in his favourite bush look: short khaki trousers, khaki shirt and jacket, and his beloved Indiana Jones hat. Earlier in the morning he added the hat as final touch to his ensemble, or so he thought. En-route to the Hill of Down the O'Daly discovered he was still wearing his slippers. There was no time to turn back, and no shoe shop open in any of the two villages on the way. On this day our skipper was going to be "slippered."

The barge was our home for most of the day: a friendly tinker's house with yellow gingham curtains at the small windows, a blue roof with two wicker baskets with a few sorry looking petunias, and a peculiar toilet the O'Daly had all to himself as only he could master the complicated pumping flush mechanism. The day was both wet and dry, and warm and cold. During the wet bits our skipper's slippers got drenched - this was not a day for short trousers, let alone fabric slippers. We didn't mind because we were inside and happy and eating Kimberley biscuits and drinking Druids Celtic cider. More or less halfway to our destination we collected another passenger – one dressed entirely in black with a crocheted tea cosy hat on the head and cigarette in the hand. After two hours we reached Furey's Pub and filled the large holes in our bellies.

On the way back we took turns to steer the barge as it chugged past Lily Pads and a line of fishermen. Every few yards a fisherman sat on a fold-up chair with a Carlsberg beer, fishing rods, fishing net and expressionless face tucked in under an umbrella. They did not like the Lily Pad because it disturbed their solitude and scared the fish. We even had to negotiate a lock in the canal: working a lock made way for roguish thoughts of leaving the lock open on our way through and imagining all the fish escaping through the lock and the water flooding the unsuspecting fishermen.

I loved the small skipper's seat, and when it was my turn to steer, I loved how my thoughts bounced off the blue roof and the chug-chug of the motor and filled the sky.

During my morning walks at Headfort the brown cows always lined up along the fence. Here they met me with their big eyes, long eye lashes, white tongues, big nostrils and cow hearts. When I talked to them, they listened. They never stopped chewing when I talked, and when I moved they moved. When there were two of them, their heads would move from left to right like spectators at a tennis match. As a city girl I struggle to come to terms with the final fate facing cows – that someday they will end up at a meat factory, their tennis heads mowed down like the buttercups at Headfort; unable to listen anymore.

Recharge

We found summer at our apartment in "*Thesi Pikragouria*" or "Bitter Cucumber" in Diminio. Rumour has it that someone once tried to grow cucumbers in the area but the crop was a bitter failure, hence the name "Bitter Cucumber." In Greece, to "encounter a cucumber" means to encounter a problem. In the bone-dry Seliandros riverbed in Diminio we found no cucumbers. Our little nest was ready and waiting with its custard yellow walls and white balconies – spick and span in the harsh brown land. On the other side of the laneway the sea was only a stone's throw away.

We arrived in Hellas at the crack of dawn one Saturday morning with the usual fuss of having to acquire a whole heap of crucial things before the shops closed at 2pm. At Coco-Mat in Corinth we found our beds and the delivery van but no driver; Kris was in Amsterdam setting up a new shop and Mrs Coco-Mat had no license to drive. So on this blistering day the O'Daly became delivery man in the white-and-green Coco-Mat van, picking up pieces in the busy streets of Corinth and transporting them to the many marble steps in Diminio. The O'Daly knew about the cryptic *kremidi* (onion) for turning left and *skordo* (garlic) for turning right; this inside knowledge always blew the minds of the locals.

I arrived in Hellas with a nasty throat infection – a cross between mumps and tonsillitis – and for the first couple of days I moved through the 40 degree heat unable to swallow. All I could manage was to lift my eyes over the balcony in order to keep watch over Ed's pair of orange armbands and Ruby's blue flippers in the water below. To the one side of the apartment is a sprawling residence with rickety chicken coop, chickens and two angry dogs; and our favourite rock beach. Every time we picked a different secluded spot to park our green umbrella – a white marble rock for back support and the clear water at our toes. To the other side is a dilapidated pink house with a geranium almost as tall as the roof, and a pair of walking boots at the front door. Here is a more civilized beach with sand, loungers, umbrellas, beach bar and *taverna.* I always wonder about the two leather boots and the many stories they hold inside.

During our first days in Diminio all we wanted to do was hide the colour of our Irish skins – we were desperate to blend in. For six weeks we followed the many familiar roads on our threadbare map of the Peloponnese; picking up strips of memories and bits of our hearts along the way. Nafplio: camping under the trees on Karathonas beach and the taste of frappes with a view of the magic Palamidi fortress at night. Monemvassia: one of our best-loved places on earth with its otherworldliness and pastel magic. Gythio: juniper, hibiscus, lemon, olives and a magnificent swim in a diamond sea next to the shipwreck on remote Selinitsa beach. According to legend a giant octopus guards the secrets trapped in the rusted belly of the wreck. Mavrouvouni: a full moon left a silver path on the sea and allowed my thoughts to dance into the night. Mani: magnificent stone tower houses against the backdrop of unforgiving Mt. Taygetus and a view of the gorgeous Messenian Gulf. And Xilokastro: the excitement of finding a new beach where previously there were rocks. Patriarch Panos left no rock unturned when he built his apartment block at the edge of the sea – he always wanted a beach nearby so he created one.

We also travelled on some new roads, and near Sparti found Mystras, an amazing fortress-state on the northern slope of Mt Taygetos. The fortress-state is crowned by the original castle on top of the hill and a network of paths trace through three tiers of ruins, descending from royalty to nobility to commoners. The walls of Mystras hold six centuries of rich and important history that kept Greek civilization alive during the dark period of 1200 – 1830. Its ruins reveal a city of Byzantine churches (with gorgeous frescoes), chapels and monasteries.

The cultural development of this fortress-state played a noteworthy role in the formulation of humanist theories and artistic trends in the 15th Century Europe. With the invasion of the Turks in 1460, Mystra's glory days were over, and by the early 19th Century the city had crumbled into ruin. Mystras managed to survive until 1825, when the fortress-state was completely destroyed by the Egyptian armies of Ibrahim Pasha. The new Sparta was built shortly thereafter and Mystras was abandoned and never resettled. Unfortunately we arrived too late with not enough time to settle in.

There was a desire to return to Ikaria, but instead we decided to meet the General's clan at their other base on the small Ionian island of Paxi. However, days before our intended departure we received an urgent SOS from the *yiayia* (grandmother) that the house was infected with man-eating rats and our safety could not be guaranteed. Paxi was not going to have us, so we moved our island hiatus to Lefkada. The kids and I left Diminio on the slow road north: a drive along the Gulf of Corinth coastline to Rio; a short ferry hop across to the mainland; and from Antirio to Lefkada through impressive mountains, green valleys and fertile countryside.

Until 427 BC Lefkada was part of mainland Greece when the inhabitants dug a canal and made their home an island, presumably to keep visitors away. However with the new bridge in place many tourists flocked to the island and as a result tour busses, roll-along suitcases, foreign languages, mopeds, and gaudy shops crowd the main spots.

The island is beautiful: a landscape smothered in green, with high forested mountains and lush vegetation that reach all the way down to the shores. There are many fertile plains with citrus trees, olive groves, vineyards and cypress trees. The coastline varies greatly: in some places there are steep white cliffs and in others magnificent beaches with fine, white sand. The price of property on Lefkada is determined by the number of trees on the property. Every inch of available land is covered by trees; they are not cultivated and allowed to roam free.

To the east of Lefkada are the islands of Skorpios – the property of the late shipping magnate, Aristotle Onassis; Madouri with writer Aristotelis Valaoritis's mansion; and Meganissi with its three caves. During World War II the submarine *Papanikolis* concealed itself in one of the caves with the same name.

I preferred the quieter places on the island: amazing mountain drives on nothing more than windy goat tracks; an unforgettable early evening lunch and *retsina* under a massive plane tree on the Plateia in remote Karia in the mountains; the sight of thousands of windsurfers at Vasiliki beach (the beach was deserted!); a swim at Agios Ioannis under the watchful eye of several windmill ruins; the solitude of the countryside; and two memorable dinners next to a grand line of yachts at Sivota. Despite the many affluent heels that move through in summer, Sivota has remained relatively unspoilt - a gem. At Kathisma beach we swam in blue with no name; a blue you could taste. With the taste of blue without a name in my mouth I knew my straw beach hat would never settle for anything other than magnificent in the future; and my swim skin for anything less than velvet. I will never forget the view of the Ionian Sea from a mountaintop: I was unable to distinguish between heaven and sea, and unable to know whether a delicate white sailing boat was in fact on the water or in heaven.

After the buzz of a summer in Lefkada it was bliss to arrive back in Diminio; back to the lightness of our home; the breeze in the candyfloss curtains; and the view of the perfect pink sunsets over Xilokastro. Our Gulf was nearly always like a gorgeous big lake and floating on the crystal clear water felt like heaven. In the wink of an eye I could lose my thoughts and senses to the sea. As far as the eye could see heads would float on the water until late into the night. But sometimes the sea would demonstrate its sea-ness with a display of waves and white foam. On those days the water's colour would change to green and the Greeks would give the sea the cold shoulder.

On our last day in the cucumber place the sea became angry because it was time to leave. It was time to swap sun, salt and sea for green. It was time to pick up the last of the summer threads in Kells. How I love the blue and brown of the Peloponnese. How I adore that harsh land.

The west

The fish arrived with a bow and a four year old birthday card and from the very first moment he became mine to mind. Our relationship was not a good one; he was gold and I did not like him or his smelly food. I often threatened to let him free in the courtyard's fountain pool but this idea horrified the O'Daly – a man who himself flushed fish down the loo in the past – and he would not hear of it. He thought the fish would like to stay mine. During our summer vacation we had to find a foster home for the fish. Friends of ours volunteered and welcomed the fish into their temporary home, a bland house that in the past had witnessed several suicides.

The fish did not behave and during his sojourn in Navan kept all members of the family running from morning till night. He would not stay in his bowl; at mealtime he tried to join them at the table and at night he tried to get to the TV. He refused to be a fish. On D-day, minutes before I was due to collect him, he leapt one last time and landed in the kitchen sink. This time there was no-one to save him. I wasn't sure whether his death was a wish not to return to his home at Headfort or whether it was the curse of the house.

During our visit to Greece Ed's daily trip to the loo became a notable event; a process advertised to the world. He would close the door and launch into a full repertoire of songs; each one sung at the top of his voice. And his little cheeks would bulge with all the notes and the noise. He always ended with the Irish Anthem, the cue that the job was done.

Also in Greece he nagged us for a small big fishing rod; definitely not a toy rod, but a small real one. We found one and he tried a couple of times to fish from the beach in Diminio. He caught no fish but plenty of amused stares from the Greeks: here was a determined little fisherman, the only boy in the whole of Greece in a one-piece swimsuit, and the only boy fishing on the beach where everyone else was either swimming or lazing in the sun.

Ed's little big fishing rod inspired his father to dig out his own rod, and collection of flies. With fishing high on the agenda we decided to end our summer in Connemara, one of Europe's most westerly peninsulas.

We followed small country roads on the back of big ominous clouds through bog-standard little places such as Collinstown, Castelpollard, Coole, Edgeworthstown, Lanesborough, Ballymoe, Williamstown, Cloonfad, Claremorris, Hollymount and Ballinrobe; places little more than a mouthful of words. The countryside was quiet and as we travelled from East to West, the wide fields and flat bogs of the Midlands gave way to the rich farmlands of east County Galway. And the ditches and hedgerows separating fields gave way to dry stone walls.

We stopped for a picnic in the tiny village of Neale, home to the notorious Charles Boycott, retired British Army captain and land agent to Lord Erne. In the 1880s Boycott tried to raise rents – and the people responded with Land League unrest. Charles Steward Parnell - uncrowned king of Ireland - organised the Irish peasantry in defiance of offensive landlords. His first such target was Captain Boycott, and as a result a new word was added to the English language.

On the narrow spit of land between Lough Mask and Lough Corrib we discovered the quaint village of Cong. Cong is home to an abbey (founded in 1128), Ashford castle, dry canal complete with locks (a failed famine relief project), running trout water and lush vegetation. The Congers are also obsessed with *The Quiet Man*, a film starring John Wayne and Maureen O'Hara shot in the village in the early 1950s. Cong is in a Gaeltacht area where they speak Irish and signposts are mostly only in Gaelic.

Beautiful Lough Corrib divides Galway in two: tame, fertile land to the east and the wild Connemara terrain of wind and rock and water to the west. The further we travelled into County Galway, the smaller the fields and the wilder the countryside became. In Connemara the landscape is a patchwork of tiny plots of land with dry stone walls, the thread that holds them together. Connemara is not about great sweeping seascapes or ancient mountains shrouded in mist, but about tiny meadows surrounded by thousands of miles of stone walls against the rugged land. Due to the poverty of the land Connemara is sparsely populated. There has never been much to attract marauders or colonizers, and any incursions have involved a battle against the terrain as much as against the people.

By the time we reached the final stretch of our journey, the ominous clouds had swallowed the late afternoon and we were left to negotiate the windy roads in a grey drizzle. In Letterfrack we turned and followed the hills to where they disappear into the Atlantic. Here we found Airde-Spéir.

Airde-Spéir is a farm so remote and so beautiful it can be described as a slice of heaven. The views from the farm are endless: a wild and wonderful stretch of Atlantic shoreline; Inishbofin, Inishark, Omey, Cruagh and Clare islands out to sea; Twelve Bens and Maam Turks mountain ranges; and a vast open area of bog wilderness. The farm consists of a stately old manor house, a family with a band of boys, forests, a lake, green meadows, a blow hole, a stone-walled garden, horses and a foal, a couple of dogs, chickens, guinea fowl, fluffy sheep and a room full of fishing gear and wellies.

The entrance to Airde-Spéir is unmarked and special instructions will lead you to it. But the moment we drove through the inconspicuous black gates, through a forest, down the long laneway lined with orange Mombretia, we knew this was special. The large walled garden is home to wild shrub beds and an organic vegetable patch with apples, pears, peas, rhubarb, gooseberries, carrots, spinach, potatoes, beetroot and curly cabbage. Every morning a big basket collected fresh produce for consumption during the day. Behind the stone wall were the gentle purple and pink of heather against the peat land; and the sheep woolly dots against the rugged hills. From Airde-Spéir the next stop is America.

Airde-Spéir is close to the tiny fishing village of Cleggan with its houses clustered around the harbour. In 1927 twenty-five fishermen from the area drowned during a freak storm while fishing for mackerel. This had a devastating effect on the local community and all that remain are poems and stories and old granite ruins exposed by weather and time.

Connemara is a place you visit for its scenery rather than its history. Augustus John described it as "the most beautiful landscape in the world": Fuchsia-flooded laneways with a spectacular red and the delicate colour of Harebells, Birds foot trefoil, Purple Loostrife, Meadowsweet, Yarrow, Dancing ladies and Field Scabious against naked stone walls.

Our few days on the farm were memorable. During the day some of the children would disappear mud-boarding down the mountainside, dodging bog holes such as the one that swallowed a horse earlier in the year. They arrived home much later, completely black, but because they were not swallowed by a bog hole, I welcomed the black. Some of us would go for a walk to the edge of the sea and others would fish in a little boat on the lake stocked with brown trout. Ed was out of his skin with excitement when his little big rod caught six fish. Dinner was in the conservatory under a vast night sky; smoked trout, parmesan, balsamic vinegar, Indian spices and fresh vegetables.

We spent our last morning at Fountain Hill beach near the black rocks of Claddagh Duff, a gorgeous secluded beach with pearly white sand and crystal clear water. In the sky a few flimsy balls of cotton-wool were attached to the blue. I floated in the gentle water and even though on this occasion blue had a name and the water was extremely nippy, this was also paradise. Diminio was a thousand miles away. On the edge of the beach were cows in the meadows; a thatched cottage with a red door; and the stone walls were bare and silent against the green. Oscar Wilde once said – "Connemara has a savage beauty."

My body tingled all the way home; in our car fresh free range eggs, six brown trout and a jar of beetroot relish. What a perfect end to our first summer in Ireland – it was time to return to autumn in Headfort. It was time to load the car with Ruby, a blue guitar, enormous green suitcase with brand new pleated tartan skirt, green jumpers, blazer, black academic gown, surplice and 144 name labels, and take her to a new life at a boarding school in Dublin.

With the beginning of the new school year, life had the habit of returning to the more mundane. As I was beginning to explore new business opportunities I needed some help with the housework. She arrived on a Tuesday in a metallic blue Mercedes 230E to clean our house. Barely three bricks high and beautifully groomed, she liked to talk about her holidays abroad. I could only afford a couple of her hours a week. When I met her first, she told me she didn't do to-do-lists and that she could quite easily quit at a moment's notice if a list of instructions was to await her arrival. Whenever her Mercedes pulled up, I put on my runners (aka running shoes) and took a long, long walk.

Autumn in Ireland can be glorious: spectacular mild days with a pale blue sky. When this happened, the pansies in our window boxes were thankful for the reprieve. They knew that when the evenings were starting to get shorter, it was only a matter of time before Jack Frost moved into Headfort. The beginning of the new school year always brought life back to Headfort School after the long summer break. I loved seeing the red and green sports shirts, white horses, helmets, hockey sticks, skateboards and children full of life about the place.

One person in Kells was never happy when the schools returned. Taxi driver Paddy Maguire reckoned the mothers on their drop off runs were like heifers in the field; all the time congregating for a little stare, pause and a chat. The school moms irritated him so much that it left him with a "contrary head." And a man with "an angry head on him" was never a good sight.

At Headfort I got my first introduction to the concept of a charity auction. The Irish love charity auctions and they sneak them into almost every occasion. At one such an event the O'Daly bought a family tennis weekend in the North, and during a school exodus weekend we took the road North through Counties Monahan, Armagh, Tyrone and over the Sperrin Mountains to Co Derry. I never realised that the two names Derry and Londonderry depended on which side of the fence you were. The O'Daly recalled the time when fighting was frequent and ferocious in the bandit country on the other side of the border. Somewhere near godforsaken Draperstown we were stopped at a roadblock: soldiers in camouflage gear with serious guns pointed at our faces while a platoon of camouflaged eyes stared from positions in the fields on either side of the car. As we were approaching the roadblock they were listening to our conversations about tennis and a weekend in the Sperrins.

After the roadblock the bleak road took us up the mountains and at one stage we thought we had landed on the moon. There was no sign of life: for miles and miles no vegetation, no animals and no people. At the edge of the plateau the road pointed straight down the mountain on a fine ski run into Dungiven. Here the landscape settled into the familiar Irish pattern of small settlements and fertile farming land.

We found our tennis family in a huge old rectory with 13 bedrooms in the stunning green countryside of Claudy. I was apprehensive to arrive at the home of complete strangers and move in with our suitcases and two outdated tennis rackets that felt all too much like shovels. Our bed was the size of an aircraft carrier with a spectacular view of the meadows and rolling hills.

We played tennis most of Saturday with breaks for tea, *ciabatta*, beetroot soup, ripe French brie and a delicious Sainsbury's spread. The coaching was intensive and good, and at the end of the day my muscles could not move. At night we bonded in front of the Aga or the big open fire in the drawing room. On Sunday we had time for a quick warm-up before the rain moved in. In Claudy we fell into such a generous welcome that we couldn't help but leave with painful muscles, an Internet address for rackets, and new friends.

Ruby took little time to settle into life in the close-knit school community at the edge of the deer farm in the Dublin Mountains. She had to make peace with the food, the new routine and school on a Saturday. And she reckoned her black gown was useful to hide her nose when there was a bad smell, or mop up the mess from a fountain pen leak. One stormy Sunday evening we attended the annual battle of the bands at her school. Ruby was the emergency bass player in the freshman band. It took us a while to understand that the emergency had already taken place and that she was indeed a full member of the band.

A week before the battle the freshman drummer broke his finger and the lead singer his voice. This meant they had to find both emergency singer and drummer. The odds were stacked high against Ruby's band, but on the evening the school hall was packed with anticipation and school kids in uniform. And then the band 'Nothing Yet' appeared on stage with its lead-guitarist half the size of our Ruby, an emergency drummer, and a rock chick with a borrowed blue base guitar. The rock chick was our Ruby.

At that moment I remembered a young girl with a blonde straight fringe, bare feet, leggings, and a voice that struggled to find the right pitch in music. The moment was surreal: a stage, Ruby's black shoes tapping on the wooden floor in rhythm to the music, her mouth at the microphone, and her fingers on the strings of the blue guitar given to her by her Oupa. I had to pinch myself in order to believe my eyes. At the end of the song all the students jumped up and cheered for the emergency band, because they were good and the students were able to recognise bravery. The moment left us stunned. The young girl with the straight fringe had grown up.

In the autumn the squirrels at Headfort scramble to collect enough acorns before the cold settles in. When the days became shorter I was desperate to keep summer inside our house with new paint. I painted with colours with names such as sunrise, laughter, summer picnic and aqua source. Painting was a first for me, and I found the process very therapeutic. I loved opening the tins, and imagining the paint on my tongue and the colours lining my mouth. I could taste the sweet memories of summer.

With the school back in session Ruby's bicycle became wrapped in the silver threads of a spider's web; no longer able to move. In the garden the Liquid Amber was dressed in red and the rhubarb leaves were gone. The O'Daly's flower bed was unfinished and looked suspiciously like an open grave. Somehow I could sense some change in the winter air – I could feel it in my bones.

Hospitals

Taking Granny to have her new knee checked out took a roundtrip of six hours. These trips were my duty because I was known as the famous driver. They were astonished that anyone could drive 40,000 miles in little over 12 months in a place four times the size of the Kruger Game Park in South Africa. So whenever the envelope with the appointment arrived, I loaded the granny and the straight leg in my car, and traipsed along the back roads to Cavan. Like in Greece, I could only ever manage one such outing in any one day.

In Waiting Area One of Cavan Hospital all eyes were fixed on the lady behind the reception desk, as if she was about to deliver an address. For a brief moment the attention moved to the glass door to inspect our arrival. Everyone sat cloaked in the hope something would happen. Tea and sandwiches were sold through a small serving hatch at the back of the room

– sandwiches with the taste of disinfectant and waiting. In the X-Ray waiting area there was a deadly silence – as if words were squeezed from the air. On a chair a young boy was fiddling with a couple of coloured pegs, locked in his lonely world of autism. He rocked and hummed, and when his rocking and humming reached a crescendo, he turned and walloped the granny next to him. When it was his turn to be called, his mother dragged him shouting and screaming from the boundaries of his world. Like everyone else, I sat as though nothing had happened.

And then a jovial old chap and his wife arrived and broke the silence with a hearty laugh and a discussion about the weather, a recent death in Navan, and the ridiculous long road to Cavan. In Waiting Area Two more rows of people were pasted along the one side of the corridor. Every time the door opened, a doctor with stylish shoes, stethoscope around the neck, and a pink file appeared and mumbled someone's name in a foreign tongue. The announcement was invariably followed by silence and blank stares. Who were all these people and where did they rest their souls at night?

We slipped off to Hampshire in England for Halloween. The autumn countryside was spectacular: pristine villages such as Nether, Middle and Upper Wallops, Whitchurch and Stockbridge; beautiful flint-and-stone and Tudor houses; stunning thatch roofs; old mils; renovated barns; rolling hills; amazing autumn trees; many rivers; small stone churches and the impressive cathedral in Salisbury; a day trip on the Wizard Express under a cloud of steam and smoke; and a wonderful display of birds at the Hawk Conservancy.

Before the arrival of Christmas I was introduced to the boarding school nightmare of head lice. I was scheduled to check into the National Maternity Hospital in Holles Street for a hysterectomy, and before I could do so, I began to understand the meaning of fine-combing required to get rid of the nits.

The welcome at Holles Street Hospital unnerved me. On our arrival we were instructed to sit on padded green bench-seating in the reception area and wait until "admissions" returned to their desk. The automatic doors did not work and they allowed the bitterly cold December air to come in and fill the room. The waiting room could just as well have been out on the pavement of Holles Street. Around us big pregnant bellies came and went. A small walk away Grafton Street was bustling with Christmas shoppers.

When we entered ward six on the third floor my heart nearly stopped. There were seven beds on either side of a large room, with one space open for me, my blue holdall and soft red cashmere scarf. I never intended to become a hyster-sister in such a public environment; I never intended to join the ranks of the sisters in an old Victorian building without a heart.

I spent my first day after the operation in a morphine haze, held together by many pipes and drains. During the day the ward would become like Grand Central Station as it stretched to accommodate the additional day cases. Beds were squeezed in and extra pillows nicked from under heads. Visiting hours were restricted but many visitors stayed chattering until deep into the night. I gave a sigh of relief at night when the big lights were finally turned off.

Every night there was some commotion; anything from the anxiety of someone's premature baby taking a turn for the worse, to the frantic search with torchlight under beds and in bins for a missing belly ring. There was always something going on. And when we felt pale and quiet Mary would arrive with her food trolley and cheer us up. She liked to stir the silence with her blabbermouth – she wanted "happy bunnies" or "happy campers" in the beds in Ward six.

In Ward six we were all private patients waiting for one of the five private rooms. Every time someone moved out I knew I was one step closer to my own space. Finally my turn came to move out to one of the small rooms, three steps wide and five steps long with high walls painted in a nowhere pink. Suddenly tea was served in a little teapot on a tray with a paper doily, and a folded paper napkin accompanied my meals. So along with the three wire coat hangers on the arm of the TV stand, the doilies, and pink walls I began my solitary confinement.

For seven days my view was one of a bleak Dublin skyline; at night the sound of sirens and in the morning the cries of the seagulls. The build-up to Christmas did not reach Holles Street – the corridors were dark and sombre. On the walls were names of people who once moved through the place: Kathleen Mooney (1923), Mary Brophy (1909), Carberry Merriman (1918) and Margaret Hennessy (1900). I wondered about these people – names without faces.

A day before my scheduled departure the O'Daly arrived in a negotiating mood and secured my early release from confinement. He dropped me at home and left for Russia. After so much pink, the green at Headfort nearly burnt my eyes.

When I arrived home a consignment of natural body products from Greece was there to meet me. I was desperate to begin a new career, and this range of products was perfect for the Irish market. The idea to import the products into Ireland landed unexpectedly during a dinner on a small balcony in Athens some months earlier. After years in the corporate world, I never thought I would become entrepreneur and distributor.

We started the New Year with the O'Daly also stepping into the deep unknown of self-employment. And we marked this change by spending New Year's in a 150 year old stone farmhouse in Connemara – a stone's throw away from Airde-Spéir. From the house we had a wonderful view of the Twelve Pins mountain range and green fields sloped all the way down to the Atlantic. We wanted wild and stormy, and we got wild and stormy.

Delphi was the perfect hide-away. At Delphi Lodge we had a memorable lunch at the stately 20-seater dinner table, once adorned by Prince Charles. The lodge is a charming country house and fishing lodge at an idyllic spot at the side of a lake, surrounded by Connacht's highest mountains. In the early 19th Century the beautiful estate was the sporting playground of the Marquis of Sligo. While visiting the poet Lord Byron in Greece, Lord Sligo saw the Oracle at Delphi and was struck by the similarity between Delphi and his fishery at home in Mayo.

Our last day in Connemara was perfect: a mild winter's morning with a landscape so still it looked surreal. Connemara is one of the most beautiful places in the world. One last time we returned to Airde-Spéir and took our *wellies*, children and dogs for a walk down to the beach for satsumas and fresh air. The kids were sliding down the mountain in a slippery, muddy heaven until they were unrecognizable, while the O'Daly and a bunch of men went hunting woodcock and snipe. As the men disappeared into the countryside they looked like soldiers on their way to war.

I was relieved to see the back-end of all the cocktail parties; mince pie and mulled wine functions; turkeys; and Santa Claus. I was happy to know the Christmas lights on the crane outside Holles Street and the flashing lights on Ed's shoes as Joseph in the school nativity play belonged to another year.

These were uncertain times. Every morning and evening a noisy formation of wild geese stirred the silence over Headfort. At night a full moon kept guard over us.

A winter of discontent

I always knew we would be moving through Greece – pausing only long enough to scratch a little deeper, getting more familiar, and claiming a tiny piece of the land as our own. In contrast Ireland was different – the move here was going to be more permanent; somehow preordained. When we blew into Ireland, Headfort was already waiting for us, and yet, for the first 18 months I felt half-visitor, half-traveller. I wondered if there would be another call for one more detour somewhere else close to the O'Daly's work. He spent most of his week somewhere in Europe. For the first 18 months in Ireland my life had the taste of limbo.

During this time we shared our home with the disruption of the O'Daly's constant travelling. When I could not bear the single-parent-life one moment more I delivered an ultimatum and he returned to Headfort. For the first time we could start making tracks other than to the airport and back; for the first time we could put away our passports and begin to integrate into the community. At last we could begin the journey of getting to know the soul of this place. The time had arrived to begin the slow process of uncovering the heart of our new homeland.

Ireland is described as the "last bastion of the white man's soul." The Irish are known to have a pagan streak deep within. They live at the edge of an ocean and they can bend like bamboo in the wind. Everything has a flow and because the Irish are out there on the edge, little things do not matter. They are not hidden deep in some alpine valley with their neuroses; they are exposed.

In this exposed place we began the painful process of putting down new roots. We started in Kells. Connecting with the place was somewhat of a hit-and-miss; like playing a game of Monopoly, without the airport and station, and without the hand-out as you pass "go." In old-time Kells the family business still rules and shops still close between one and two for lunch. There is a dullness in the streets, a feeling of hopelessness. Shops are shy to display their wares and instead hide deep behind their inconspicuous shop fronts. One such shop sells knock-out soda bread, an award winning selection of wines, and funerals. A fresh batch of soda breads usually arrive on a Tuesday, and whenever we asked for a loaf of it on one of the other days, Mrs. Mac would refuse to sell us one as she did not think they were fresh enough to impress blow-ins. The shop counter is always jam-packed with freshly baked apple pies, coffee cakes and *fat frogs* on special. In the little room behind they keep the coffins. People shuffle in and out of the shop and depending on the day, you could be ordering your bread while someone else is sizing a "box." The septuagenarian Mrs. Mac loved to hold forth with the O'Daly on the "shockin" grammar of Ulysses and how to kill a mockingbird. When the two of them got going, they wouldn't even notice the frail old man trying to squeeze past with his soda bread in a Hennessey's cognac box.

Many of the shops are from a bygone era and sell anything from old-fashioned shoes and clothes, curtains, bed linen, knickknacks, solid fuel, loose sweets in glass bottles, and ice-cream wafers in "thrupenny", "six penny" and "nine penny" sizes. Ice cream and wafers are big business in this part of the world. It is a Sunday thing – the thrill of building your own wafer ice-cream.

The people in this part of Meath make up for the colourlessness of the place. Eccentric people can be found around every corner; like the actor who faithfully followed his dog to the bookies in Kells once a week, as if his dog was a guide dog. Or the neighbour who refused to go anywhere at Christmas because he did not want to leave behind his Christmas tree, dog, and parrot that rings like a telephone. Whenever he went away on business his parrot would ring non-stop to try and get him back.

Further afield in Navan a friend's clothing shop was so overcrowded, he was resigned to following the phone cable to locate the phone when it rang.

When he got a new cordless phone and the cable was no longer there to lead him to the handset, his phone ended up ringing in shirt boxes all around the shop. Or another who is obsessed with death and funerals – at the first whiff of a pending death, he drops everything and rushes to the scene, whether he knew the person or not. One night he almost got killed at the removal of a body and he responded with: "Sure wouldn't it be shockin if I went to see the dead man and there I ended up dead me-self." He always answered every question with "sure ye know yourself," or "sure ye don't know the half of it." Like wafer ice-creams, funerals are big in Ireland – people appear to die here all the time. At the first word of a death everyone rushes out to get a Mass card; "must get a mass card, must send a mass card."

In Dublin we found a business world so completely different to anything we had ever experienced. The similarities between Ireland and Greece were uncanny – and I began to understand why the Greeks refer to the Irish as the "Greeks of the north." The O'Daly was met with tepid enthusiasm; he discovered he was overqualified for the Irish market and was told his CV and experience befitted a Methuselah. In my case I felt a deep sense of insecurity – I had no idea who I was or what I wanted to do. The universe had pulled me out of a stream, and here I was no longer certain of what I was capable of doing. Joining the ranks of the "family" business was a new experience. In one go I became chairperson, personal assistant, IT manager, sales manager, warehouse manager, financial and delivery person; depending on who I was when I answered the phone.

Stamina was needed to settle into Greece; I never realised that the process of settling into Ireland would require a fresh dose of endurance. I was totally unaware that patience was beginning to weave its teaching through my life.

The winter of 2003 turned into a winter of discontent. We were both without an income; we had one computer between the two of us; one car to share; and I was slowed down by a recuperation process after Holles street that took its toll. We spent a month in hibernation from the harsh winter weather.

When a consulting job came, the business opportunity took us to Monaghan. In County Monaghan the countryside consists of many rounded mounds of land left by retreating glaciers at the end of the last Ice Age; small green drumlin hills like eggs in a basket. The hedgerows stitch their way across the hills – marking out the fields, and here and there little lakes provide change from the sameness of all the eggs in the basket. Historically Monaghan was part of Ulster, during the Partition in 1921 it became part of the Republic. In Monaghan almost everyone is either a McKenna or a Treanor, and it is not unusual for a McKenna to marry a McKenna and a Treanor to marry a Treanor. Because all the surnames are the same the locals are known by nicknames such as Willy of the Hill, Skin the Goats, Pat Fat, Suffer On, Concrete John, Toeheads, Heap of Clay, Red Owenie and Fagaharley.

Here we found the aristocratic pile of Castle Leslie where Paul McCartney got married, and Yeats and Winston Churchill once stayed. And the Castle became one of our favourite places. I even dreamt about living somewhere around Glaslough.

During our winter of discontent the children fortunately settled in and Ruby took up playing the bass guitar with a dream of becoming one of a handful of female bass guitar players in the world. At the Montessori school at Headfort Ed started ballet and he came home with words such as oesophagus, isthmus and "epigogelis" in his mouth. It appeared as if he was running the school and that the principal was only there to assist him.

Our home became an open place where people could fall in: train tracks and little boys in pirate boats in the living room; meetings in the dining room; Greek personal care products in the guest loo; candlelight dinners on a table guarding stationery and files; peat fires; vanilla tea in mugs; *Bobotie* and wine; laughter until wheeziness sets in; and a headmaster stretched out on the carpet over a cup of Barry's tea.

The winter was followed by the rhododendrons in glorious bloom, and brand new lambs in the fields. There was always something to remind me how precious life is.

Rainbows and a blue summer

When I opened my eyes to the warm touch of the Diminio's Bitter Cucumber I was in heaven. I spent the first six months of the year trapped in a fog of post-hysterectomy exhaustion. A fog so dense that not even a visit to Africa, or the arrival of the long days, or the colours of the rhododendrons could lift it. A fog so dense it swallowed me. And even the old toilet seat O'Daly tossed into our cozy fire one night and almost exploded our chimney, making all the neighbours came running to tell us our chimney was on fire, could not shift the fog.

But somewhere on the way from Ireland to Greece we tiptoed over the watershed and when we arrived in the Cucumber the horizon was clear. And what better place to start a post fog era than at the edge of the beautiful water. In the bittersweet blue of the Cucumber I could think again. And remember our brief trip to Africa.

My parents were at Cape Town Airport to meet us. Seeing them at an airport or a station broke my heart; I felt angry over lost time, and sad that I could not be with them to hear the days leave their marks.

We arrived with a little boy who no longer recognised his roots. For Ed it was all about an exciting journey to visit his *Ouma* and *Oupa* in Africa;

about seeing their neighbour John; about Ouma's special treats; and his small tree-house and ladder in the park behind the house in Rosenheim.

Rosenheim greeted us with a display of stunning late summer colours and fresh apple crumble and moist chocolate cake with caramel filling.

We spent our first few days near the southernmost tip of Africa in the shadow of the magnificent mountains at Hermanus. Between June and December a large number of Southern Right Whales flock to the shores of the Western Cape to mate and calve. I was hoping to see them, but unfortunately we were ahead of the giants, and instead enjoyed the beautiful coastline, the *fynbos*, white beaches and gorgeous sea at Walker Bay.

In Hermanus we discovered gems like Bientang's cave, a seafood restaurant in a cave at the bottom of a steep rock cliff at the water's edge. The cave is named after the last known Koi San Strandloper to have lived in the cave. According to legend Bientang lived there at the turn of the 19th Century and is said to have disappeared mysteriously. While living in the cave she was totally self-sufficient with access to the rich supply of seafood and running water at the entrance to the cave. Bientang was a very spiritual being with supernatural powers – she was able to communicate with animals. Pods of whales would return year after year to the cave; and remain there for months on end. Did Bientang's spirit attract the whales to Walker Bay each year? And how can I ever forget the taste of Cape *Snoek* basted with a caramelised apricot sauce grilled over the coals?

When the wind tried to blow us away we would disappear to the wine estates in the nearby Hemel-en-Aarde Valley for wine tasting. Alongside the famous Hamilton Russell Vineyards we discovered a number of sassy new vineyards.

Every day in Africa was measured; in the background time was always ticking by. When time is measured there is no reprieve – the minutes and the days race as if there is no tomorrow. We had no schedule, demands of expectations and for once enjoyed riding on the back of the flow. We enjoyed silly pleasures like Sodacream Sparletta fizzy drinks, speckled eggs, pink angel's kisses, Chomp chocolates, Provita crisp bread, Kellogg's Strawberry Pops, Damascus nougat and milkshakes in every possible flavour.

There was a memorable lunch under the pergola in the heart of old Stellenbosch; a view of Table Mountain at night, magnificent and serene in the soft light; a meeting with cheetahs at Spier Wine Estate; and precious time to catch up with all the family.

And then one grey morning we arrived at Bellville station for our train to Johannesburg. A short, round coloured woman with no front teeth greeted us with a big smile and announced that things were going well as "by the grace of God she was still on the right side of the grave." When we said our goodbyes she sobbed with us through the gap in her teeth. We waited in the cold for the colourful Shosholoza Meyl train to arrive. Behind the tall security fence my family waited to wave a last goodbye; a fence, a station and a train. The train arrived, picked us up and took us away.

We planned the train trip for our own train enthusiast, and because we wanted to experience the land and not simply fly over it as if the countryside did not exist. We wanted to see how much we remembered. So we spent 24 hours in the friendly company of the Shosholoza Meyl. Crowded shantytowns lined the railway all along the way until we reached the open spaces. As we moved through the land, small children with little or no clothes would wave at us and sometimes some of the little ones would show us the middle finger because we were in the train and they had nothing.

We snaked through the first autumn colours of the Hex River valley and through places such as Touwsriver, Matjiesfontein, godforsaken Leeu-Gamka, and Kimberley. In the Karoo we were rewarded with a glorious sunset on a vast, quiet land and through the open train window the African night was palpable. Like a *shongololo* (earthworm) the train passed through fields of corn and yellow sunflowers; and past the exact spot where some years ago an inebriated woman arrived at our picnic spot at the side of the road, removed her red stiletto, filled the shoe with rainwater from the brown puddle and proceeded to drink it. There are so many memories locked within the borders of my heartland.

On our arrival in Johannesburg we did not recognise the station – now presentable and secure. We arrived on a Sunday and the city was quiet. There was time for a fine banquet and a small top-up of Indian food before returning to the long days and end-of-school-year merry-go-round at Headfort. Besides, our summer holidays were waiting around the corner.

Our visit to Greece was going to be a short one; we wanted to do what every other Greek was planning to do – get as far away from Athens before the start of the Olympics.

We joined friends for a day trip to Arcadia province with its dense forests, light sprinkling of red-roofed villages and lonely monasteries. Our trip took us to Dimitsana, a little village perched on the side of a steep, rocky pine-covered mountainside. The Greek Revolution started in Dimitsana and the village claims to be one of many unofficial first capitals of Greece. From there we proceeded on to the narrow, irregular cobbled streets of Stemnitsa. Stemnitsa also participated actively in the war of liberation, serving as a repair centre for all guns used in the Revolution. Stemnitsa too claims to have served as the first capital of Greece. We made a small detour to godforsaken Karitena with its crusader castle and where nothing moved in the heat.

Our drive home took us through small roads in lush forests – we could just as well have been in the Alps. In every clearing there were large congregations of coloured beehives. The O'Daly became obsessed with the hives and stopped every few miles to take photographs; trying to get the picture perfect grouping of hives. Not only did he have a thing for bees, but he also liked to banter with puns. For the entire journey the O'Daly inflicted "to bee" or not "to bee" on us and it nearly drove us insane. In Vytina – a ski resort in winter – we paused for delicious *tiropitari* – fried cheese pie, similar to a calzone pizza. We ended the perfect day under the night sky in Nafplio with *patates* with cheese, grilled lemon chicken, grilled pork and boiled zucchini flowers.

One of the highlights of our brief stay was the Euro 2004 football finals. We joined the Coco-Mat family at the Corinth beachfront to watch the semi-finals between Greece and the Czech Republic. The beachfront and *tavernas* were strangely quiet but we decided to mix football with dinner. Suddenly there was a goal and in a split second chaos erupted: a chap from the next table took off and ran across a number of other tables into the night; people were hugging and screaming; and firecrackers exploded all around us. We drove home on the back of a cacophony of hooters. Everywhere droves of people were draped in flags.

We re-joined the Coco-Mat family for the final. During the game a large truck went round and round the block sporting a huge Greek flag and an almighty hooter. After a nail-biting second half the unthinkable happened: the Greeks won the finals and an even bigger chaos erupted all over the place. For days after the victory blue and white covered almost everything and everyone. We loved being surrounded by such joy.

During every visit to Greece, we became more and more entangled with the place and the people. And it became increasingly difficult to leave. My life is in pockets, scattered over many places. And bits of my heart are stuck to each of those places.

Connemara menagerie

The doormat says "beware of the kids" and the moment you arrive at Airde-Spéir you know this is not a run-of-the-mill farmhouse. In fact, the moment you enter the gates and drive through the leprechaun woods, you know this is a magical place. A place where no-one will find you.

At the end of the long driveway is the grand old house. Once a hunting lodge, the house has high ceilings and many rooms – its face turned to the vast Atlantic. Airde-Spéir is home to a menagerie of animals: hamsters (some with sight and some without sight), tropical fish, a gundog, an old lady dog with a bad bladder, a German Shepherd called "Special K", farm cats, chickens, guinea fowl and chicks, horses, sheep, a gorgeous brown foal called Piglet, and a cockatiel named Charlie.

We were asked to house-sit the menagerie and to master the recycling and feeding routine. From the beginning Charlie liked the O'Daly and spent the entire induction time on his shoulders nibbling his ears. On our first morning on duty, Charlie lured the O'Daly with his charming collection of songs and as soon as he got out made his way to the tops of the cupboards, refused to get back into his cage and kept the O'Daly captive for four hours. He was never given another chance to rendezvous. But we still loved Charlie when he called us in the mornings, sometimes getting stuck on the high notes.

Morty, the farm manager at Airde-Spéir, knew everything "had a name on it" but didn't always know what it was. Morty didn't care because he had no desire to know the names of things. His wife was part-time housekeeper and sometimes she unpacked the dishwasher before the washing cycle had a chance to take place. This didn't bother her because she was unaware that the crockery and cutlery were still dirty.

In the big walled vegetable garden broccoli, broad beans, potatoes, carrots, peas, cabbage and every other vegetable imaginable grew within the seclusion and peace of the stone walls. On a clear night the moon came to check on their progress.

Everywhere Mombretia mixed with purpleloostrife and heather coloured the late summer countryside orange and purple and pink. We swam at Claddagh Duff under the blue sky until we had brain freeze and raced on the beach in view of the cows and the thatched roof house with its red door.

A short drive away we discovered the beautiful Renvyle Peninsula where ancient stone walls hold together long narrow strips of fields and keep the green from spilling into the sea. Blackberries, a calm blue ocean and the sweet smell of silage; what more could we ask for?

We also visited the busy little fishing village of Roundstone in the heart of Connemara. A beautiful drive took us past the spot near Clifden where Alcock and Brown landed in June 1919 after the first ever non-stop transatlantic flight; through Ballyconneely and on to Roundstone. The road follows the rugged coastline, past beautiful bays in turquoise. The countryside was crammed with wild flowers and in places resembled a moonscape with the silver grey of the rocks framed by golden furze.

In Roundstone the stone harbour has a view of the Twelve Bens of Connemara. Roundstone is home to the world's only full-time bodhrán maker, Malachy Kearns. A bodhrán is a goat-skinned drum-like musical instrument renowned for its perfect tone which produces the haunting, rolling rhythms in Irish music. Malachy's workshop is in a 16th Century Franciscan monastery and according to him "the sound of the bodhrán got me in the gut, because the sound of the bodhrán goes through to your gut, rather than your head." His mantra is "I know how to breathe, so I can drum," and he works to the rhythm of the ocean waves.

From Roundstone we followed the frilly coast of isthmuses and islets on to the vast open bog plain and home to Airde-Spéir. We planned our excursions around Piglet's feeding times. She always called for her food and afterwards would give the O'Daly a big milky kiss. In between we climbed the hills, followed the Olympics, or read in front of a big fire in the orange room.

I felt privileged to spend time in the folds of Connemara; to be close to its raw landscape. Back at home two schools and autumn waited for us.

Our little boy started at primary school. On his first day he skipped to school in his grey uniform and his tiny freckles looked like pin pricks on his cheeks.

Oberrieden

The first time I saw her in my Greek class in Kifissia there was something special about her. Something I could not explain – meeting her was not a mere coincidence and that our ways were meant to cross in that classroom over a foreign alphabet.

She was one of the top students in our class; being half Italian, half French, and married to a German gave her a knack for languages. Over many cups of coffee a careful friendship developed until we both left Greece more or less at the same time. She and her family returned to the order of Switzerland, and we traded chaos for green.

And then on one cloudy Thursday morning two years later, I boarded a plane and flew the short hop to Zurich. She was at the airport to meet me and from the moment we met we might as well have been back in Ekali or Dionysos or Politea. We were oblivious to the fact that it had been two years since our last meeting.

For two days we compared stories, photos, mid-life challenges and our children's growing pains. I told her about a little boy who believed he was half-African, half-Greek and half-Irish; who needed reassurance at bedtime that the Romans were not planning to conquer Ireland; and who thought the gravy at Headfort School was revolting. I told her about a bohemian girl who collected plectrums; and loved orange, Doc Martins and Jimmy Hendrix. I told her about the many boxes of Greek products that arrived in Kells and tried to squeeze us out of our house. And I told her of mending stands and flittered cardboard boxes, trying to make them look respectable before sending them out into the world; like straightening a child's clothes before you let them leave home.

The house in Oberrieden was high against a hill at the edge of a forest and overlooked Zürichsee. In the house breathtaking art and carefully selected pieces of furniture looked striking against the neutral shades and modern, stark lines of the architect's design. Everywhere bits of dazzling colour flirted with concrete and glass. And for a moment the bliss and perfection of Zurich was a wonderful change; a place spotless and serene; super and suave.

On the first day we did not leave the patio, afraid that if we moved our catch-up would slip away; afraid if we budged we would lose sight of the beautiful lake.

The next day we did Zurich. We parked in an underground parking garage where little red or green lights above each bay indicated availability, and a floor so spotless it could be licked. From a vantage point we could see the city, the Grossmünster and Fraumünster churches, and St. Peter-kirche tower with Europe's largest clock faces; the Linmat River and the beautiful rooftops. The last of the summer flower boxes were filled with red or pink geraniums; always in a single hue. We walked along the narrow cobbled streets; ate sushi in the Altstadt; walked over the Rathaus and Münster bridges; and got lost in Frans Karl Weber's toyshop and Jelmoni's fabulous deli. In the sun people were pausing at cafes over coffee; slick and sophisticated.

Back in Oberrieden we visited the local bakery, cheese deli and vegetable shop. Heidelbeer yoghurt, Zopf bread, conserve and a view of the lake for breakfast; pain paillasse and moschbrot, fresh Gruyere and a truffle brie that makes you groan for dinner; and for a treat Luxemburgerli, delicate small round meringues with a butter filling.

From their front door the green fields and forest were barely one hundred and fifty steps away, and corn fields and ordered allotments where the apartment dwellers lived out their garden dreams. Some sheds had a pizza oven on its small deck, and Italian and Ferrari flags on its roof. The little patches of garden looked like an organised shantytown hidden from the world.

I left the order and precision of Zurich with more Luxemburgerli, a tractor and three-axle-tipper-trailer, an orange Swatch, Sprüngli Grand cru chocolates and forbidden cheese in my bag. Back home the sky at Headfort was grey and grumpy. On the courtyard walls millions of black flies stuck to the warmth of the grey paint like pebble-dash. A sea of flies desperately trying to claw their way into our cosy home; frantic to get in so they could be somewhere safe to die.

In another corner of the courtyard at Headfort grounds man and caretaker Patsy was scratching around looking for the missing bit for his ladder. He was a familiar sight on the grounds, and he always stirred up a chuckle in me.

Green chaos

When we moved in we had a long list of improvements we wanted to do to our house. For more than two years we nurtured this list, at times some of the things on the list drove us barking mad. One day out of the blue the O'Daly announced it was time to make a start with the list, if only to give us hope that one day the list would no longer exist. He thought the way to a woman's heart is through her wardrobe, so he decided to replace the cupboard in my dressing room with a slick Sliderobe.

In addition to being home, office, meeting place, juncture, occasional healing centre, guest house and warehouse, the O'Daly thought our house needed to be building site as well. And without much notice boxes of products, stationery, and who-knows-what-else had to find space where there was no space to be found.

One night, with barely enough time to remove the last of my clothing from my cupboard and pile my shoes in the safety of a corner, Donal arrived with his blue toolbox and his silence, and ripped out the cupboard and chucked the debris out of the window. He did not stop with the wardrobe however. Like a man possessed he also ripped out walls, floors, tiles, shower, basin and toilet until the two rooms were one, naked, and wardrobe and bathroom were in a heap in the garden. Donal made an awful racket. The noise drew our neighbour out of her house with her bad head and fierce anger and she ranted until a bad taste was left in the air. At the end of the first night I found one room instead of two and a large mountain of rubble on top of my shoes.

Without any prior planning we found ourselves with a sizeable project and more than enough, as the Irish would say, to "do our heads in." We found Willy the tile mason in hospital with his irregular heartbeat and he had to check his diary through tubes and monitors. We also discovered that finding a plumber in this part of the world is near impossible; solid wood needs time to acclimatize in its new environment; containers do drop on and shatter ceramic tiles; Sliderobes need to be designed, measured, re-measured and made; and bathroom pieces need to travel for weeks before they arrive on site.

In typical O'Daly enthusiasm, as soon as the project started, work stopped again. He preferred the spur of the moment and did not like borders and boundaries; he was a Meath man with a big African heart.

The bitter cold of winter arrived before the warm colours of autumn could get a chance to settle into the countryside. In the autumn grounds man Patsy had to spend most of his day blowing away leaves. This was a particularly busy time for Patsy – he moved slowly and he gasped for air in the middle of his sentences. So he complained and gasped a lot when talking about the new leaves that awaited him every morning.

Winter is the time of year for coal fires, fleeces and hunts. On a grey, drizzly morning I attended my first hunt meeting as a spectator: there was mulled wine, lots of excitement, red cheeks, jodhpurs, riding boots, hounds and the most beautiful horses. The air was thick with pedigree, anticipation and steam from the horses. On this occasion I did not spare a thought for the "foxy gentleman" – I hoped he remained elusive, but I would be lying if I said I didn't love the drama, tradition, and the beautiful horses.

Winter is also the time of year when the men go pheasant shooting and the rock-chick became a beater for the first time; the time of year to receive home-grown chilies in a mail goody bag from friends in Greece. In winter the dark fell early on our chaos.

Grandfathers

I never knew my maternal grandfather – he died before my second birthday and all I have to go on are his diary and the stories and memories of others. In 1902 when he was only six, a band of British soldiers arrived at their farm and bundled him, his mother, siblings and two goats onto a wagon and took them to a concentration camp near the town of Klerksdorp in South Africa. They had to beg the English, who they referred to as the "Tommies," to allow the goats to come along because they needed the milk for their infant twins.

In the scramble they were given a few minutes to grab whatever they could find: small pieces of furniture and a few precious possessions. The last view this little boy had of his home was a house engulfed in smoke and flames. He was filled with fear and sadness and all he could do was cuddle his little dog, whom he had tucked away in his lap. As they left, a few remaining chickens and farm animals not slaughtered by the soldiers ducked for cover in the grass.

The journey to the camp was long and the little boy nearly died of hunger. He could not stomach the bully beef. He could not understand why they were taken away from their freedom. And for a period their home became a tent behind a barbed wire fence; their days filled with long queues for coal, food and milk rations, boredom and a bitterly cold winter. They shared their tents and their prison with annoying white ants. When the boy was not queuing for rations he spent his time playing with his little dog, Topsy. One afternoon two soldiers appeared, grabbed the dog from his hands, pushed him aside and disappeared. He searched for days but never found Topsy. This event traumatised him so much the pain never left his heart.

One quiet day his father and older brother arrived to collect them and they returned home with nothing. On the way there his father bought a packet of lemons and in his journal my grandfather describes the bittersweet taste of a first fruit; and freedom.

And then out of the blue my maternal grandfather's voice arrived on a CD all the way from Africa. After his death in the early sixties a recording of hymn singing during a synod meeting in Natal was heard on the radio, tracked down and copied onto disk. Above the crackles and rustles left by time his beautiful tenor voice came alive and filled our house. If only this little boy could have known that almost 100 years later his voice would reach a house in Ireland, thousands of miles away from the suffering of a concentration camp.

I also never really knew my paternal grandfather. *Oupa* Wiid was a stern man, always dressed in khaki, and wore thick spectacles and well-worn oxblood leather boots. His chest was always heavy with emphysema. Rumour has it that he went to school for one day and that on this day the teacher was absent. He was a formidable man who taught himself to read and write. He never managed to escape the farm to develop his intellect but instead remained stuck in the drudgery of farming in a remote part of South Africa.

I remember him sitting on the veranda – staring into the distance, or resting on the bench in the afternoon. At these times we had to be quiet so as to not wake his heavy breathing. After the sheep was slaughtered, my Oupa would sit with a razor blade and scrape the sheep's head for hours until the skull gleamed snow-white. The next day the head appeared on the dinner table and looked at me with two glazed eyes from under the mumbled blessings of grace. For the rest of our time on the farm I could not walk past the place where the slaughter took place, afraid to step on the death spot.

We always said goodbye to my paternal grandparents at the gate next to the avocado tree. And my Oupa would stand there with his walking stick, bad ankles and braces; inside his heart was breaking over our departure.

Ed does not remember his Irish grand Dá. At one stage he thought the Boss was God's assistant in heaven and that he looked after God's garden. When we took him to see the Boss' grave he started to dig because he wanted to find him and see him. Ed enjoyed telling his friends and his teachers about his *Oupa* in Africa; about his "big Mercedes" and that he loved the car because the inside smelt so fresh. He told them that his *Oupa* made him a tree house with a little ladder. The three languages confused our boy, and once he referred to his *Oupa* as his uncle. Uncle *Oupa*.

The O'Daly was grandfather to Ed's soft toys Ted, Donkey and Bunny. When Ed was a baby, green Ted joined our family all the way from Nottingham. He was loved so much that his hands became empty with all the loving, and his ankles heavy as the stuffing gathered in his ankles. Donkey was a Greek addition and when we lost him in the new Ikea store in Athens, Costa had to phone to enquire about the missing donkey. The switchboard lady dropped the call when she thought Costa was making a prank call; looking for a donkey in Ikea. We never got that donkey back – he disappeared forever in the Ikea maze. Santa Claus scooped up Bunny in the UK shortly before Christmas and dropped him in Connemara. The gang followed their "father" wherever he went, and they had to say "hello" and "goodbye" to their grandfather – the O'Daly – every day. He did not care when his friends would slag him at school about it.

Thinking of my two grandfathers I wonder how far Ed's reach will be one day.

Rainbow Easter

For three weeks the sky belonged to Africa. For three whole weeks we were able to fill the many gaps left by thousands of kilometres. We left a late winter in Ireland for our usual Easter break in South Africa and a desperate drought in the Western Cape. In the days before we departed a brutal cold spell arrived, robbed the rhododendrons of their first colours and left many of us sick with the flu.

I travelled with the horrible bug and spent the first week in a stupor of antibiotics, steroids and pain killers. During this stupor we visited the annual Afrikaans cultural festival in Oudtshoorn, capital of the Klein Karoo. We travelled on Route 62 through friendly, fruit growing, wine producing places like Worcester, Ladismith, Montagu, Robertson, Calitzdorp and Barrydale. The road took us through the Swartberg Pass with its impressive cliffs, craggy rock formations and beautiful scenery.

Oudtshoorn is synonymous with ostriches and there are 400 ostrich farms in the region. Oudtshoorn also has wide open spaces and broad streets and during the festival every inch of open space is filled with heat, people, music, aromas, art, crafts, high spirits, talent, colour and language.

We spent our last week catching up with my parents during a little break in Arniston, at the southernmost point of Africa where the Indian and Atlantic oceans meet. We travelled through countryside where both sheep and land were the same scorched brown. Arniston is named after one of the many sailing ships that foundered over the centuries on the wild Agulhas reef. In April 1815 the British troop ship *Arniston* set sail from Ceylon with a complement of wounded soldiers and some officers' wives and children returning home from the second Kandyan War. When the *Arniston* broke up on the Agulhas needles, only six of 378 passengers and crew survived.

Arniston (aka Waenhuiskrans, "Wagon-house Cliff") is best known for Kassiesbaai (its 200-year old restored fishermen's village and national monument), and its caves (as big as the barns in which the early Dutch settlers housed their ox-wagons) which are exposed during low-tide.

Arniston delivered white-washed houses, lush bottle-green shrubs, birdsong, seagulls and glorious peace. We spent our days on the soft white sand and rocks next to the blue sea. We raced on the beach and rolled down the big dunes. For a while the rock chick became a child and the two children built a mansion on the rocks amongst the rock pools. They dreamed up bedrooms, en-suite bathrooms, lounges, a swimming pool and even a garden. They knew that if they jumped off the garden into the sea they would jump off the heel of Africa.

We swam until well after the sun had disappeared. We were unable to tear ourselves away from the sea and the perfect day and leave behind the sea anemones, blue bottles, crabs, perfect round pebbles and our bright red starfish called Roy. At night we would be too frightened to close our eyes; scared that the blue would run out.

When it was time to leave South Africa we always scrambled to collect treats and special things. On this occasion we left with biltong (dried meat) leaves, speckled eggs, dried peaches, hundreds of bead bracelets and necklaces, township art and a striking painting of Ashkam-in-bloom in the Kalahari Desert. Also in my suitcase was my parents' 1946 Funk & Wagnalls College Standard Dictionary with its pages so brittle, barely able to hold the black ink between the two worn-out covers; on its pages were whispers left by two sets of fingerprints.

On the day we left the sky was blue. The plane took off and turned over False Bay, Cape Point and Bloubergstrand on its way north. As we crossed over the brown land Ed spotted Robben Island and the prison. On our visit to the island he was very taken with the place. He did not understand the significance of reconciliation or that the inmates were not robbers. He was eager to get one last look. I turned the other way.

Blue summer

Our consulting business swallowed both the O'Daly and I in its hungry mouth. The business swallowed me so completely that before long only my two feet were left sticking out. I was not able to write; for months and months my words simply bottled up, unable to get out.

By the time the summer holidays arrived we were in desperate need of sun and sea so we packed our business, kids and suntan lotion and moved to Greece. For the month of July our upstairs balcony became both command centre and creative den for our business. For the entire month a mobile data pipe was positioned over our house in Diminio.

At the Bitter Cucumber each day fell in exactly the same way: fresh bread from the local bakery for breakfast, stripy umbrella at the rocks for swim and sun, lunch, siesta, swim until the sun disappears into the sea, dinner and sleep. Some of us swapped the swimming and siesta bits with work. But what a pleasure to work against the turquoise backdrop of the Gulf of Corinth; what better setting to colour in the grey and blank spots of our clients' businesses?

During the first week or so a ferocious wind blew non-stop and stirred the sea into a mass of waves. On these days the locals would not venture out – only we Africans were brave enough to ride the waves. And then one day the sky held its breath and the sea became a mirror and stayed like that for the rest of our stay; at the Bitter Cucumber the days were pure paradise.

In between work we took time off to visit some of our favourite places. We toured the Laconian province and found new gems like the delightful Akropolis *taverna* in Sparti where *saganaki* (fried cheese) arrived in a flame of Ouzo, and where an entire feast for six cost less than two coffees and three Panini's at Starbucks in Ireland. We found the gorgeous whitewashed cottages on the beach at Selinitsa near Gytheio, where the day started and ended on loungers at the edge of the water. We returned to the small balcony against the rock at Monemvassia for classical music, a sunset and freddos; to Mystras and Dimitsana; consuming olives, fresh bread, cheese pies and more freddos on the way. And we found Kayak, the ice cream parlour where the aim is to have a few flavours of drop-dead home-made ice cream and freshly fried donuts, dripping in honey.

We made a couple of trips to our African Coco-Mat family in Corinth. Dinners in Corinth were special and our laughter and bantering made the waiter's day. I never saw Greeks roll with laughter, or guffaw; they were very composed when partaking in the fashionable dinner parade. We also celebrated a name day with dinner under a full moon at an amazing fish *taverna* at the edge of the sea in Neas Skios near Nafplio. This fish *taverna* was completely hidden from the world and only the locals knew where to find it. A number of stylish nightclubs lined the coastal road to the taverna where Athenians go to listen to their favourite performers without any restrictions on noise. We discovered during full moon there was no big fresh fish to order because at night they can see the nets and they know to hide from them. The little fish were silly enough to go looking for the light and then ended up in the nets, and on the dinner table. Across the bay, the Palamidi fortress was lit up against the night sky.

This time we took a ferry across the Gulf of Corinth for *freddos* in the gorgeous village of Galaxidi at the foot of Mount Parnasssos on the southern coast of the mainland. We meandered home via the coastal road to Nafpaktos where in 1571 the famous naval battle of Lepanto took place and then across the amazing Charilaos Trikoupis Bridge at Rio that connects the mainland with the Peloponnese. This bridge has the world's longest cable-stayed suspended deck and is considered to be an engineering masterpiece as the bridge has to deal with challenges such as seismic activity, the probability of tsunamis and expansion due to plate tectonics.

During our stay the O'Daly made a couple of trips back to the UK and Ireland. On one such trip he flew on a new direct flight on Malev Airlines from Dublin to Athens. He was the last passenger to board this flight and ended up on the last seat between a yob from Dundalk and an autistic lad from Belfast. The autistic lad was on a Seventh Day Adventist healing journey to Athens and the yob on his way to join his brother in a pub in Paros. The O'Daly did not feel like talking to either of the two guys so he made up a language and became the Hungarian, Janos. This baffled the yob who thought the autistic lad was a Seventh Day "Adventurist," and who had never before met a real Hungarian. When asked if he spoke English the O'Daly would respond with a mishmash of Greek, Afrikaans, German and the suffix "ski." The yob never detected that the O'Daly understood all the questions. Half-way through the journey the autistic lad's holy water started to drip from the overhead hold onto the O'Daly's hands, and when the Hungarian air hostess came to investigate, she almost blew the O'Daly's cover. The dripping of holy water on a pair of Hungarian hands freaked out the man from Dundalk as he reckoned this was some sort of holy sign. With this drama the four-hour journey became legendary.

While we were at the Bitter Cucumber our Chinese toilet seat broke. We discovered that in rural Greece they did not do toilet seats; in fact it seemed as though the Greeks had very little need for new toilet seats. Not only were toilet seats scarce, but we were unable to find a seat with the specific dimensions of a Chinese posterior. When we were about to give up we contacted our Greek HQ and command centre in Nafplio and late one Saturday afternoon – a moment before closing time – the O'Daly and Costa found a seat at a store on the outskirts of the town. The salesman was perplexed that a fellow countryman of Thin Lizzie and Skid Row could travel all the way from Corinth to Nafplio to buy a Chinese toilet seat. After dinner under the moon next to the Wisteria-covered wall we could go home and restore our Chinese throne to its former glory.

Our last Sunday was spent over a late lunch on our balcony. Friends from Athens came to visit and we did something we've never done before – have two lunches, one immediately after the other. Our friend produced a meal that some years ago landed her a husband. The moment we finished the last crumb of the first lunch we could not settle down until the men returned from a mission of finding more of the same ingredients so we could repeat the repast.

Life at the Bitter Cucumber was uncluttered and simple. The days were light and uncomplicated; the biggest challenge often whether or not to take the Lilo and beach chairs to the beach or how to last until nine o'clock when the *tavernas* open for dinner.

When we had enough of *karpousi* (watermelon), *aubergine*, *dolmadakia* (stuffed vine leaves), espresso ice-cream, *freddo* coffees, goggles and flippers it was time to go home. And when our souls were filled with enough sun to last us through winter we packed our creative den, command centre, kids, mobile data pipe and moved back to the small green place. This time I left with a copper Masai bangle and stunning red and blue glass vase in my bag.

Loss for words

I stopped using the dry cleaners in Kells. They wanted to analyse every spot and stain with a "What's this?" and "This!?" The person at the counter wanted to discuss each stain and then check with someone in the back of the tiny shop to decide whether or not to accept the spot. And all I wanted to do was drop the clothes and run – I never wanted our spots and stains exposed on a shop counter in Kells.

When Ed's first tooth fell out I spun him the story of the tooth mouse that uses little teeth to build houses, and he came home from school completely confused because in Ireland the tooth fairy reigns and he was not too sure whether this was all a lot of nonsense. So he decided to hold onto his tooth and no mention of money could change his mind. I forgot that the tooth mouse lives in Africa and somewhere between the fairy and the mouse Ed lost his faith.

Earlier in the year, around Easter, the O'Daly was attacked by gall stones. Some nights he nearly died with the nausea and pain. At first the specialists were unable to find his gall bladder, but several attempts and investigations later the stones were diagnosed and an operation was scheduled to fit in with his busy work schedule. Before we could say "Jack Robinson" the local network kicked in and gallstone cures appeared from far and wide. Ireland is full of cures for this and that and who-knows-what: Paprika with lukewarm milk; a legendary magic potion from a chap up the country somewhere; and a concoction made from Butcher's Broom. The latter cure came from a friend and rumour has it that the cure healed a friend of the family whose participation in the Moscow Olympic Games was threatened by gall stones. Rumour also had it that there was only one butcher's broom bush in Ireland and that it grew in a garden in the village of Tyrrelspass. So one day a packet arrived with 12 sprigs - each exactly two inches long - and a paper with instructions. We had to boil the sprigs for four hours and when our whole house smelt of pungent green, the liquid was mixed with an equal quantity of whisky. The O'Daly took the "muti" and became as drunk as a skunk, and the man who hardly touched alcohol had to be put to bed. In a green alcohol haze the stones went quiet.

Shortly after the drunken episode we met with the Offaly faith healers and they announced that the gall stones would be "zapped" and healed. On the eleventh hour the operation was cancelled and that was the end of the stones.

I went for my first bone density test in a mobile trailer – little bigger than a portable loo - next to the Catholic Church in the main street of Kells. At the mobile "Drop in for a breast-bone-blood pressure-cholesterol test" facility a guy with peroxide hair and the cut of a bouncer invited me in; a mobile phone was stuck to his ear and his trousers pulled up much too high over his belly. He continued to talk on his phone and pointed to a chair next to a small desk. Every time a vehicle passed the entire trailer would shake. I placed my foot in the scanner – it was shaped like a foot spa. He assured me the process would only take a few minutes and when nothing happened he became a little edgy, grabbed his mobile phone, and made a conference call for help. After a couple of "hmmm's" and nods he announced that the sole of my foot was too thick for the scanner and that never before had he come across anything like it. So I had to press down extra hard on one leg while the traffic on the N3 whizzed past. I chuckled because he did not know about my barefoot days as a child; he obviously did not see the label on the soles of my feet which reads: "Real leather – made in South Africa."

At the end of summer my parents came on their final visit to Ireland. I often wondered if they would be able to make this last trip, so I was overjoyed when they came and I could show them around our homeland. We shared two glorious weeks in gentle weather. I showed them where the McEntees sell their brown soda bread and coffins; where Jimmy does his stains; where the kids go to school; and where a neighbour keeps his 5,000 red hens. Every morning my father prepared a ruby grapefruit with precision, especially for me.

We visited the beautiful North Antrim coast, a land steeped in myth and legend. Our base was a comfortable inn north of Bushmills. The view was spectacular: rolling hills and shoreline fields that end abruptly in the sea. There was no gentle fusion between land and water - the green fields simply disappear down sheer drops and sharp cliffs into the sea.

During our two days in Antrim we explored the shoreline between Portrush and Ballycastle; and on our way saw sheltered harbours and slipways, small fishing hamlets, isolated ruins, kelp walls, limestone cliffs, impressive rock formations and magical headlands. The sky was open and the sea calm.

Our Inn was a stone's throw from the sea and the intriguing Giant's Causeway - an amazing array of some 40,000 basalt columns. The Causeway was formed 62–65 million years ago over a long period of igneous activity. At the time the causeway area would have been situated in an equatorial region with hot and humid conditions and the fascinating pattern in the causeway stones formed as a result of rock crystallization when the molten lava came into contact with the water. According to legend Finn MacCool, giant and reputed leader of the guardians of the King of Ireland, tore large pieces from the cliffs to build a causeway that would bring him to his Scottish adversary on the other side of the Irish Sea who was mocking him. When the causeway was built the Scottish giant had no choice but to come across the causeway and challenge Finn face-to-face. However, Finn's labour tired him out and he was not ready for fighting so he made a large cot, disguised himself as a baby and climbed inside and waited. When the Scott arrived he noticed the crib and the baby inside and full of fear of meeting the father of the massive baby he turned on his heels and fled back across the causeway to Scotland, destroying it as he went.

A stay in Antrim would not be complete without a visit to Bushmills distillery, and a taste of whiskey. The village of Bushmills developed with the water powered industries of the 1600's and became one of the main centres for corn, flax, spade and whiskey production. At one time the river Bush powered seven mills along its stretch through the village.

Every morning I went for an early walk while the countryside was still asleep and only the black-and-white cows were awake. This was quiet time. For miles and miles the coastline rested like a jigsaw puzzle piece in the water. I experienced sadness in the land and I wondered about the pain trapped within its soul.

On our last day the countryside was covered by a dense fog. We took the scenic road home through the Glens of Antrim; via Fair Head with its vertical dolerite columns rising to 600 feet above sea level where on a clear day you can see Scotland and the Mull of Kintyre across the Irish Sea. The tides that run below are some of the most treacherous in the northern isles; twice a day the Irish Sea ebbs and flows, sending billions of gallons of water between Ireland and Scotland. The sea looked scary and the small roads lined with pink fuchsia on the edge of the mountainside were nerve-wracking. Woolly sheep stuck to the mountainside like ticks on a dog's back. The scenery was breath taking. After espressos in Cushendall we headed home.

In Antrim my father's borders between Durbanville in the Western Cape and Ireland became blurred. He became anxious when he could not remember; and names, numbers, places and faces all became confused.

During the last two days the prospect of flying made him increasingly agitated. This made the last hours awkward and by the time we arrived at Dublin Airport my father was difficult because he did not understand why he was leaving or whereto he was going. Seeing such a fine mathematical brain unable to connect broke my heart.

At the airport the goodbye was swift. A friendly chap in a high-viz jacket arrived and bundled my father into a wheelchair and took him and my mother away. The send-off was a matter of load-up and go. Saying goodbye happened fast, and as the chap left with my parents all I could see was the back of a wheelchair and a flat-cap and my mother's trolley suitcase and her silver hair. Suddenly an airport departure gate separated me from them. I was unable to follow. On the way home my car was empty and I realised future visits to my heartland would be forever changed. The very next day the fall started in all earnest.

Piestany

We crossed over the Danube well after eight in the evening. A dense fog had claimed the land and all we could see was the darkness on the other side of the windscreen. It was mid-January and -10 degrees and we were in a burgundy car on our way from Vienna to the Slovak town of Piestany.

A close friend of mine had convinced me that a stay at a health spa was what we needed to lift the winter out of our spirits. And that is why four of us found ourselves in a foreign world with a taxi driver who could speak a few words of German and who drove like a maniac. During the hour-and-a-half drive to our destination in Piestany we spent as much time overtaking as we did driving in our own lane. Fortunately the road was as straight as an arrow.

Piestany is a spa town in the broad valley of the Vah River in south-western Slovakia. The health spa is on a resort island between two branches of the Vah and at the site of several hot springs (with temperatures between 67-69°C). The healing sulfate-carbonate water originates in a tectonic break 2,000 metres deep and bubbles up from the river banks. On the island tall trees and a large number of grand hotels and spa houses (with a capacity of 2,300 beds a night) line the footpaths.

We arrived at the Balneo Esplanade in fits of laughter, like four giddy teenagers on a school trip. And for one week I became "Madame Please," "Madame," "Please Madam," or simply "Please". On our first day the lack of spoken English, registration rigmarole and many treatment locations in the different spas overwhelmed us, and I was convinced I would never be able to know the "where", "when" or "how" of the place. My spa week started with a 9 a.m. visit to a physician, a brusque old bag who barked from behind her mask. Getting started meant waiting in front of a number of padded brown doors until called for; and then fumbling through the formalities until I received my program with completely random timeslots. Due to the affordable cost of the Slovakia Koruny, we were able to book loads of special treatments in additional to the ones included in the basic package. From that day on our lives revolved around our paper printouts.

Before we arrived in Slovakia we realized Piestany is not a beauty spa, or a place that would appeal to yuppies or fashionistas, or even appear in the luxury getaway features of glossy magazines. The place had the feel of a spa boot-camp for the masses. In Piestany they come with walking sticks, curved spines, wheelchairs, wrinkles and frozen knees; and they shuffle around in tracksuits, white gowns and Birkenstocks.

My first proper full day started with a Scotch jet bath at seven in the morning. I arrived in a large, bland room reminiscent of Auschwitz with a number of open cubicles - each with a green bath and a naked woman inside. While the rest of the world was asleep I stripped naked and marched the length of the room to a white tiled corner and positioned myself in front of the firing squad of the therapist and a jet machine. No music or soft lighting, no friendly smiles or small talk. While I held on to a bar on the wall for dear life, the therapist aimed a gush of water at me and every time she said "Madame, please" or "please" I had to turn. Whenever the hot water changed to icy cold, all I could think was "Jesus, Mary and Joseph – have mercy on me!"

I learned early on that marching around naked is part of the landscape at Piestany; and that nobody notices the jelly bellies, droopy boobs, cellulite or operation scars. The only cover available was a crisp white heavy-duty cotton sheet with the smell of a hospital. The cotton sheet was used to wrap patrons in a cozy, brown blanket-envelope after treatments. I was surprised to find the comfort of cotton on my wet skin.

As the days passed, my program sheet became more disheveled with all the opening and folding, the sulphur started to settle on my skin, and I began to feel new. I loved the stillness of the mirror pool and its hot natural sulphuric thermal mineral water; the time on a lounger in the microclimatic iodine salt cave made of natural sea salt from the Red, Dead, Black and Baltic Seas where 45 minutes inside the calm space equals a 3-day stay by the sea; and the amazing sulphur mud wraps.

My mud wraps always happened in the late afternoon when the facility was half-deserted and both men and women had to use the same section. The place looked like a ramshackle operating theatre with bright neon lights and as I hopped onto the bed in anticipation of the arrival of the mud man, I felt a sense of trepidation.

The mud man approached his "subject" like a surgeon, wearing gloves and white Wellington boots. He used a big hosepipe to spurt many kilograms of brown sulphur mud all over my arms, legs and body until I could not move. The treatment ended with a shower under a dribble of water behind a mud-stained plastic shower curtain, and a dry wrap under a warm blanket. And for days afterwards I had to remove bits of black mud from the smallest of crevices and creases all over my body.

The meals and set-up of the dining rooms were so dire that we abandoned them after the first two days. In between treatments we used to hang out in the hotel's coffee bar, or at night weather the below zero temperatures and leave the island across the rustic suspension bridge for a meal in one of the cosy restaurants in Piestany's city centre.

On Sunday we hired a taxi and took a trip to Bratislava. The landscape between Piestany and the capital was flat and soulless – all I could see was a dead straight motorway heading into the horizon. Shortly before World War One Bratislava functioned as a place of relaxation for the people from Vienna and the two cities were even connected by a high-speed tram. Bratislava was bleak with painful scars from communism very visible: a poor place with blocks and blocks of uninspiring, crumbling apartment blocks. We visited the castle which dominates the city on a hill overlooking the Danube; the castle stood guard over the city and it looked out-of-place above the incessant grey sameness of the many other buildings. The place was so drab and so cold that we went shopping in one of the city's few modern malls.

On the last day I braved a carbon dioxide bath. The carbon dioxide baths took place in a white space: the roof, walls, curtains, linen and therapist's clothes, clogs and hair were all white. Even the plastic bag I had to climb into was a thick white; the only colours were a red hosepipe and brass tap against the wall. Once in the bag the therapist secured the top of the bag tight around my neck to make sure I was completely enclosed in the plastic "oven" bag. And because I couldn't move I fell onto the bed like a bag of spuds. The therapist fed the hosepipe through the tight closing around my neck and opened the tap and filled the bag with carbon dioxide. Once during the treatment the gas was topped up. The thought of being found asphyxiated in a white bag in Slovakia briefly crossed my mind but within minutes my body was enfolded in a bubble of gas and I drifted off to a wonderful peaceful place. Next to me the heavy contended snores from a total stranger tore small cracks in the white space.

The carbon dioxide is supposed to increase the circulation in the limbs and improve the capacity of the heart. My treatment ended with a swift roll-down-removal of the bag (so that no gas could escape), a couple of minutes to catch my breath, and a drink of orange liquid; the orange a welcome centring point as I tried to return from the bliss of my white cocoon.

I smelt of sulphur when I boarded the plane packed with Slovaks, newly minted EU citizens en-route to a better future in O'Briens coffee bars all across Ireland. I felt brand new too; and I could never look at life in exactly the same way again.

There was something deliciously liberating in being lost in a space where there are no names or titles; no expectations or criteria; no noise or status; no pose or pretence. In the treatment areas there was very little spoken. In this mute place there was nothing to crowd out the soul. I loved the anonymity of the island and the fact that on the island the world did not matter. At the time I didn't realise Piestany would become a marker in the ground; that there would be a before-Piestany and an after-Piestany.

Back home reality greeted me with a "bang." When I discovered how unhappy Ruby was at her boarding school, the Piestany sulphur on my skin evaporated at once, and for a couple of weeks I was speechless. The timing was tense as Ruby's mock and Junior Certificate exams were looming on the horizon; they make such a big fuss about these in this part of the world. I reacted with Chinese herbs, reflexology, acupuncture and more traditional remedies to help her broken spirit. She had reached a point where she could no longer cope with the lack of me-time in the 24/7 schedule; where she could not fit into the "our community" mould; where she could no longer face a bitter and conniving bully who would not leave her alone; and where she was tired of a school so full of its own importance.

I began the process of trying to unlock the code of our Libran child; to try and understand her deep soul.

Rainbow Easter

We retreated to Africa for Easter, and for the first time in a long while spent a few days in Johannesburg. We stayed in a friends' house with a beautiful secluded garden and a blue pool, while they withdrew to the Natal coast. I was back amongst familiar voices, well-known pavements, vibrant colours, and energy of the people I love so much.

We had planned to visit a game reserve for Ed's sake, but in the end the prospect of a comfortable home won out and we ventured as far as the Krugersdorp Game Reserve. During a game drive at Haia Safari Ed thought he was deep in the African bush; we saw loads of animals and it didn't matter that the big white Superdome and the edge of the city were visible on the horizon. The Highveld air tasted good.

We reconnected with old friends, new friends we made during our stay in Greece and who have since returned to South Africa, and of course our old nanny Johanah. I stepped through these moments with care – savouring each one by one, and making them last as long as possible.

In Cape Town I saw my parents for the first time since my father lost his memory. This part of our trip weighed heavily on me as I was not too sure what to expect. At the house in Rosenheim on the edge of the Durbanville vineyards things were on an even keel. Outside the house due to a harsh drought the colours in the flower bed were not as abundant as usual, and inside there were fewer words and more activities packed away in cupboards and drawers.

During the first few days I spent a lot of time sitting with my father in the lounge – just the two of us. He would sit on his favourite blue chair and the whistle of his breathing would stir the silence. No *La Boheme* or *Pearl Fishers* or *Figaro* in the room with the big red carpet. No reminiscing and laughing over things that happened in the past – only a quiet sadness. And I remembered many, many years ago when he would lie next to me on the red and blue of the same Persian carpet in silent closeness. But now the carpet was threadbare in places and the tassels almost worn out; its rich royal colours muted.

When our gatherings became bigger and one-on-one was no longer possible, the chatter and noise would push my father to the edge of our conversations as he struggled to find his words, and he would withdraw into his own world. He managed OK in the safety of the familiar patterns of his own environment.

On our first Sunday we took him out for a drive along the Stellenbosch wine route in search of a place to eat. The day was glorious, and when we pulled in at the Boshendal Estate we were unbelievably lucky to grab a last minute cancellation for a *Le Picnique* on the stunning grounds. Our lunch under the tall trees was a triumph. In the family picture taken there Ed's face was painted in camouflage.

Two days later my father's breathing became more laboured and he needed to be hospitalized. He left the house in his favourite denims and sheepskin slippers, turning around once to look for his penknife on his bedside locker – as if one would need a penknife in hospital. The rest of our week revolved around visits to ICU where my father was either both very confused and/or difficult, or heavily sedated. We learnt that any new situation or setting has a severe impact on a person with dementia. At times they had to tie him down: he was struggling with riots and demons and wanted to sort out the staff because they "were not qualified to look after him." He hated being in ICU, all the time wanting to pull out the pipes and cables. I was shocked to see him so unsettled and without peace.

Within days his once imposing frame became frail, his shoulder bones and spine protruding and his silver watch looked big and out of place on his wrist. Back at Rosenheim the house was speechless - on his bedside locker his torch and penknife remained untouched.

We left Cape Town on my mother's birthday. My father did not know or understand when the time came to say goodbye – his forehead felt so cold. But I left with a wonderful memory: during his last night at home, after he had said goodnight, he returned to tell me something, but when he opened his mouth all that came out was gobbledygook. Even so, I saw the words in his eyes and somehow I understood what he was trying to say. In that precious moment I was able to crack the code. My father never returned home; from hospital he moved to the best available sick bay in a retirement home which was never meant to be his final residence.

In the beginning of June I got another opportunity to visit my father during a business trip to SA. Most of the week was spent in Johannesburg with only 72 hours in Cape Town. I found my father in a soulless place behind a fence where the large, neat garden pretends to soften the edges.

The place has long passages and old worn-out chairs with crochet cushions in colours that don't match; frail bones; sinewy hands; eyes that stare into space; and the smell of life when the breath has almost run out.

I could not believe the deterioration in the space of two months. During visits my father and I would sit in the passage against the bland wall and share a mandarin orange or two - one segment for him, one for me. Eating the mandarin was a process: I would wait while he meticulously removed the fibres from the fruit – one by one, placing each fibre in my hand before attempting to pick at the next one. His fingers never stopped pulling at the fibres on the fruit or the piping on his gown-pocket when the mandarin was finished. Watching him broke my heart; all I could do was sit with the taste of salt in my mouth. In his world I was nowhere.

I left, heavy with the rawness of not being able to support a lone parent who after more than 50 years of marriage, was now in charge. Of not being there for a brave parent who is finding the daily trips to the sickbay heart-breaking. And of not being there to take a turn to sit with him in one of the worn-out chairs.

Blue summer

The first six months of the year left a hole inside of me and only the blue and the salt of the Bitter Cucumber could soothe it. So we rolled up our challenges, our work-in-progress, weary bones and relocated to Diminio for the month of July.

This time our travels took us to the very north of Greece - an area we've always wanted to see. We had one week for a small taste of the North, but we were in the good hands of our friend Costa as excursion leader. He is also our local guru, head of communications in Nafplio and in charge of air traffic control over the southern suburbs of Athens. He is a man with a black folder and a heart the size of Mount Olympus - someone you know you want to keep forever.

Our travel plan was well thought out and we arrived in Kells months before via several iterations of Google Earth detail. Throughout all the to-ing and fro-ing of building the perfect plan our meeting and separation points never changed. As with most fine excursions, ours started at Goodys in Agios Stefano, a stone's throw from Dionysos, where we used to live. Goodys is the Greeks' answer to the golden arch, and its Flo Café makes a damn fine coffee. But this time the place was closed so we commenced our trip north on empty stomachs, a book on Salonica (to study), and a walkie-talkie radio for staying in contact between the two vehicles.

The O'Daly had an obsession with rainmaking, and true to his reputation as Rainman, as soon as we pulled up at our meeting point, the skies opened up over Agios Stefano and rained cats and dogs - or as they say in Greek, "priests and chair legs." The rain did not stop for days afterwards.

Our first base was at the Hotel Philippion in a pine forest high above Salonica. To get to the waterfront we had to enter through the arch in the old city wall and wind our way down the narrow streets of the upper town ("ano poli") with its beautiful wooden houses that overhang the streets. The upper town is what remains of Ottoman Thessaloniki and whenever we traveled down the winding roads the locals would hoot incessantly at our Athenian number plates. Like most north/south divides, the Thessalonians have little regard for Athenians. We spent both our two nights at wonderful *tavernas*; one in the charming old Jewish quarter known as the Ladadika, where they used to store olive oil and the other further along the waterfront in a quiet neighbourhood. How can I ever forget the taste of eggplant with sesame and yoghurt, humus with sundried tomatoes, artichoke with feta and lemon mustard sauce straight out of the oven? Or the mellow sounds of Cat Stevens, the Eagles and "*Stairway to Heaven*" and the warm, friendly company in a *taverna* in Salonica?

I loved Thessaloniki – a vibrant city with a large student population and a place with a wonderful laid-back atmosphere.

During our week in the north we travelled over 2,000 kilometres and along the way dropped into some fascinating places. Our excursion took us to the top end of Sithonia in Chalkidiki; along the modern Egnatia Odos – a highway which closely parallels the ancient Via Egnatia the Romans constructed in 146 BC to link up the Roman colonies from the Adriatic Sea to Byzantium; and along the Gulf of Orfanou to Kavala; and all along the way the outline of Mount Olympus was visible on the horizon.

In Kavala we stayed at a hotel perched on the side of the mountain like a bird's nest. From our balcony we could see over the whole city and we could even get a glimpse of the magnificent aqueduct in the old town. Dinner on the rooftop under the stars was a triumph: delicious food, the soft yellow light of the city below us, Merlot from Mount Pageo, and a fabulous view over the Thracean Sea. In these perfect surroundings we stroked the rims of our wine glasses until a hum chorus filled the night and the waiters were mystified because we sounded like members of a druid's convention.

At Fillipi we walked in the footsteps of St Paul and Lydia and on the vast Thesian plane in the shadow of Mount Pageo relived the battle between Mark Antony and Octavian versus Brutus and Cassius, the assassins of Julius Caesar.

We took a day trip to the Ottoman market in Komotini - a city at the cross-roads of civilisations - and got stuck in a shop with hookahs, icons, jewellery and other paraphernalia. The O'Daly broke out into German and when he asked about a fez the shop owner summoned her shop aide - an

Ottoman Geriatrix - to take us fez hunting. He took off, and we struggled to keep up with him as he marched on past the smell of almonds and tobacco like a man possessed. He never looked back to see if we were still there; his knees didn't bend and his trousers were pulled up high. Once he had dragged us the length and breadth of the market he stopped to ask three patriarchs on a bench and all you could see was their "oxi's" ("no's") and utter amusement at the foreigner-in-search-of-a-fez. At the market Converse lives next to fake flowers; fire extinguishers next to lace; nuts and Turkish delight next to glitzy evening dresses; brooms and bright beach balls next to flip-flops; and linoleum next to nougat and *koboloi.*

At night we left the tourists behind the big fortress in Kavala and travelled to the edge of the sea for smoked mackerel, grilled fish and watermelon. Being close to the borders with Bulgaria and Turkey, we regretted not having gone the extra few kilometers to cross over.

On our long trek back to the Bitter Cucumber we stopped at Vergina close to Aigai – once the royal capital of ancient Macedon dating back to 650 BC, in search of King Philip II's tomb. In the searing heat I became irritated with a king that selected such a miserable, dusty, godforsaken town as his final resting place. Nothing was moving in the heat. But once we entered the Great Tumulus we knew the great trek was worthwhile. Greek archaeologist Manolis Andronikos dug for 25 years until in 1978 he came across the find of a lifetime: the graves of King Philip II and the son of Alexander the Great's son King Alexander IV – undisturbed and not plundered. Andronikos knew this was big and according to rumour he loaded the bones of Philip II in the boot of his car and sped back to the university in Thessaloniki. On his way he was stopped by the police and once the officers got over the "I've got the bones of a king in my boot" explanation, escorted him with flashing lights the rest of the way.

We saw lavishly decorated wall paintings and amazing artefacts; the gold casket which contained the remains of Philip II and golden myrtle wreaths so beautiful and so delicate they looked unbelievable – as if they were faux and bore the label "Made In China"!

Our last stop was a return to one of the most special places on earth – Meteora. As the sun was setting on a long day we sat in silence and awe on top of the mountain and savoured the mood. The last leg of our journey took us to Mouzaki at the foothills of the Notia Pindos mountain range where Costa grew up. From there we took a spectacular route through the Vardousia, Gkiona and Parnassos mountains to our separation point at Itea. Here we handed back the walkie-talkie and followed the route where barely a year ago we disposed of bits of our old Health-Walker exercise machine in municipal refuse bins along the way so as to confuse the Greek steel bone collector and to make sure they could never trace the bits back to the Bitter Cucumber, and back to us. The O'Daly gave me the Health-Walker as a birthday present when I was pregnant with Ed. The contraption moved with us from Johannesburg to Dionysos, and from there to Diminio, where the only place it could fit was the balcony. What was once a good idea became a bother, so we dismantled the machine and wherever we could, dropped the bits in municipal wheelie bins along the roadside. This birthday present stayed true to its promise and made us work until the last minute of its existence.

Most mornings in Diminio began with a swim before the world awoke, and a work day punctuated by a swim in the late afternoon. We took turns to work on one of the balconies, at the desk, or on a lap somewhere - depending on the creative need of the moment. The O'Daly was followed by nagging belly aches and pains, and we experimented with excluding bread and baklava, and this and that. In the middle of paradise he was surrounded by a summer of discontent; he was dealing with his own bitter cucumber.

A trip to the Peloponnese was not complete with the customary *patates* and lemon chicken under the night sky in Nafplio. This time our Rainman did not deliver rain but he made up for this by tapping into an unsuspecting neighbour's wireless network and downloading some massive work files, and data showered down over Costa's olive and orange groves. Costa's neighbour in Nafplio was a tad eccentric and also very nosy. Whenever Costa was down from Athens, at the very first stirring, neighbour Gianni would drop in to satisfy his curiosity. On this night our plan was to baptize the hookah, but when the 70-year-old alleged nutcase neighbour fell in for meze we feared that the sight of a blond half-Irish, half-African girl with a hookah in a Greek setting could be the final missing puzzle piece that would send him home to blow his brains out. So we changed our plan.

Asterix and Obelix traveled with us through Greece. Ed lost his two front teeth in one week and all the way he was really bothered as to why we never named him Asterix. The young entrepreneur started a "back-whacking" business and whenever he whacked our backs with two sticks, he would hound us all day long for payment in cash.

Our neighbour in Diminio introduced us to a magnificent old water mill tucked away in the hills of Upper Diminio; the mill had been converted into a *taverna* and the setting was perfect to spend our last evening. We were a complete spectacle: foreigners hosting a local guru in a place meant for the locals. That night 85-year-old Aunt Poppy taught Ed how to become a pro at bread-ball-shooting. They made little balls with the soft insides of the bread and then launched them at the unsuspecting diners.

Over the years we found that in between meeting and separation points with our Greek family (from Corinth, Athens and Nafplio) the heart only grew fonder.

As we headed back to Green, our local guru Costa was checking the co-ordinates of our flight plan, and making notes in his black folder.

PART 4: THE RIVER FLOWS

Ithaca has given you the beautiful voyage.
Without her you would never have taken the road.
But she has nothing more to give you.
And if you find her poor, Ithaca has not defrauded you.
With the great wisdom you have gained, with so much experience,
you must surely have understood by then what Ithacas mean.

K. P. Kavafis (C. P. Cavafy), translation by Rae Dalven

Birth day

Friday the 15th was a beautiful autumn day, unusual for mid-September in Ireland. Outside the kitchen window a soft blue sky watched over a new herd of brick-red limousine cows in the field. The 15th was also the O'Daly's birthday and in the morning I whipped through the house to make sure everything was spotless for the occasion. There was a smell of lavender in the kitchen, and sandalwood in the lounge.

September was the beginning of a new school year and Ruby was starting her final two years at a college in Dublin. Things were settling down into a new pattern – a new phase was about to unfold. Late in the afternoon the O'Daly arrived home from work with his computer case in one hand and a bottle of Moët & Chandon in the other. He loved good champagne, and whenever he presented the Moët I sensed there was something to celebrate. But on this occasion his face looked drained – grey, as if he had seen a ghost. As he handed me the bottle, I sensed something unsettling lurking inside him; something so dark that not even a bottle of bubbly could hide. The O'Daly tried to make small talk, to divert attention, to pretend that nothing should interfere with the celebration of a birthday. He tried to lift the remains of the day. And then he dropped the bomb.

He told me his consultant had called him on his mobile phone on his way home from work with the diagnosis of an aggressive stomach cancer. The O'Daly received the news while driving – there was not even the buffer of a stop. We were about to join friends for dinner at our favourite restaurant in Carnaross; the kids were watching television in the lounge. The O'Daly's words fell on a normal day with such ferocity and so out of place, that they almost needed translation to make sense. At that moment a thick panic filled me and threatened to overwhelm me. I was in a small boat on a vast ocean – a boat with no bottom. Looking at the ocean around me was terrifying.

In the presence of the news I was unable to find a point of reference, an anchor point; there was no safe place to land. At that moment the soil under my feet felt foreign and I felt root-less. I was standing at the edge of someone else's life, looking in. And at that moment I felt completely alone.

All I wanted to do was talk to someone in South Africa – my family; I had a desperate need to connect with my tribe. I was unable to face the children; face the friends who were joining us for dinner; or face the O'Daly. I was unable to hold him, or console him – in the space of a couple of words I felt as though I had lost the ability to nurture and protect.

When I said to the O'Daly "I cannot face dinner like this, I cannot do it," he responded with, "I want to go – I do not know when next I will be able to enjoy a good meal." So we left the children, travelled the familiar road to the old forge, pretended we were celebrating a birthday, and braved our way through the three course menu. The night passed in a blur, and all along I struggled to hold back the tears.

I don't remember when or what we told the children. There was no big meeting, or gentle discussion - we tried to shelter them from the blow. I was trying to cope with the moment. And with the news a schedule kicked in – we were now in the hands of appointments and procedures. The treatment program started with a full CAT scan and operation.

On Sunday afternoon before we left for Dublin we took some family shots with the usual rigmarole of one child not wanting to appear in a photograph and the other facing the camera with wit squint eyes and a silly smile. En-route to the hospital we stopped for whippy ice creams in Dunshaughlin. The O'Daly loved 99 whippy ice creams – he had a thing for them and every so often he would search them out. We consumed our ice creams as if everything was normal. By the time we had the O'Daly checked into hospital and we were ready to return home, the city was completely clogged with thousands of All Ireland Football final fans.

Ruby and I picked a B&B in Drumcondra so that we could be close to the hospital as the O'Daly prepared for his surgery. The operation coincided with the Ryder Cup week and accommodation was as scarce as hens' teeth. As is the case with most B&B's in Ireland, this red brick Victorian house on the other side of the Royal Canal looked charming on the Internet but in reality ended in the usual disappointment of out-of-date burgundy, velvety wallpaper, sombre dark wooden furniture, gaudy green carpet and a bed that felt like a dining room table. What we had planned as some comfort during the first two tense days became a drab, dark space. Ed was in the hands of friends – he was only seven and we wanted his days to be as untainted as possible.

Until that Wednesday in September I had never met the consultant – I had no idea what the man looked like. I knew he was the O'Daly's surgeon and that he came highly recommended. I also knew he delivered some shocking news to the O'Daly on his birthday; over the phone - a bolt from the blue that pierced our lives and shattered our world.

First on the hospital list was a CAT scan, and later that evening when the results came back the news was good: the cancer was contained to the O'Daly's stomach; in particular to the bottom half of his stomach which meant only half (instead of the whole) of the organ needed to be removed. This was good news; a glimmer of hope – we could manage this one.

On the morning of the operation, Ruby woke up covered with bites all over her body – she appeared at the breakfast table like someone with the pox. We were not sure where the attack came from: fleas, bed bugs or even spiders. As I headed for the hospital she took her bite-covered self to her new College.

After a four hour long wait the O'Daly arrived on a trolley, in one piece – under the weight of a huge bandage. A friend tip-toed in to keep me company and we spoke in whispers to each other so as not to disturb the haze of morphine in the room.

At some stage in the afternoon we stepped out for a cappuccino and when we returned to the 3rd floor I saw a man leaning on the counter of the nurses' station, in a very open, public place. He was dressed in a dark jumper and trousers; his face downcast. He looked like he could be a Meath farmer, or the chap behind the counter at Kells Stores selling building tools and materials. He was not charming.

While we were still some yards away he started to talk: "It was really bad. I've never seen anything like this before, we couldn't do much." I thought: "Who are you? Do you have the right person? What are you saying to me? Is this real? Someone help!" He made no eye contact. "When we opened him up it was everywhere – we could not operate, we simply closed him up again." "But the CAT scan was clear – how was this possible?" He responded with silence. "You have two options; one is chemotherapy and the chemo will be fierce and he will spend weeks at a time in hospital and this cancer does not respond well to chemo, and the other is to go for quality of life for what time is left."

I wanted to sit down somewhere – my legs felt wobbly and I felt ill to the pit of my stomach. I did not know where to begin. Ed was in someone else's home; Ruby on her way from school with a pair of new Marks & Spencer pyjamas for her dad; and my car in the hospital car park that would be closing at nine pm sharp.

He told me "I'm going to see the O'Daly now; I'm going to tell him - come with me." Did we really need to tell him at that moment? How does one recover from news like that, with the taste of anaesthetic and major surgery still fresh on your breath? "I do not believe in lying to someone – he needs to know." Lying never crossed my mind – I was trying to cope with the news, with the shock of the moment. And I was frightened beyond belief. I was unable to face the O'Daly – totally powerless. All I could think of was where to begin.

The nurses suggested I move to the privacy of their little office. "We've ordered a plate of sandwiches for you." Sandwiches – who needs sandwiches when a life is in the balance? I wasn't there when the O'Daly received the news; instead I made a call to South Africa and a call to Granny. And then the O'Daly asked to see me. "I cannot see him now; I am not able to see him now." I passed – not sure because I was unable to witness his fear or my own was too much to deal with. At that moment all I wanted was someone to pray with me.

At some stage the consultant appeared again; I did not want to see him but he joined me and stood before me looking somber. All I could think of saying was "where there is life there is hope." He responded with silence - nothing. At that moment the man robbed me of my hope: I had no choice but to start this journey from someplace below zero.

Somewhere in between the panic and the silence Ruby arrived with the pyjamas. And she received the news still covered in those gruesome-looking bites.

As I was trying to find that point from which to begin and to stop the free-fall, the trolley ladies were handing out trays with cabbage and ham, tikka masala chicken, onion soup and chocolate roulade to patients in pyjamas. Outside a junkie was squatting with his back against someone's car; his eyes half-closed – a hoody for protection, a fag for warmth, and a paper cup half empty with coins.

And back in Headfort Ed was learning Latin and looking forward to his "tuck" on Thursday.

The dreaded bites transferred to me and I became covered with them. They were everywhere – hideous wine-red blotches that itched and burned. With the slightest movement the bite marks reminded me of the hole in my heart; as if they were the stains left by an indescribable grief as it tried to make its way out of my body.

Once again there were two beds in a hospital room: one for the patient and one for the unidentified patient. This time I was in the other bed. The two weeks in hospital was a rollercoaster ride; there were a couple of bleak turns, a number of scary moments, poignant silences, and hours in the presence of the charcoal black of panic and despair.

When the time came to take the O'Daly home, the world looked very different on our slow drive home through road works, potholes and bumps. Life at Headfort would never be the same again. We had won the cancer lottery: Adenocarcinoma, a particularly aggressive beast. Only one in a thousand stomach cancers happens to be this one. What are the chances for a dice to fall this way? We had a battle on our hands.

Life it is!

The arrival of Adenocarcinoma caused a complete stir in our home. The O'Daly's cancer came like a tsunami and wiped out old habits, comforts and eating patterns, and gave us the impetus to clean the slate – start all over again. In its wake I was like a rock climber unable to get a proper grip for my fingers and toes to hold on to. The rock was right against my face – I couldn't see left or right; or up or down. I was in limbo, and this place was very, very scary.

Overnight a whole range of alternative healing methods crossed our threshold. We experimented with alternative herbs and concoctions; Burdock root, Sheep sorrel, Slippery elm inner bark and Turkey rhubarb root. This complete turnaround left me bewildered. We switched off the TV and one-by-one discarded the toxic traps and things that managed to find their way into our lives. We embarked on a major de-cluttering process. At times the clearing out was frightening and I couldn't dwell in those scary spaces for too long. The terrain ahead was unknown, and all I could do was find a place where I could put my feet for the next step.

Palliative care arrived at our doorstep, and I was introduced to the word 'palliative' for the first time – a word with the colour of tar and the taste of fear. We decided not to have the word, but instead welcomed the wonderful community services which included a dietician and an elegant nurse with a brooch and a big smile. We wanted to re-brand "palliative" and change its colour to blue.

Cygnet Adenocarcinoma is a brute as the cancer is almost impossible to detect. The presence of the cancer can only be detected during surgery and with the naked eye. Monitoring progress in fighting the brute is done by comparing the results of one PET scan with the next; and even so, the comparison provides an indication, not certainty. We had no real way of knowing how well the treatment was working, or not. And for a brute of this nature there is no blood marker or medical cure – it is a mysterious monster that lurks in the deep.

The O'Daly began a wild scramble to find a cure or an alternative treatment, and his Internet search took him to Brazil, Germany and America. He was looking for a glimmer of hope. So when the huge green hospital folder slipped into the bottom of the suitcase for its trip to New York, we realised we were about to embark on a challenging journey.

We arrived at Newark at noon and slipped into the Big Apple through the Lincoln tunnel - six of us and a number of suitcases all squashed into a yellow mini-van with four seats available to sit on. There were no limousines or real vans available on the day, and we had to make do with discomfort. Outside an icy wind brushed the pavements.

The doorman Dino was there to meet us when our overcrowded taxi pulled up at the pavement canopy. A friend of a friend came up with accommodation with the feel of home - we had to undergo a process of vetting before we were allowed to stay at this very fine address.

The apartment was straight from a Raymond Chandler novel: 1940's décor, regal colours, ornate Victorian and gilded furniture, heavy paintings, Persian carpets, valuable sketches, interesting artefacts, and a green Ireland-shaped telephone. This was a place with a serious pedigree; but also a very tranquil space. We got to know the doormen, superintendent, and were even invited to tea with the president of the building.

We also got to know the pavements around East 74th Street: the well-heeled dogs and their owners; many polished Lincolns; the acceleration of automatic car engines; steam rising from manholes in the streets; the sirens and constant honking of horns; diners with excessive portions and bad coffee; and the craziness of endless choice. We clocked up many foot miles up and down town. When the O'Daly was with us we walked slowly and always stayed within reach of our haven. We were in the folds of generosity and the grace that surrounds generosity felt incredible.

Several times during the day the heating pipes would grunt and groan, and "bang" and "clang" under the weight of the winter sky. When that happened I wondered if someone was trying to axe their way through the pipes and into the apartment.

Finding something the O'Daly could eat and drink became my focus – I scoured the convenient stores around the Upper East Side for food and drinks with no colourings, preservatives, strong flavours or intolerant textures. My attempts were hit-and-miss, and I longed for the days when there were no such complications. How we take the simple pleasure of being able to eat food and drink liquids for granted. Every mealtime became a nightmare, and I could not bear to see the O'Daly struggle to find something – anything - to swallow.

The Rockefeller Outpatient Pavillion at 160 East 53rd Street is an impressive building: 11 floors, each with its own area of cancer focus. At reception we were greeted by a larger-than-life African-American gentleman; his vocation was to welcome the depths of pain and despair. This man's being painted the word 'palliative' with white.

The place was full of light, friendliness and calm. And although there were many very ill people around, the place did not feel heavy or sad. The patients came from all over the world; they arrived with green folders, wigs, wheelchairs, bruises from needles, and stories full of pain.

When the specialist arrived in the examination room she was even more petite than what I imagined – her beige court shoes held her feet with a full finger's space at the heel. I wondered if they slipped off when she walked on the streets of Manhattan. She was open and professional, an expert in the field of stomach cancers, and she happened to be from Ireland. She confirmed everything we already knew about the "brute," but added that the disease was treatable and that miracles do happen.

The specialist confirmed the treatment plan – the cocktail of chemo drugs prescribed for the O'Daly was developed and trialled at Sloan-Kettering. The O'Daly's cocktail consisted of a mixture of three or four of the most toxic chemo drugs on earth.

At the end of our Sloan Kettering day the O'Daly and I walked the three blocks to 5th Avenue and sat on a bench at the edge of Central Park. Here we were on a park bench in New York – my first visit to the city. We sat in silence; nearly 20 years of marriage compacted into the space between us. There was a half-moon in the sky and we watched in silence as the city moved non-stop around us; cars, people, prams, busses, poodles, joggers and sounds. And every so often an autumn leaf brushed past us and landed on the pavement.

He bought himself a beautiful Italian-made hat in a shop on Lexington Avenue, off 74th Street; an olde world shop that caters for gentlemen with pedigree and old money. The O'Daly has always loved his hats, in particular the Indiana Jones type. After all, how can you confront a Brute without a hat?

In the streets of Manhattan images of scenes from some years ago landed like a movie reel – I remembered when I tried on wigs at the bland Cancer Association building in Johannesburg (South Africa) before the commencement of my chemotherapy. The place was desperate and the wigs awful. All I wanted to do was bawl because the wigs were ridiculous – they weren't even new. These were not wigs for ladies with dignity or pedigree - but then again, at the time we didn't know anything about wigs and cancer, we only knew about hats.

However, that is where the similarities ended. At the Johannesburg General Hospital my chemo arrived in a brown paper bag: one toxic drug.

The O'Daly on the other hand was faced by a wall of chemo: Cisplatin, Irinotecan and Bevacizumab (a monoclonal antibody meant to 'lock in' cancer cells) plus a multitude of other drugs to counteract side-effects. The mention of any of these names would drain the colour from the faces of those in the know.

We took a limousine to the airport – the four of us looking like celebrities. There was sadness in the car, and each one of us sat in silence; our words remaining as thoughts. We slipped back into Dublin with confirmation that we had a battle with Goliath on our hands.

There was something about the O'Daly and chemo; at the first whiff of the stuff he became a demon – a man with a mission. This time the building project was even more ambitious than before. I arrived home one evening from the hospital to find our house wrapped up in building works. Men with drills and saws and noise had moved into our only haven. From his hospital bed and with his trademark "O'Daly fever" he commissioned a renovation project of epic proportions. My mother was visiting at the time and when we returned from a blissful mother-and-daughter day at a country spa I discovered our two baths filled to the brim with wall and floor tiles. On the landing two toilets and washbasins were lined up next to the box with Joseph, Mary, Jesus and all the wise men. Somewhere in the rubble my mother's face cloth and soap were missing. As if being without bathrooms wasn't enough, the builders also ripped out three bedroom cupboards and filled every open space with a mountain of clothes, ring-binder files, a long history of books, and bags full of rag dolls, rhinos, teddies and ducks from days gone by. In the mayhem there was nowhere for the tears and the toll associated with the cancer treatment to land. There was no space to breathe.

The O'Daly's chemo happened in the day oncology ward of the Mater Private Hospital – a small basement room that could hold nine patients at any one time. Most of the time the unit was overcrowded and understaffed, and as a result the space was jam-packed with noise and constant activity. In this unsettled space hats and head scarves were put to one side; tough battles were fought; and the fine line between life and death was very visible. In this space earthly possessions had no place and the only windows were in the mind.

Chemo happened on Wednesdays for two weeks in a row with a break on the third Wednesday. Each treatment took between five and seven hours to administer. The side-effects of the treatment were horrific, and living by their side became torture. Every meal became a small victory – we focussed on oats porridge and chicken soup with dollops of full cream, Mars bars, boiled eggs, crackers, and bread-and-butter-pudding. This was while we were still adhering to the hospital nutritionist's food pyramid programme; they wanted to "fatten him up" and "give him energy." Sometime later we discovered how inappropriate sugar is in the presence of cancer - we scrapped the nutritionist's lead and instead made our own way through the wealth of information we found in books and on the Internet.

We drifted between panic and despair on the one hand and sheer delight on days when small miracles happened. All we could deal with was one moment at a time. I do not know which was tougher, going through the pain of the illness and the dreadful side effects of the treatment, or to watch someone suffer and to see how Levi leg pipes become too big for legs and eye sockets too big for eyes; and to feel completely helpless.

As a patient I had withdrawn into myself, but in my role as witness I was unable to do so. How can the observer do anything but observe? The O'Daly's suffering happened right in front of me and his pain filled every corner of my being. The pain was with me when I went to bed at night and the pain waited for me in the morning when I opened my eyes.

But with the yin of a cancer journey came the yang of blessing: the generosity of friends that were present to support with messages, food, fetching and carrying and to provide each of us with time-out from the drain of the very stressful regime. There was also a steady stream of healing directed at us: meetings with healers, from ordinary folk to famous people-with-special-gifts – they arrived on our doorstep. We received hundreds of Mass cards, prayers from all denominations from all four corners of the globe, and enough icons, holy water and oils to fill a shrine shop at home. They came from the highlands and the lowlands; from the north, south, east and west; and they prayed on mountaintops and in rivers, in places such as Lourdes, Fatima, Medjugorje and further afield. The outpouring of love and support blew us away.

Alongside the building project at home the O'Daly created a charitable Foundation from his bedside. With so much passion and determination I was sure he was going to be OK. I could not help but take my hat off to his bravery.

Battleground

We soon became familiar with the after-effects when the *nuclear bomb* of chemo - Cisplatin – hits the body. On chemo days all we could do was grit our teeth and hold on for dear life. At every treatment we had to refortify our resolve so that there could be no way for courage to slip out.

Before every chemo session blood samples were taken to determine whether chemo can in fact happen that week – so we were never quite sure if chemo was going to take place or not. As can be expected from a man-with-a-hat the O'Daly's bloods baffled the oncologists; from treatment to treatment his white and red blood counts climbed instead of declining, and after the first few cycles reached the level of a healthy person. This was unheard of. If someone was going to win this battle, the O'Daly would be the one.

On many occasions over the years the O'Daly tried to watch the vintage film *It's a Wonderful Life*, but for some reason he never got round to it. The movie is a regular stand-in on Irish TV at Christmas time. It was therefore poignant when a friend handed him the movie totally random and out of the blue. On a particularly raw day the O'Daly settled in front of a big peat fire and finally watched the movie. I was working nearby and got a fright when I heard sobs over the muffled sounds of the movie and the fire. When I peeped in to investigate I saw the line "No man is a failure who has friends" on the screen, and for the first time in his life the O'Daly found rivers of tears; tears he never knew he had.

We thought we had a script for our life; that we were well into the roll-out of the plan. But midway through the performance we received a new script. This meant that each one of us had to take on a new role, and settling into these roles involved a lot of fumbling as we got to know our lines and expressions. We had to find our way on a new set, and we had no way of understanding the Director's vision. But as they say in Ireland, "you don't know the half of it": locked within the lines and performance of a new script was always the potential of banking an Oscar.

When Christmas arrived we bought a lush dark green tree that looked as close to the real thing as could be. The decorations came out, but somehow the mood remained muted. I couldn't view the red and gold of Christmas in the same way as before. To add to this we were exhausted – tired of holding up the wall of courage. I was still unfamiliar in the fragile space of hope and surrender – and relying on an unconditional faith that all is as it is meant to be, and that we would be O.K. Too often despair would knock on the door and try to upset the truce. The winter felt extra dark and cold and we longed for the sun and warmth.

We broached to prospect of a break-away and the doctors responded with a small radius of possibility. The O'Daly was the one who introduced me to the "road less travelled"; whenever we went away, we always chose a location somewhere out of the ordinary. We did not do the package holiday thing, and we liked to explore far flung and off the beaten track places. We soon discovered that the radius of about two hours' flight from home did not leave us far flung or with much choice. A week before Christmas we escaped to the black moonscape of Lanzarote, one of the Canary Islands 70 miles off the coast of Africa. We were after the sun and a small reprieve from the relentless program of chemo.

During our week we never ventured too far from our sun loungers or beds, except for a visit to the Timanfaya National Park. The Park's Fire Mountains were created between 1730 and 1736 when more than 100 volcanoes rose up and devastated a large part of the island. Travelling through the desolation of the red, ochre and black volcanic landscape was both fascinating and eerie. Standing on a place where a few meters below the surface the temperatures reached between 400°C and 600°C felt strange. As I stood close to the large hole in the ground where the El Diablo chefs cook the restaurant food, the smell of grilled meat mixed with the fumes from the belly of the mountain swamped me and wiped out my appetite. The island did not provide a soft landing – the place had no soul. Instead, its starkness only served to highlight our journey – an internal one with the same harsh landscape as the external one. Large hotels and package deals were lined up and gave the place an impersonal, mass-produced feel. We did enjoy the quiet, the sun and the endless view of the ocean. After months of not being able to drink much the O'Daly feasted on a tall *Erdinger Weißbier* every day.

We tried to move through the Christmas period without disturbing the tinsel, fanfare or hullabaloo too much. For Ed's sake the one not-negotiable requirement was to stay with the tradition of Santa Claus and his chimney delivery. Ed had done his homework in the Argos catalogue, and all he wanted for Christmas was a "Golden Retainer dog and her playful pup." Under the circumstances, a golden retriever and a pup soft toy was a modest request.

In the New Year we received very encouraging PET CT scan results, and contrary to expectations, the ferocious cocktail of chemo drugs had knocked the tumour action very hard. We could not celebrate this good news – after four months of mucking through some very treacherous terrain we were simply too exhausted.

As cancer settled in to our daily routine, the O'Daly took Ed along to one of his chemo sessions. Here the young lad discovered the real reason for the O'Daly's illness. He asked many questions and when the O'Daly explained the meaning of "oncology" his whole body stiffened when he found the word too big to swallow. We didn't realize that he was introduced to cancer at school, and that this introduction had a negative connotation. From that day on he made sure that he always kept one eye on his father.

One day out of the blue the O'Daly announced that he had a surprise for me, and true to his adventurous nature, the surprise was big. Without consulting me he had gone and signed up both of us to join a group of doctors on a three-week trek to Everest basecamp. We had four months to prepare for the expedition. I was flabbergasted – here I was barely able to come to terms with the big changes in my life and he had committed me to a significant physical challenge. With so much on my plate I received the O'Daly's surprise with a certain amount of resentment and anger; I was not sure I could handle the extra load.

I was unaware that Everest was on the O'Daly's bucket list – we never had time to discuss bucket lists. I should have known; the O'Daly was a man with vision; he was a man who always held a dream or two.

In the midst of winter I started my training in the Wicklow Mountains. This first walk took determination of the kind I didn't know I had within me – it had been years since my last hike. Here I was in the hills, in the sleet and the cold, stretching my muscles and unfit lungs to the limit. The O'Daly was still too weak to start his training program, and in the bottom of his cupboard was a brand new box with Meindl boots still waiting to be cracked open. My own preparation for Everest base camp became a mirror of what I was dealing with from day to day.

After the encouraging results we sailed into the oncology day ward for the O'Daly's first treatment of his new lighter chemo regime. There was a new bounce in our step - after all, we had Cisplatin and a cocktail with the colour black under our belts. But when the O'Daly nearly collapsed under the weight of six hours of treatment, I was reminded that there are no rules when dealing with a brute and its treatment. The O'Daly was admitted to hospital, and once again I could taste the familiar salt that came with panic and fear. In the new cocktail the doctors kept Irinotecan, dropped Cisplatin, and replaced it with Fluorouracil and a monoclonal antibody that was still on trial. There was big excitement when one of the new drugs delivered a skin rash – this meant the drug was doing its work. For the O'Daly a skin rash was another thing to add to the long list of side effects – what was a skin rash anyway when every other part of your body had already been hammered to a pulp?

One of the blessings, of being gripped by a serious illness is the fascinating people that fall into your life. We opened ourselves to the flow of healing that is particularly prevalent in Ireland. One gentle soul travelled from Carlow to Kells once a week to lay his hands on the O'Daly. He always appeared without notice and without words. The three hour roundtrip on country roads did not bother him – and he always arrived with a wonderful warm energy. We knew nothing about him, but that he came through a friend of a friend, and his departure was as unassuming as his arrival. This Carlow man cared with his whole heart. Then there was the serene-looking physiotherapist with a red beard, acupuncture needles and healing hands. We found him behind an unpretentious shop-front in an unassuming suburb of Dublin – a matter of synchronicity. He adopted the O'Daly as a friend. And there was Poonam, a wife of a colleague of a friend, who came to our house a number of mornings to give of herself. She brought Pranayam yoga to our house and after the session she would settle into our kitchen and cook special meals with fennel, fenugreek, naan, chickpeas or red kidney beans. With her delicate nose ring and broken English she assumed responsibility for the O'Daly's wellbeing.

There was so much love passing through our home. Unlike the surgeon, these people brought hope.

When the driving from Meath to Dublin for chemo treatments and college runs became too arduous, we signed up for a small pad on the edge of Dublin's Phoenix Park. We were still in the thick of the property development madness and the developer allowed us to move in before the building was ready. We loved the 1752 acres of beautiful parkland and big herd of wild Fallow deer in the park on our doorstep. The apartment was a welcome halfway base and hide-out from where to digest the blows of our battle. It provided an uncluttered space with vanilla furniture, vanilla walls and clean lines where we could be anonymous. The place was filled with vanilla of the Bourbon type. This was our adult space with no TV or radio, no telephone or knocks-on-the-door. The apartment somehow kept the heat of the battle away from our home.

But in the first couple of weeks the place remained a building site, and on a number of post chemo nights we were left without electricity in bitter-cold darkness. In the vanilla environment we struggled to find vigour, satisfaction and real comfort. These were low moments – desperate, forlorn and raw. Once again the environment reflected my internal world every step of the way.

Ed became a boarder at the school at Headfort. His bed in the Utopia dormitory gave him a little space between him and the battleground – in his world things were more or less normal. On weekends we all reunited at home as if nothing had happened during the week.

As the treatment sessions continued the O'Daly got thinner and thinner; he lost a third of his body mass (30kg) and became skin and bones. He was so frail that if I had to, I could fold him up in my arms and carry him.

But he soldiered on and at times the O'Daly was convinced he finally had the brute by the scruff of the neck. He was still not strong enough to commence his training for the trek to Everest Base Camp, but instead he spent time assembling our first aid kits and collecting all the bits and bobs needed for our three weeks in the mountains.

The days were getting longer and all along the green trellis fence at Headfort a yellow row of daffodils appeared, and there were new lambs in the fields. Around the corner an expedition was waiting with baited breath.

We took an orange train to Galway for our first meeting with the Everest Base Camp team. The expedition was a special event of the Cardiology Foundation and at some stage we had to present ourselves to the Team Leader – a fine and very serious doctor – for inspection. Prior to this meeting we were required to complete very detailed medical questionnaires, and needless to say, the O'Daly did not complete his for fear that he might not be given the green light to travel to Galway and fail at the first hurdle. Patient confidentiality meant that no-one in Galway had any knowledge of what they were about to meet.

The Team Leader was a medic from his crown to the soles of his feet. During his studies he won all the gold medals from the west to the east coast of Ireland; he specialised in high altitude medicine and became the best in Europe. Leading expeditions to high altitude was his thing. When it came down to business there was no place for humour – his aim was to get the group to base camp and back without any casualties - and that was what he intended to do.

After an hour-and-a-half discussion of 144 ways to die at altitude (from blisters to DVTs to acute mountain sickness to heart attacks) we stepped into the small meeting room to meet with him. He went pale when he saw the O'Daly's medical history: a terminal illness with a best-before-date. Never before had he been confronted with a trekker with such a distinctive label. But he did not flinch and without mincing his words he talked about death as though death was the fourth member in our little meeting. We listened and the O'Daly negotiated, presenting worst and best case scenarios, and by the time we left the doctor was perplexed and undecided as to whether to allow the O'Daly to travel to Nepal.

Our trek to base camp was meant to coincide with mountaineer Gavin Bate's world record attempt at a solo north/south traverse of Everest without supplementary oxygen or any camps on the mountain. The plan was to meet with Gavin at basecamp and deliver his supplies and clothes. Gavin spent his life either on an expedition or planning one – he is very familiar with the outer edges of challenge.

We left Galway with the realisation that the mountain would always be there and that unnecessary risks were are not worth taking. The chemo had not affected the O'Daly's gift of the gab and we left with wonderful new friendships in place.

We spent St Patrick's Day weekend snug and tucked away at Headfort. The day was bitterly cold and we only opened our front door long enough to get more peat and coal for the fire; the gap never big enough to let the jolly of St. Paddy's Day sneak in. At the end of the weekend there the leftovers of green and white and orange were scattered in the streets.

Paddy's weekend also happened to coincide with the O'Daly's "Best before date" – given by the inimitable surgeon. We celebrated with a bottle of Chablis but never quite got into the spirit of things. It was difficult to be festive when at the other side of celebration there was the weight of uncertainty, the 'brute' and chemo.

On the other side of a bottle Chablis two worlds lived side-by-side: the one regulated by chemo schedules, a blue Healing Code book of do's-and-don'ts, media interest, well-wishers and a medicine box; and the other one a mystical one without any rules and regulations. These two worlds often collided in the midst of the battle and in the small sips of celebration when a milestone was reached. Ultimately the battle is a solo one – most of the wrestling happens inside, and fully sharing this inner world with another is impossible.

One morning we arrived at the chemo ward to find the O'Daly's platelet count so low that they were not sure whether to continue with the treatment or not. After a huddle and a discussion they took the chance and proceeded with the chemo cocktail. In the cancer ward many of the milestones involve numbers and on this occasion the oncologist named the number that would be required to continue with the next treatment. True to form the following week the O'Daly exceeded that number – he continued to play havoc with the medical world. Somewhere in the treatment cycle they gave the O'Daly a precautionary blood transfusion that left him unsettled and overwhelmed by someone else's nightmares. And for a period the foreign blood disconnected him from his own technicolour dream world.

While we were waiting for the final verdict on whether or not the O'Daly would be allowed to fly to Kathmandu, and on to Lukla, my walking boots took me to the Mountains of Mourne in Down, Wicklow, Cuilcagh in Cavan and Fermanagh, and Slievenamon in Tipperary. Preparing for Everest was a lonely process – many a time I loaded my backpack with tins of organic cherry tomatoes and chickpeas to add some weight and pretended that I had a full load on my back. Rain, sleet or snow did not make a difference – I had a very limited time to get expedition fit. Meath is a rather flat county and one suitable place I could find for my daily walk was Loughcrew, or Slieve Na Calliagh, the highest point in County Meath. Here amongst the scattering of passage tombs that date back to 3300 BCE I became the lunatic who walked up and down, up and down the hill in full gear when most sane people were still tucked into their warm beds. And I was resentful – I had never anticipated training for an expedition in the midst of chaos, in an Irish winter.

We kept all four pairs of hiking boots in the back of the Landrover – there was a gentle restlessness about us. True to our gypsy nature (albeit high-tech gypsies) we had a serious bout of wanderlust – there was so much we wanted to do. When it became clear the O'Daly would not be able to make the trek to base camp, he adjusted his vision to a hike from Lukla to the Sherpa capital, Namche Bazaar, where he would park himself and write. His dream was to be based somewhere in the presence of Everest; somewhere he could feel the pulse of the "Mother of the Universe."

The news we'd been waiting for came late one afternoon: a clear PET scan; one that showed no clinical evidence of any cancerous cells in the O'Daly's body. On one of our visits to the faith healers in Offaly they saw a clear scan. The oncologist was blown over – he had the scan interpreted by several specialist radiologists and they all confirmed the results. This was near impossible – we were over the moon. And with the good news came word that the O'Daly was given the green light to join the Everest Base Camp expedition, but only as far as Namche Bazaar. He would be given his own personal porter, and the two of them would wait in Namche until our group reconnected with them on our way down the mountain.

After a tension-filled time we headed for Paris for a reprieve – we wanted to take Ed to Gaul, the birthplace of Asterix, and we wanted to see the Eifel Tower. My first visit to France passed in a blur. With the O'Daly too drained and too weak to walk too far, I saw the main sights alone. I wasn't able to engage with the place, and the beauty and romance of the place passed me by like a stranger in the night. Fresh croissants and baguettes did not taste the same when one member of the clan was locked in a world of pain and discomfort. The O'Daly was so frail.

Once back from France I had to check in with the other man in my life – my father. I arrived in the Western Cape surrounded by the pressure of the Everest expedition, by now around the corner. I had to keep up the training, and climb something; so the most obvious choice was Table Mountain. My guide for the morning was a gentle soul with long hair, a beanie, copper bangles and long tanned legs – a gorgeous chap with a passion for green, lizards and abseiling. He fetched me at the V & A Waterfront in an old, yellow VW Citigolf; one of those little cars that drive on a wing and a prayer. By the time we arrived at the base of the Plattekloof Gorge, steam and water were pouring from the engine.

The day was perfect, absolutely perfect: 30 degrees, no wind, blue skies, a mirror ocean, and the smell of *Fynbos* in the air. I started the hike fresh off the aeroplane, full of bounce and with an avocado and espresso under my belt. But the mixture of altitude, bounce and heat caused my head and gut to spin out of control, and my legs to feel like lead. On our ascent the guide suggested twice that we might want to turn back; twice I looked at the gap in the rock where the blue was waiting, and twice I said: "No, let's keep going." A third time I urged the guide to turn back but he simply shook his head – by now it was too late to turn back, and that the only way forward was the way up. So I climbed Table Mountain with many pauses and at times stretched out flat on my back; my skin against the calming cold of the rocks.

I've been to the top of Table Mountain several times before, but this time the view tasted so much better. After all, my footsteps were all the way up the gorge on the city side of the mountain.

Then there were the visits to the sickbay in Durbanville where my father was in care. I arrived at a time when they were ripping out the old biscuit coloured linoleum and replacing it with a new grey. In order to protect the old folk broken by dementia and Alzheimer's from the chaos in the passages, they parked them in the dining room all day long. In the same corner was the old lady in a pink tracksuit – she held her head in one hand while the other one scratched relentlessly. Somewhere else Ouma Saar would shuffle from table to table collecting side plates and sandwiches and placing them into a bag attached to her walking frame. And in another corner my father would sit on a brown chair with his eyes closed – locked in his own world.

I would collect him from the confines of the dining room and take him outside into the sunshine, or into the library. He walked with great difficulty and hooked his arm into mine for support. I instantly recognised the feeling of a frail arm hooked in under my arm as if to find strength in the hollow. Here I was, providing a strong arm to both my father and my husband at the same time. Did my dad even know of my lonely battle back in Ireland? On a few occasions my father recognised me, and then for a moment his eyes would light up and smile.

I wasn't used to visiting my heartland without the O'Daly and the kids; this was not how I wanted it to be. I wondered about this heartland of mine: is there ever a tipping point linked to the amount of pain, or the size of a battle experienced in one place versus another, whereby one's heartland is replaced by another? Is the heartland even a place? Or is it perhaps a collection of all the memories gathered in the heart? Maybe the heartland is merely the place I am in my journey?

When I returned to Ireland there was only enough time to pack my boots, layers, platypus and plasters for Nepal.

An expedition amidst chaos

The night before my departure the O'Daly became unwell and I had to take him to the hospital, where he was instantly admitted. The chemo regime that was so successful in beating back the tide of the cancer had unfortunately played havoc with his digestive system. For 12 days he was unable to eat or drink, and by now severely dehydrated it was unclear whether he would make the trip to Everest at all. I was overcome by panic. In between trips to the hospital I attended to the final preparations required by three weeks away in the wilderness: a trip to the airport to collect our old *au pair* from South Africa who undertook to take care of the children in my absence, grocery shopping and house cleaning. Packing happened around midnight and consisted of throwing things into my duffle bag; I had no idea what was in it and what I was leaving behind.

All along I was torn in two as to whether to go or stay. On the one hand there was the matter of the effort expended in getting ready for the trek and achieving my goal, and on the other there was the O'Daly fighting for his life. When I veered towards staying, the O'Daly begged me to go; his deep wish was that I make the trip, and in any case he was still hopeful that he would be there to meet me in Namche. If he could not, he said I could show him pictures on my return.

In the end I decided to follow my gut, to go ahead with the expedition, and to trust that if I needed to stay, something would prompt me to do so. I decided to trust that I was guided, and that if I had to stay, things would work out that way. At this point I surrendered, and I gave over to that indescribable force that was holding me.

On the morning of my departure I collected the O'Daly from the hospital and headed for Dublin airport to meet the team for our midday flight. Here I was in the car with my two children and husband of nearly twenty years on my way to a send-off. But this send-off involved a solo adventure – one fraught with risk. All along the way I said to God: "Stop me if you must; please stop me if I should." I had no frame of reference for any of the things that were happening to me – I was in a river, and this river was flowing toward the ocean. I was unable to stop the flow of the water.

The airport was a blur; I don't remember the goodbyes and I don't remember the look in their eyes, their faces. One image stayed with me and became a painful reminder of the suffering: two frail hands desperately trying to hold on to a dream. Nothing felt right about what was happening. Somewhere in the chaos I lost my mobile phone and as a result the rest of the team were already checked in by the time I arrived at the airport – they simply thought I wasn't going. I commenced my journey on the outside of the group. In my gut I knew I had to make this journey, and I trusted that it was meant to be.

It was dusk when our plane flew over the hills and landed in Kathmandu. And in the low light the place looked magical - like something I had never seen before. Long delays in London and Doha with airplane problems meant we had lost an afternoon in this intriguing city. As we left the airport building crowds of locals were pushing and jockeying for a slice of the action: to carry a bag, take us to our hotel, or beg for a dollar. We were escorted through the crowd, bundled into two minibuses and taken to the Kathmandu Guest Lodge, originally a Rana palace and oasis in the centre of Thamel. Driving through the city was something else: cars, tuk-tuks, bicycles, motorcycles, people, goats, dogs, cows, trucks, minibuses, and rickshaws all use the same narrow roads. Noise and cramming; complete chaos - and yet somehow in between the non-stop beep-beeps everything worked.

My one vice is a not-negotiable requirement for a hairdryer. Born with super-fine hair there is no other way of making any sense of my hair but to blow it, so upon our arrival I left the big gates of the Guest Lodge and went looking for an adapter and hairdryer in the cramped little supermarket around the corner. I found an adapter from a bunch of second hand adapters in various states of decay. As I was going through them to pick the best of the lot I couldn't help but wonder who they once belonged to. The hairdryer was more difficult and required the help of the person at the till. I was taken to the shampoo shelf and when I tried to explain I did not want shampoo but a hairdryer, the shop lady kept pointing at the shampoo, until I got it: a special offer with shampoo-for-black-shiny-hair-and-get-a-dryer-for-free. The girl at the checkout looked at me with a big smile and told me that I was so lucky to be getting a big bottle of shampoo-for-black-hair as well as a hairdryer. The dryer was the size of a matchbox, had a cable the length of a ruler, and a plug with dodgy points. This made blow-drying tricky as I had to hold the dryer with one hand, hold the plug into the wall with the other hand, and somehow find a way of holding the brush, while doubling over so that my head could reach the dryer.

During our day in Kathmandu we visited the ancient Stupa at the Boudhanath Buddhist site - one of the biggest in the world, and the Pashupatinath Hindu temple on the shore of the holy Bagmati River. Here we witnessed several cremations – done so matter-of-factly that the normalness stunned me. I come from a world where funerals were sombre, private affairs. There was no engaging with the body of the loved one in any way – from the moment of death until the actual burial the body was out of reach, kept somewhere else. Cremations were done out of sight – as if the body had to be veiled; as if the body would only remind us of death's cruelty.

In the murky Bagmati river a bunch of kids were searching for coins, and monkeys were leaping in-and-out of the water, unperturbed by the ashes of the dead floating by. Above the river the sadhus (holy men) live in ramshackle huts stuck in gaps and caves in the vertical rock face.

In the evening we walked through the busy streets for dinner at a traditional restaurant - handpicked by a local expert. We spent one busy day in Kathmandu –much too little to connect with the place, and I felt as though I was in a dream.

On our way

The shutters of the many little shops were still drawn over the hustle and bustle of the previous day when we left Kathmandu Guest House for our flight to Lukla. Our two minibuses were crammed with people, back packs, hiking boots and navy duffle bags; on the roadside a group of kids were practising martial arts. We travelled with ease through the relative quiet of the crack-of-dawn morning with excitement in our bones. Away from the daytime chaos our expedition was finally under way.

At the domestic terminal of Kathmandu airport I was amazed with the speed at which they turned around the little Yeti Airways planes; they landed, were emptied, loaded, and made ready for departure back to the mountains in record time. We were bundled into two twin Otter planes and a beautiful air hostess handed us each a hard sweet and some cotton wool for our ears. For the duration of the flight she sat as quiet as a mouse in the very back seat.

The sky was overcast and much of the flight was a few thousand feet above ground with a view of the terraced landscape and river valleys below. And then we broke through the clouds and arrived in the space where the big ones live. Above the clouds we found a wall of spectacular peaks, one higher and more impressive than the next; an incredible surreal world.

Lukla is the gateway to the Sagarmatha National Park and southern half of Mount Everest. The village is situated on the side of a mountain - and at 2,840m Lukla is at a point higher than Thabana Ntlenyana (2,390m), the highest point in Southern Africa. There are two ways to get to Lukla, by small plane like we did, or else a 12-hour bus drive from Kathmandu to Jiri and then a week-long trek from Jiri to Lukla. Flying into Lukla is not for the faint of heart: as we approached the village the wings of the plane skimmed the foothills and all you could see was the pilot heading straight for the side of a big 4005m mountain. At the very last minute the airstrip became visible. The strip is only 475m long, at an awkward angle against the side of the mountain, with a sheer drop of nearly a kilometre to the valley below on one side, and a mountain wall on the other side. The pilot landed with precision – only the most experienced pilots are allowed to land in Lukla.

Once off the plane I was awestruck by the amazing beauty of the landscape; the white peaks that tower over you; the total silence; wonderful fresh air, a welcome change after the pong, noise and pollution of Kathmandu; and by the sheer scale of everything. We were met by a crowd of would-be-porters - each one hopeful for a job and a meagre income to support a family for six months. We were also met by our own team of 18 porters and Sherpas.

The great trek

After tea and a chance to stock up on chocolate in Lukla we walked the short distance along a beautiful valley to Phakding. We walked through tiny Sherpa villages, and in the silence of the mountains all I could hear were birdsong, the occasional clanging of yak bells, the rush of the Dudh Koshi River, and the gentle chatter of a group that had only been together for two days.

I loved arriving at our lodge for the night. There was the welcoming ritual of hot tea or lemon water upon arrival, the handing out of our room keys, settling into box rooms, straightening out of sleeping bags, removing of contact lenses, slipping into pyjamas or tracksuits, and taking off hiking boots. In Phakding we were given a minute or two to drop our backpacks before we were taken up a very steep hill to the Thulo Rimiskung Gumela monastery. The aim was always to go a little higher than the sleeping place – this was to prepare us for altitude. On our way to the monastery we followed the gentle rhythm of our Sherpa, Tshering – we followed the colours of the rainbow umbrella attached to the back of his backpack. At the monastery there is a Buddha so special only a select few are able to see him. We paused in the silence and warm, rich textures of the place. On our walk back to our base for the night the darkness filled the valley; somewhere in the dusk I could hear the call of a lone cuckoo.

We spent our first night in the mountains at an altitude lower than at our starting point at Lukla. And from the word go I became acutely aware of going lower, because dropping in altitude always meant the very next stretch would involve climbing.

For the six miles from Phakding to Namche Bazaar we followed the rushing Dudh Koshi through forests of birch, juniper, blue pines, firs, bamboo and rhododendron. As we criss-crossed the river over several hanging bridges, the views were spectacular. Some of the bridges were so high I was unable to look down at the dizzying heights below. I remembered the photos the O'Daly printed of Namche to get us focussed on the expedition – they gave me nightmares as no matter how I viewed them, they involved heights of a vast scale. And here I was, crossing hanging bridges and walking on the edge of mountains with a void of vast proportions one footstep away.

After a large rice-lunch there was an enormous two-hour climb of some 600m to get to Namche. I wound my way up the side of the mountain at a snail's pace – the climb never-ending. There was no view of the end-point – all I could see was a wall of mountain to climb. On the way to Namche I realised that similar to the fight against a brute, climbing a mountain is a lonely process. The climb was all about me and will.

Namche Bazaar – or "Dark Forest" – is in the shape of a horse-shoe and perched on the side of a mountain at an altitude of 3,440m. Namche is the gateway to the Khumbu region and also in the high altitude zone. At the first signs of the village I felt energized – it was as well that I did not know that our lodge was the very last lodge at the top end of the village, which meant crawling up many, many steps to reach base. Here I felt the lack of oxygen for the first time – moving took effort to breathe. High altitude also meant strange dreams, sleeplessness, battling to fall asleep, headaches and nausea.

Namche is a fascinating place: how did it manage to hold on to its position so dangerously close to the edge and not slip down the side of the mountain into the deep valley below? Jho – a cross-breed between yak and common cattle – linger in the pathways and little shops are crammed with anything and everything – strange brands of suntan lotion and white chocolate a couple of years out of date. Most of the shops had loads of mountain gear hanging from their roofs, walls and shelves, and around every corner hikers were haggling with locals desperate to make a sale. In Namche two internet cafés competed for business – one with familiar golden oldies music and the other with an owner who popped chewing gum bubbles. There were several notices for telephones and even a bakery with fresh pastries. In the narrow streets the little children played as if they were in the best play park in the world.

We stayed in the luxury of the Khumbu Lodge – a place with one shower and two loos with toilet seats to be shared by 20 of us. We had two music lads in our group, and on our first morning in Namche their trademark wake-up chant came at 5.30 for a short walk to a viewing point for our first glimpse of the Mother of the Universe. This was meant to be a rest and acclimatization day, but we were taken up a steep ridge (the height of the Empire State building) to the Everest View Lodge (3,880m), built by the Japanese and where oxygen is installed next to every bed. The lodge is the highest hotel in the world and after some five hours of strenuous up and down we could finally start our rest day.

In Namche I became aware that all was not well in Dublin. Every attempt of mine to contact anyone back home failed: all I got was voicemail and my inbox remained empty. This was my last chance of having access to email and phones. Not being able to reach anyone made me frantic, and from this point on I became obsessed with getting to a phone. I became desperate for information.

We left Namche and its phones and internet cafes, and headed on a gentle contour path for Deboche (3,820m). I had no idea of what was going on in Dublin, and we were about to disappear deeper into the wilderness. After lunch at the banks of the Dudh Koshi River we had a mammoth climb of 600m to the monastery of Tengboche. Stopping at a river bed was never a good sign; a river meant a valley, and in the Himalayas a valley meant a long way from the top. I was amazed at how I managed to climb for hours at a time – putting one foot in front of the other; one in front of the other. Tengboche was planned as a stop on our way down the mountain, so on this occasion we stayed long enough to watch a documentary about the place that put us all to sleep. I was exhausted and longed for a good night's sleep.

The Tengboche valley is so beautiful and peaceful I could have been in heaven. The monastery is encircled by snow-covered mountains, open meadows, gentle rivers and lush forests. People from all over the world come to see the place – and here I was numb and unable to feel the beauty. There was no time to pause here as we had to get to our lodge in Deboche before dark.

This was a low point for me – I felt unconnected to the group and I was heavy with sadness and worry. There was no-one to share with; pairs and trios had formed based on shared backgrounds and in any case, no-one wanted to be burdened by anything over and above the demands of being pushed to the limits. Like me, every member of the team was on some mission or other. After all, I had made the choice to go.

We started our trek to Dingboche (4410m) with a walk through a forest. There were wild purple flowers in the grass and the rushing sound of the Imja Kholo River in the background. Rain had fallen the night before, so the countryside was cool and refreshing; for the moment the dust was gone. At some point we crossed the Imja Khola and followed the steep climb to Pangboche above the tree level. We left green behind and entered arid Alpine terrain, and the further we walked up the glacial valley, the more barren and inhospitable the landscape became. Some six hours later we arrived at our overnight lodge in Dingboche. By now the lack of oxygen caused my movements to become very slow.

Dingboche is well into the high altitude zone, and very chilly. During the winter the entire village closes. Our lodge was a haven: we spent the two long evenings in the warm dining room playing cards, chatting or reading. The big ones - Ama Dablam, Nuptse/Lhotse wall and Island peak - never broke through the clouds. There was no need to see the big ones to know I was in a special place; somewhere above the ceiling of mist some of the greatest peaks in the world loomed.

Our second day in Dingboche was another rest day which we spent climbing up a steep, narrow ridge (600m up) where the mist thankfully hid the vertical drops on either side of the footpath. Back at base I had a wonderful, warm 250 Rupee shower in a makeshift outdoor hut where there was nowhere to put shampoo or hang knickers, socks and clothes. I stood in a bowl on the ground and throughout the shower I wondered if there would be enough water to rinse myself. In Dingboche a hot shower requires enough notice for the water to be boiled, carried outside and the bucket filled.

The moment we landed in Dingboche I asked about a phone, so Tshering Sherpa took me on a difficult 30 minute walk, dodging yaks (which can be a nuisance) and traversing on rough footpaths to the only phone in the village. Our lodge was on the edge of the village which meant that the moment you left the lodge you were immediately on remote mountain terrain. I managed to reach Ruby, who could not give me any information about the O'Daly. Instead she said she would text me when next she was at the hospital. God love her – here I was in the middle of nowhere and she wanted to text me. The call frustrated me and left me with more anguish; I couldn't help but wonder if she did not know or did not want to tell.

That same night one of the lads wanted to phone home, so I used this as an excuse to brave the cold and go along for another try. I could help show the way – after all I had walked the way to the lodge earlier. We left with down jackets, hats, gloves, young Dawa Sherpa and one hand torch. Within a couple of minutes the torch died and suddenly the three of us were alone in the pitch black night. Every bush looked and sounded like a yak. We were unable to find the footpath on the uneven terrain, tripped over rocks and bushes and could not figure out how to get to the distant lights of the lodges. We became completely disoriented. When Dawa Sherpa announced: "I am lost, I don't know where to go" we panicked. Back at the lodge no-one was aware we had slipped out. We had to work hard to convince the lad-on-a-phone-mission to turn back, but after a tricky journey we finally reached our lodge. When the lad still insisted on speaking with his family, Dawa Sherpa suggested another house in the village with a phone, and we decided to give it a try. We tried for a long while to wake the owner, and then he had to unroll the wires, dig out a box, connect the wires, and wind up the phone. He never got a signal – and we never managed to make that call.

Our next stop on the route was Lobuche. In the overcast conditions we did not see many peaks, but after the first hump the mountain wall which forms the border with Tibet came into view. For the first time the goal post was in sight. Somewhere between Dingboche and the Thukla Yak Lodge, in the middle of nowhere two amazing things happened: during one stop a small group approached us and all I could hear was the familiar sounds of "*Al lê die berge nog so blou…*" – a song about a blue mountain. Hearing my mother tongue in this faraway world nearly knocked me over, and when huge African hugs followed the members of my team looked on in disbelief. During another stop our music man whipped out his tin whistle for an impromptu play; when another group passed by, their Sherpa surprised everyone by producing his own whistle, and under the blue sky the magic of a memorable whistle-off took place.

I didn't get to Lobuche with the group and when I was told to turn back I could not hold back the tears. Tears come easily in that part of the world: the stakes are high and Everest is the place where dreams are made, or lost.

"Siga-Siga" (slowly-slowly)

On our last morning in Dingboche I woke with an almighty headache; one that really got my attention. I checked with the team doctor – he wasn't too perturbed and so I trekked on. Halfway up a steep 200 metre rocky hill I realised I could not continue. The decision was made to send me back all the way down to Dingboche. I told the doctor that if I was to return to Dingboche that I would simply continue on to Namche Bazaar where I would wait for the team. I could not contemplate the thought of having to re-trace every step down and then up again the next day.

The doctor was unsympathetic, a little irritated by the interruption. Chiring Sherpa stepped in and we conspired that I would go back to our lunch stop-off point at Thukla lodge, start Diamox, take a rain-check in the morning, and then catch-up with the group the next day. So Dawa Sherpa and I took the lonely route down. No-one in the team offered to walk with me – all eyes were focussed on reaching the end-goal.

Dawa Sherpa stayed with me in my box room and talked non-stop; he told me about his college course, his dream to see the sea, and his love for the mountains. Dawa Sherpa's brief was not to leave me alone, but all I wanted to do was curl up under the thick, garish blanket, and close my eyes. I did not care who had slept on the sheet and under the blanket before me. My duffle bag with my own sleeping bag was due to arrive with Chiring Sherpa and a porter later that evening.

As I was warming up I struggled to shake-off the feeling of complete desolation. The afternoon at Thukla Yak lodge was one of the longest: all the lunchtime hikers had moved on and there was no-one left at the place. I was concerned about my head, concerned about developments in Dublin, and I was without my gear. As the sun was about to set an Irish chap and his Austrian girlfriend checked in. They were on their way down the mountain – an expedition done without Sherpas or porters, one completely made up as they went along. They were followed by two more victims of acute mountain sickness. As the darkness moved in a handful of the locals joined us around the stove for a little light and warmth. In this small gathering the other two couples shared their stories of incredible adventures. At bedtime I had to find my room in complete darkness.

The next morning a bright blue sky and amazing white peaks were waiting for us. After an early breakfast we recommenced the steep one-foot-in-front-of-the-other climb up to Chukpilhara, the Memorial site where a long sombre line holds the many rock formations, monuments and statues which mark the deaths of climbers who died on Everest and other peaks in the Khumbu region. For a moment in this inhospitable land, the sound of birdsong was interrupted by the humongous thunder of an avalanche.

At the top of the climb were the endless moraine heaps – piles of stones and debris brought down by the Khumbu Glacier. The glacier moves at 200m per year – a phenomenon that boggles the mind when standing by its side. We were surrounded by peaks, peaks and peaks: Pumo Ri, Nuptse, Lobuche, Chumbu and Ama Dablam, all of them over 6,000/7,000m. Behind the Nuptse/Lhotse wall Mount Everest stood in hiding. In this magical world I learned that anything below 6,000m is classified as a foothill, and often not worthy of a name.

We reached the overnight stop of Lobuche, a small settlement at the foot of the giant Lobuche peak, at mid-morning.

Mountain days

Our days on the mountain started around 8-8.30 a.m. and on average we walked for six hours. Somehow the wake-up call started in one place and then the stirring would roll through the paper thin walls: either a tin whistle, someone talking, the lads' signature chant which became recognisable by everyone up and down the valley; or a knock on the door. Then the process of squeezing everything back into the duffle bag and backpack started: sleeping bag into its small bag; contact lenses into eyes; night clothes, first aid kit and other stuff into various plastic bags; and water into the platypus. The porters always left 30 minutes before us and once they were off we could settle into breakfast. Each porter carried at least two duffle bags on their backs. There was always someone who ended up carrying the many dozens of eggs, and pots and pans.

From the moment I woke up I started with my four litres of water for the day. I tried to get the whole lot under my belt long before bed-time. This made sense to me as the thought of trying to balance over a smelly hole-in-the-ground in the cold dark of night, with one hand to hold the torch and the other to remove layers, without getting my house shoes full of sewage, was to be avoided.

The lodges varied from adequate to comfortable. In some of them the rooms were the size of a shoebox; the bunks consisting of a rough frame with a foam pad covered by a sometimes-changed sheet and that was it. In this solitary space I dumped my sleeping bag and at bed-time as I waited for the sleep to come, I could hear the whispers and breathing of the persons next door. This was not the place to break wind – the sound would travel from shoebox-to-shoebox, from one end to the other. There was generally one toilet downstairs and sometimes the only shower was a cold one.

I loved the food, but our group's Irish palate struggled with the Himalayan diet: mo-mo's; heaps of pasta or rice; garlic soup; potatoes; dahl; cabbage; high altitude barley, wheat, buckwheat and spinach; scrambled eggs or omelettes; and the odd treat of Tibetan bread or prawn crackers. The Sherpas served us our food and once the hungry lads had their seconds they would sit down in the cramped kitchen and tuck into the leftovers. Black tea or hot lemon water was served at 6 a.m., after breakfast, before and after lunch, upon arrival at the lodge; and before and after dinner.

At each of the lodges there was always a saucepan of boiled water ready for drinking and the brushing of teeth. The taste of this water was vile and like me, most of us ended up buying many, many bottles of water. As we moved up the mountain the price of water went up, and consuming the minimum requirement of four litres a day became quite expensive. Chocolate was similar, the higher up the mountain the more out of date the bars became. We found bars more than a year-and-a-half out of date. Sometimes I didn't care when the chocolate was white with age, but other times I was getting more than what I had bargained for. At times I couldn't know for sure whether I was eating coconut or weevil. For this reason I could never eat a Bounty bar again. The selection of chocolates was limited: Mars, Bounty and Snickers bars. Our team doctor got some of us hooked on Bounty bars and the addiction proved expensive. Fortunately, as we reached above the tree line we hit the very out-of-date-bars. The Bounty bars thus became dubious, and the addiction was resolved.

Our expedition took place towards the end of the climbing/trekking season which meant the foot paths were relatively quiet. However, from Namche on both human and pack animal traffic increased, and we became like trails of ants going up and down the footpaths. The sound of a yak-bell meant a yak-attack was imminent, and at the first warning sign you had to get out of the way of the yak-train; the yaks did not budge – the trail was theirs. This invariably meant scattering up the side of the mountain as fast as possible to get out of their way.

Washing of clothes was not a big priority – there were no guarantees that the clothes would dry and I did not want bits of damp clothing hanging on the outside of my backpack in the dust. I rotated my socks; each pair of socks was aired during the night, ready to be worn the day after the next. Showers happened every other day and most of the lads grew beards. As the expedition progressed we became a scruffy bunch

With the consumption of several litres of liquids a day, toilets became a big issue. And along the way there were disgusting long drops - rackety shacks most of the time perched on the side of the mountain with exposed drops; more discreet long drops; holes in the ground; and sometimes nothing other than an awkward angle somewhere in the open. Squatting and using the stick and straw method to cover up became an art form.

We met the most interesting people on the way: one such group was from Idaho and on their way to a wedding at the Tengboche monastery. In their group was a hippy soil scientist who trekked in Levi jeans and cowboy boots. So taken was he with our group that he joined us for a couple of our music evenings and became an honorary Irish. Our group became famous as word spread up the valley about the "Oirish"-who-make-music-at-night. In every village our music lad always managed to find a guitar.

In the evenings we fell into song and music, and ended up with lengthy card games late into the night. For brief moments I imagined everything was normal – that Dublin did not really exist and that I was whole.

All along the way Mani, or prayer stones, are piled into cairns and left at hilltops, mountain peaks, auspicious places, outside temples, holy sites, crossroads where travellers pass, or anywhere prayers are offered. We always walked clockwise around the Mani stones, and we adhered to this ritual throughout.

Everywhere in the Khumbu region "The North Face" gear can be found – almost every Sherpa, porter and villager wears it. I was impressed by the wide presence of the brand – but a few days into the expedition spotted that the name was spelt "The Hortn Face" and I realised that these clothing pieces were indeed fakes. In the authentic world of peaks and nature there was the little pleasure of being able to also sport a branded product; even if was muddled up.

Amazing people

The Sherpas assigned to our expedition were incredible; they were gentle, humble, friendly, caring, patient and wise. There was always a smile concealed in the lines of a weather-beaten face. The porters were a lot shier and other than carry our bags, they did not interact with us. They were the enablers for our expedition – the pack-horses. I often wondered if they were fed during the hard slog, and where they slept at night.

Foreign tour operators often exploited the locals and seeing the hardship on their faces unsettled me. I saw numerous porters carrying over fifty kilograms up near vertical trails in all weather conditions, often wearing flip-flops or worn-out shoes. The weight on their backs would slow them down and I passed the same ones again and again on my way uphill. Here I was with a daypack on my back, working hard up the mountain – how must it feel for them? We were all faced by the same hill, yet we were all lugging different loads on our backs; a different experience for each one of us. Is it not about recognising the fact that my load is unique, translating this own experience into empathy for the other, and ultimately being thankful for my own load?

Sometimes I found a porter sprawled on the side of the footpath looking as if he was dead – but he was only taking a quick nap. The bands that go around their heads to secure the unholy loads to their backs often cause their eyes to go squint. Let alone the effect of the load on to the neck – that tender place where the voice and expression reside. These people were paid a mere pittance for their crucial role in the business of expeditions. I saw one young boy fall over under the weight of his back. He was a few bricks tall and desperate to earn a wage.

On the route the dull thud-thud of the wooden sticks the porters use to stay upright became a familiar sound.

For the children, life in the Khumbu region is carefree, and seeing two youngsters playing badminton over the back of an unsuspecting *Jho* on their porch was as normal as Ed kicking a soccer ball in our back yard. The only difference is that children in the Khumbu region grow up in the most beautiful garden on earth.

A brown helicopter

In Lobuche, Chiring Sherpa, Dawa Sherpa and I were reunited with the rest of the team, who were on a rest day. As much as I tried to convince myself otherwise, my head was still aching, but there was to be no mercy and once we said our hello's Tshering Sherpa took me up a very steep ridge to a look-out point over the massive Khumbu glacier. He wanted to take me to an altitude higher than our sleeping altitude. For the first time I could see base camp in the distance. I was desperate to be well enough to continue on to Gorak Shep with the group.

We had just finished lunch at the lodge in Lobuche when a messenger arrived with a note. This was proof that "Everest mail" really worked – this man had walked from Namche Bazaar to deliver the message. He handed the piece of paper to the head Sherpa, Chiring. For some strange reason I noticed him slip in and my eyes remained fixed on Chiring Sherpa as he opened the note; I watched him stroke the paper, stare at the words, stroke and stare some more, and then get up and walk straight to me. Before Chiring even opened his mouth I could feel myself going into free-fall.

Things were not great in Dublin – the O'Daly had taken turn for the worse. An operation to bypass his stomach and an obstruction in his small intestine was unsuccessful, and his intestines could not recover after the surgery. He went into major surgery weakened by the chemo – a second operation was always going to be a gamble.

I know this was a difficult walk for Chiring; the previous evening he returned to Thukla – a few hundred metres further down the mountain – to take care of me. At Thukla I was in Chiring's charge: a gentle, compassionate man with loads of mountain experience. His goal was to re-unite me with the others at Lobuche the next morning; not to deliver the blow that would pull me from the group and the mountain.

I was paralysed by panic: it would take four or five days to walk down to Lukla before (weather permitting) I could catch a flight to Kathmandu, and before I could begin the 20-odd hour journey home. My hair had not been washed in days, my clothes were a week old and I wondered if the O'Daly would hang on until I got there. The team immediately jumped into action and before I knew my head was dunked into a bowl of cold water, hair washed and towel dried, my gear packed and we were waiting for the sound of a helicopter engine.

After the messenger's bad news had spoiled lunch, we were on constant standby for a helicopter. All afternoon at regular intervals the lodge owner made ten-dollar-a-minute calls with his satellite phone - but the helicopter could only land early the next morning and I spent one last tense evening in a tiny room with partitions and no floor; where the legs of my bunk were smack-bang on the outside moonscape. Not even the garish blanket could provide any consolation. The night was painfully long. Was I in the eye of a storm, or in the part of the river before the water bursts into white rapids? Or was I in that place in between two moments? I was a very long way from home.

There was much consternation in the tiny village when the brown helicopter approached the faint "H" on the rocky surface and touched down next to the wreck of another helicopter. The chopper first dropped a Canadian climber with a scrap of paper with my name on it, and then disappeared back to Base Camp to collect the body of the most famous Nepalese female mountaineer, Pemba Doma Sherpa, who had fallen down Lhotse and take her body to the monastery at Tengboche.

When the chopper returned, one porter grabbed my duffle bag and another one my backpack and my hand, and with the rotor blades whizzing over our heads they bundled me into the back of the chopper. Chiring Sherpa had 10 seconds to put in a request for a base camp detour; this was after all the goal of my expedition. The army pilot and co-pilot were in a rush and in no mood for smiling or talking. The back seats were folded away so I ended up next to the Canadian flat on my bottom with my bags on my lap. The Canadian climber had failed his attempt to summit Everest; a climb he was documenting in memory of a friend who had died on the mountain the year before. Thick pieces of skin were peeling from his sunburnt face like wallpaper.

The chopper was filled with a great sadness; and not even the various shades of army brown could camouflage the sense of loss.

Outside a send-off committee of team members, Sherpas and porters waved us goodbye. In order to send me off, the team had postponed their departure for Gorak Shep. As we lifted into the air the chopper made a U-turn and flew to base camp – I was going to see base camp after all! As we turned over the colourful tents at base camp the Canadian was showing me the way from the Khumbu icefall up the South Col to the summit. I handed my camera to him as I was unable to aim or focus or capture the moment on film – for the first time I gave in to the tears that had been collecting behind my eyes. For the first time in months I was being carried – by a brown helicopter. When the surly co-pilot asked me if I had fallen down the mountain, all I could say was "no"; he was unaware of the hospital room that was waiting for me back in Dublin.

The detour only took a couple of minutes and when we flew past Lobuche for the last time, I spotted a pair of orange arms waving from the group. I noticed the co-pilot pointing at the fuel gauge – the tank was near empty. I was not sure which was more frightening – being in a helicopter at altitude with an empty fuel tank or the unknown that was waiting around the corner in Dublin. We stopped at Pheriche to refuel and collected two more Canadian climbers. The four of us sat in squashed silence in the back of the helicopter during the one-and-a-half hour flight to the army base in Kathmandu. I discovered much later that both resident doctors at Base camp and pilots loathe helicopter flights at high altitude, because they are so dangerous.

My departure from Everest was equally chaotic as my departure for Everest. It was unexpected, rushed and very traumatic. I was pulled from the mountain.

Going home

My long journey home started at the army base in Kathmandu: I had no idea who would be fetching me or how and when I would be leaving for Ireland. My information about the O'Daly was sketchy and I had no idea if I would arrive in time. But someone appeared and back at the Kathmandu Guest Lodge I had a shower, tuna salad, and a gin and tonic. I used my little hairdryer for one last time.

Pure panic propelled me through the torturous negotiation to get a seat on a plane out of Kathmandu. I caused someone else to be bumped off the plane and in doing so avoided a 16-hour stopover in godforsaken Doha. There was some time left to brave the colours and smells and busyness of Thamel for a few last minute mementos; I had to haggle hard to buy a gorgeous red cotton throw with elephants on it with the last of my Rupees.

The gardens of the guest lodge looked so peaceful – a bubble of calm under the watchful eye of a Buddha.

One moment I was in the breath-taking Himalayan world of peaks and sky and space, and the next I found myself in the dark confines of Room 443 in the Mater Hospital. Everything happened in the blink of an eye and for a number of days after I wasn't sure which of the two worlds were real, and which imaginary.

The O'Daly never made it to Everest. Fate would have it that unless two sets of Meindl shoe prints could be left at base camp, neither of the individual sets of shoe prints would do so on their own. I wasn't sure whether it mattered that I never got to base camp, that I came within four miles of completing my mission, and that all the cost and effort was in vain. Was there going to be a part of me that would be driven to return and complete the mission?

I finally arrived at the hospital after midnight, two-and-a-half days later, and started my 10 day vigil at the O'Daly's bedside dressed in my smelly mountain clothes and the silk Sherpa-send-off scarf still around my neck. I could not believe that so much had happened since I left for Nepal - an operation and almost impossible recovery process. I could not believe how much the landscape of my world had changed during my absence. I found the O'Daly in severe post-op pain; unable to eat or drink anything other than water (and this would be the case until his intestines kicked into action); unable to walk more than a few steps with almost superhuman effort; unable to speak in more than a whisper; drained of every ounce of energy and all reserves; and his spirit totally crushed.

As we took turns at his bedside it became apparent that his intestines were not going to work and all we could do was watch as he simply faded away. In the cocoon of Room 443 there were the little sips of ice water – how he loved the smell of Espresso in a paper cup; big eyes in a bony face – how he loved to listen to our chatter beside him; the constant gurgle of oxygen and noise of a fan in the corner; desperate prayers; the smell of antiseptic gel on our hands; a bursting patient's file at the door; images of Sky News, "Deadliest Catch" or "Forensic Detectives" on the TV in the corner; swollen ankles in big fluffy socks; the regular 'whirr' of the morphine pump; and towards the end a very distinctive, deep-deep, sweet scent. We didn't see much of the world outside – I wasn't even sure that there was a world outside the hospital walls.

When I felt the voice of despair, I dropped down to the little chapel on the ground floor for a conversation with God. I held on to the story of David and Goliath and believed that all I needed was to find that one small pebble with which to hit the vulnerable spot on the giant's forehead. If there was one person on this earth that could beat the brute, the O'Daly would be the one. Here I found moments of calm, and here I could pause away from the world. And here for the first time I became aware of a gentle spring, a delicate source of life budding from the place beneath my heart. I didn't understand what was happening to me.

On the last Saturday Ed visited his father and when he was told that the O'Daly would not be coming home, he was sceptical as he could not understand how someone could be staying in a hospital forever. His last goodbye was a kiss on the O'Daly's hand – unable to hug his frail body. Shortly afterwards the O'Daly slipped into a coma and as if the atmosphere knew, a grey rain filled the sky.

Ruby and I spent precious time at the O'Daly's: we remembered and laughed and cried. Sometimes we talked nonsense and when we were totally fed-up with the four walls we played hopscotch in the passage. I could never understand why they combined salmon pink and lime green in a place of pain.

The time to say goodbye came quickly. We lit candles, placed a photo of the O'Daly's favourite Connemara on the bedside locker, draped a silver shawl to cover the bright bedside light, and played some of our favourite songs such as *San Francisco* (Scott McKenzie), *As tears go by* (Rolling Stones) and *Malaika* (Harry Belafonte). We could do nothing but observe as the O'Daly's breathing became shallower, his feet colder, and his hands lost their touch. Before I could make sense of anything, we were in the time of *after*. The staff told us we could stay as long as we wanted, but suddenly the words "staying" and "being together" had different meanings. The magical song I shared with the O'Daly was over; he was gone.

Around six a.m. I stepped out onto the wet pavements with a leather holdall and a big green refuse bag. Dublin was still asleep and it was only a matter of time before the day would begin its usual cycle of movement and noise and life. And I did not feel part of that day. I had never felt such numbness before; never-ever experienced such a total lack of sensation.

Then the To-Do-List kicked in and processes took over: the planning of a funeral, like you are planning some social event; the breaking of the news to a little boy; and the opening of doors at home. Emptiness; a pair of Camper shoes; a toothbrush; an e-mail address; a mobile number; a passport; a hat; a box with medicine; hiking boots; an unopened Amazon parcel; a Vodafone award for a person who cared; a newly framed photo of Boss Daly; African daisies still-in-nursery-pots; an unfinished book; and a brown bag with unused mountain gear.

I entered the surreal world of "gone forever" where total disbelief and brutal reality live side-by-side. When Ed heard the news the words fell on him like artillery shells, and he responded by retracting and curling up into a little ball. When he was brave enough to return, he headed for his Lego box and built a coffin with dead person inside, hearse, pall bearers and a priest. He drew his family of four, and under each person wrote a date next to the label "born", except his dad, who also had a date next to the label "died". He announced "you are a widow with two children now" and told total strangers "my father is dead." He wanted to know every detail about tombstones, cremations, fire and what was going to happen to the O'Daly's pyjamas. At night he went to bed with a row of photos and photocopies of photos of his daddy (including a mobile version for his pocket) in handmade paper frames.

As I stepped into no man's land I came face-to-face with the Irish obsession with all things to do with dying, death and the departed. Nothing could have prepared me for the ferocity of this obsession.

The unrest started during the hours before the O'Daly's passing; his siblings gathered in the hospital passage behind a cloud of muted whispers. These were siblings whom we didn't see from one end of the year to the next. I was bombarded with "Isn't this terrible!", "Oh, isn't this just awful"; these dark words tried to colour my sense of hope. At the time I was still holding on to the possibility of finding that one small pebble needed to destroy the giant cancer brute. The family had lost touch with their son and brother– they had no idea the O'Daly was not into the whole business of funerals and wakes. They didn't know he never subscribed to the obsession around death and dying, and that he was all for living.

I was in the small waiting room catching my next breath of hope when a text arrived to ask about a wake for the O'Daly at the family farm. Here I was holding on to life, still believing a miracle was possible, and the family was already preparing a wake.

The day of the funeral arrived like any other day. I was to step into the experience without the benefit of a manual. There was the matter of religion, an unfamiliar protocol around Irish funerals, a seething family, and the wishes of three remaining hearts. Over the years the O'Daly often joined me in the folds of the more modern Protestant congregations in South Africa, and although he remained Catholic, he was reluctant to attend the Catholic Church.

So we arranged a beautiful service for a special man: an inconspicuous coffin with three single sunflowers and three letters from a boy addressed to his daddy; the long walk behind a black hearse from the mortuary through the main street of Navan to the Protestant church on the hill; passers-by blessing themselves; shoppers stopping to look and see; a church full of people; a proud young boy leading the way with the coffin pretending to rest on his shoulders; a canon and a priest; e-mail messages from around the world; and a Celtic Tenor and three beautiful songs he made ours forever. There were tears and hugs outside the church, and when the hearse left with the coffin reality hit home – this was not a dream.

An undercurrent of tension with the brothers interweaved the day, and an invitation to sandwiches and tea was rebuffed by most of the family. Neighbours and the local farming community were told not to attend the funeral, and there was a general disregard for our wishes. The Irish family was determined to reclaim the son that left home when he was thirteen; first to boarding school, followed by university, and then on to a faraway land. He was theirs and not ours. Did regret perhaps fuel the animosity? Did the family finally discover the value of the "possession" once it was lost? Were they even aware that the O'Daly could never be possessed in the first place?

The chapel at Mt Jerome cemetery and crematorium was an anti-climax. We waited for our slot in a soulless primrose yellow canteen, and when we finally entered the chapel the coffin was waiting for us. We sang *Amazing Grace* as the coffin disappeared behind a bland, beige curtain. Ed was concerned about the fire – he believed that the cremation involved a plane to take the O'Daly to his African home. Before I could say "Jack Robinson" the whole affair was over, and a handful of us gathered at the Hole in the Wall pub for a glass of chilled Chablis. We were surrounded by an avalanche of condolences, cards and personal letters. I don't remember much about the first two weeks – the river carried me.

And then one day, in the grey drizzle, it was time to follow the vague instructions to the wrought iron gates of the Funeral Director's home in the countryside. A couple of miles this way, some turns, a couple of miles that way, until we found the house with the water feature in the middle of the lawn and a congregation of gnomes and figurines in the garden. He welcomed us with a warm smile and an invitation to join him for coffee. The kitchen was cluttered and I could not see a space big enough to fit coffee. He told me how difficult our funeral was – "very sad," and how beautiful our funeral was – "very unusual," and how I really must fall in for a coffee sometime in the future. We left his driveway past a bunny with a carrot and a smiling sailor next to a light tower. On the seat next to me was a green box with a printed label on the one side – on the box was the O'Daly's name.

A place, a time, a car and a green box – none of this felt real. All I could do was take those same small steps that worked so well whenever I was faced with a huge hill in the Himalayas. Was the time in that special place my preparation for the journey ahead? Retracing my steps through the colours blue, white, red, green and yellow that represent space, air, fire, water and earth inspired me. I stepped into the days after, held together by someone, and fortified by that indescribable little spring below my heart.

At times I could not believe that the O'Daly was no longer around, and I expected him to walk through the door from a meeting or chemo session at any time. But his keyboard and leather wallet remained untouched, and his mail unopened. Sometimes his calling card of that unique deep-deep scent became so palpable that I knew he was about.

We did not crack an invite to the O'Daly's Month's Mind requiem mass. Instead this became the local community's big moment and the church near the homestead burst its seams – well out of sight of anything foreign or Protestant. Without explanation two children were left out of an important event at a time when their hearts were still red raw. From that moment on our mourning and rebuilding happened separately.

I travelled down to the healers in Offaly to chat through the clear scan they saw when the O'Daly was still in the thick of his battle, and the healing they envisioned when an image of a near flat-lined electrocardiogram came to life again with flickers of some peaks. They were devastated by the death of the O'Daly; he was both friend and apprentice to them. At one particular point in time there was indeed a clear scan: for that moment the cancer had been beaten into submission. But the chemo had taken its deadly toll and it became obvious that had the O'Daly survived, his quality of life would have been abysmal. The real insight I got was that the healing they saw took place on another level – the healing happened in another realm, where soul returns to Source. That was all that mattered.

As the pair of them walked me to the door faith healer Pascal Delaney stopped me and said: "I don't know how to say this but there is another man on the horizon." I smiled, because somewhere in the ashes of my mourning I realised that I was only at the halfway point in my life, and that another life was very possible. Somewhere inside there was a knowing that I was on the cusp of a new beginning. At that moment I said "yes" to life.

My brief stay in the shadow of the "Mother of the Universe" touched me in a very special way – I could never be the same again. My heart was filled with peace – I had no regrets leaving Ireland at a most trying time to join the expedition. The expedition to Everest Base Camp became a watershed in my life; from that time on I knew that the sheer scale of the mountains would forever influence my vision.

Itchy feet

One thing we always did was plan our trips abroad well in advance; sometimes the plane tickets for the next trip or two would be tucked away in the drawer. We wanted to be sure they were there on the horizon and that they couldn't escape. In the top drawer were four tickets for our annual summer trip to our Greek homeland. Barely three weeks had passed since the hole appeared in our lives and once again I was faced with the heavy decision to stay or to go. I was not sure we were brave enough to face the place that held such special memories. Once again I followed my heart and decided to go. I am sure my decision was incomprehensible to some; how could I leave my mourning and travel somewhere else? But our mourning was scattered over several places, and in order to mourn we needed to confront these places. I needed courage to meet *our* places – a courage that could only come from a deeper source. Besides, the river was flowing – the water was transporting me to the next point in my journey.

For the first time we were able to fly directly from Dublin to Athens – and what a difference this direct flight made. We left in an emerald green plane with one empty seat.

Hellas waited for us with her blue colours, mountains and sea, and her Bitter Cucumber. In her familiar brown lap we were confronted with the blunt reality of "then" and "now"; of "was", "is" and "can never be." The experience was to be direct and without any soft nuances; difficult but hugely cathartic at the same time.

We arrived in a hot Diminio after dark, and for the first time I was in charge of the rental car, keys, rusty locks, electricity switches, dusty patios and dealing with a burglary on our first night. The thieves got away with our mobile phones (with a last text message from the O'Daly), camera, data card and cash. We started our days at the Cucumber disconnected from the world. If that was not enough to contend with, shortly after our arrival the sewage pipes in the building became blocked and flooded the apartment one floor below. A sudden knock on the door pierced our fragile peace, followed by a Greek rant that contained only two familiar words: "shits and poohs." We were mortified – were we really responsible for the mess in the apartment below? I couldn't help but wonder: "how much calamity will it take to finally break my being?"

In the apartment we found the aqua we painted on walls the day before our departure the previous summer by now well dry; and upstairs the O'Daly's desk, running shoes, Swiss army knife and khaki shorts were left untouched.

Dear friends stepped in to accompany us on our journey and in order to accommodate our visitors we rented a six-seat vehicle and for our trouble got an ugly Fiat Doblo. The Doblo became our home as we "tinkered" through the vast, striking landscape of the Peloponnese.

We travelled down familiar tracks to places of the heart. Our first stop was at a stone house in an orange grove on a working farm in Vathi at the edge of the bay of Laconia: mandarins, lemons, olives and figs; Willow and Poplar trees; terracotta pots filled with colour; and evenings with the smell of cow parsley and sea.

Next we returned to a beautiful house on the rock in Monemvassia: white lace curtains; dark wood; a rooftop patio; Jimmy still serving in his bar; a Romeo and Juliet window with an endless view over the sea; and the surprise of a bright red full moon sliding out as if from the bottom of the sea, and then painting the water silver.

We ate under the sky, at the old water mill in the hills above Diminio, at the water's edge and under trees; watched an Orthodox christening taking place in a 1,000-year old little white church somewhere along the Attica coast; roared on a thrilling donut raft ride behind a speed boat off the Mani coast; floated in the unbelievable lightness of the blue Mediterranean; enjoyed bitter cherry spoon sweets and special ice cream on a balcony in Paleo Faliro; danced to the beat of 1970's Swahili music that filled the Corinth night; and fell into the arms of our Greek family that simply stepped in.

I drove the Fiat Doblo from Diminio (near Corinth) through congested places like Keratsini, Moschato, the port of Piraeus and Kalithea to the Athens suburb of Nea Smyrni. From there I made my way to the airport through the city centre, skimming the Acropolis on my left and the old Olympic stadium on my right. For most of the journey Ruby the co-pilot couldn't find us on the map, let alone translate from Greek to English. This achievement left the locals pale with shock and awe and they made me an honorary Greek for passing the biggest test of all – the test of driving through the congested Athens city suburbs. By the time we returned to the Bitter Cucumber later that night I was in need of a strong tipple.

Our neighbours embraced us and where before we struggled to communicate, we all understood the meaning of tears, warmth and hugs – they needed no translation.

2,000-odd kilometres later we left Athens with a supply of Sparta olive oil, a set of new bed linen, a golden silk and leather clutch bag, a pair of silver starfish earrings, a decorated mirror with wishes in Greek and two little Matchbox cars-on-loan from Costa. In my suitcase was an icon-for-protection – taken from a neighbour's wall in Diminio for a wall in Headfort. We left with the treasure of friendships strong and brave enough to embrace new bonds in a new context, and the knowledge that we were blessed.

Leaving Athens did not happen without one last small hitch; the wheels of our plane got stuck on a runway light, as can only be expected to happen with an aeroplane painted in the colour green. We landed in Dublin well after midnight; the northern sky line was bright and for a brief moment I felt unsure about returning to a foreign land where the prime link no longer existed.

Dealing with loss

The minute we arrived back at Headfort, Ed constructed a wooden cross from bits of scrap wood. There was urgency about this job – as if he had to put into place a plan that had been brewing for some time and was about to boil over. He painted the cross green and followed this by engraving the first two letters of the O'Daly's name. Then he turned to a paint brush for the remainder of the letters and smudged the "y" because he "got a little distracted." He finished off the task by building a small holy circle around the cross with bricks, and filled the centre with flowers and petals from the flower boxes and gardens of neighbours.

He wanted a place he could go to remember his father. For Ed the experience at the chapel of St. Jerome's was unsatisfactory: for him the O'Daly disappeared behind a beige curtain and vanished.

Our return from the Greek pilgrimage signalled the beginning of a mopping-up phase; of letting life return to a new normal. I made a conscious decision to connect with my pain and to engage with the enormous changes that were inevitable. In between the huge drain there was the wonder of feeling little sparks of life-force. A new season was waiting for me, and from this moment on I decided that I would raise the sails and let the wind carry me.

The healing that started in Greece continued in the openness of Connemara. Summer in Connemara is montbresia, wild fuchsia, blackberries, backpackers, cyclists, ponies, bustling towns and foreign languages. The summer landscape was a feast of orange and cerise, and the purple-blue hues of harebells, foxglove and heather.

For the month of August we were given the freedom of Airde-Spéir on the edge of the Atlantic. We moved into the secluded paradise with headland and hills; kayaks and lake; sea and caves; a horse-shoe bay; and a walled garden with everything organic you can imagine: broad beans, peas, artichoke, beetroot, potatoes, apples, nasturtiums, corn flowers and garlic.

Summer at Airde-Spéir is fresh wild salmon; rocket and coriander salads; homemade gravlax; impressive barbeques; snakes and ladders and draughts; a swinging chair in the Buda garden; chats in kayaks the length and breadth of the lake; a bonfire with marshmallows, red wine, goofy teenagers and private thoughts; and long, long evenings.

We were the first ones to stay in the brand new cottage in the yard, where thoughts and emotions were able to move freely in the crisp white space. We were so blessed to be given a safe place to fall - the grace of being able to pause in the folds of such generosity, sincerity and love.

We shared the yard with two horses and a family of fowl. In the evenings the chickens, guineas and one white dove would return to their coop – the four guineas always last to enter as it would befit those at the top of the pecking order; and every morning they would squeal to be let out. And so they became part of my daily ritual.

Our west coast days took us down to the Burren in Clare and a wonderful day in New Quay where we were spoiled with fresh lobster and crab claws; a wild trip around Galway bay in the *Yellow Bastard*; a meeting with the resident sea lions; and a half pint of Guinness to toast the day. The owner of the *Yellow Bastard* was a true rib connoisseur and we had to hang on for dear life as he took us around the bay; thrills, shrieks and views of the Burren which can only be seen from the water's side. From there to the beaches around Ballyconneely for body boarding and a picnic under a threatening sky; back to the icy sea of our favourite Fountain Hill; and to new friends and the abandoned village of Aillenacally.

And our west coast days also took us to a long row of white stepping stones across a vast bog to a little stone cottage and a hermit. There is something about arriving and leaving on stepping stones. On arrival the curiosity of following the steps into the unknown, the hidden; and on departure following the steps away from the wonder of discovery, of sharing, and still depending on each step to find the way back. There is something about meeting a very special man who has lived in isolation for 26 years without electricity and running water - and all you want to do is spend more time listening to him. This man made the choice to step out from civilization and he never looked back. His weekly trip over the stepping stones, via the bus to the local village, and the church service was enough to nourish him. In between he lived on prayer, very little food and peat logs to keep him warm.

But most special were my daily walks across the purple hills. Whenever I got to the highest point, I would lie down on the heather with an endless view of the sea, total solitude, and the sky the only limit.

There is no better place on earth than Connemara to find healing. The rawness of the landscape allowed me to peel off the many, many layers left by 20-odd years.

Saturday the 15th *September* marked the O'Daly's birthday and also the day he received his shattering diagnosis. We celebrated this day in the seclusion of the beautiful American garden at Headfort. We formed a small circle on an opening on the far side of the Handkerchief tree: the day was perfect and the green space a fitting place to be remembering an extraordinary man.

We were hidden from the world as 47 balloons floated off into the sky; and we watched until the purple and red of the balloons melted into the blue. There was a toast with champagne, some words, some longing and recollection, and some silence. And for the moment when the sky melted the colours, time stood still.

My way of dealing with the immense changes in my life was to engage with the pain. Before I could begin the process of a re-birth, I had a strong urge to get back to basics and re-discover who I was. I had no roadmap – there was my intuition and an indescribable compulsion to move forward. For some reason seeing a therapist or counsellor never crossed my mind. I didn't know at the time that I had embarked on a treasure hunt.

Very soon after death left a hole in our home we tackled the O'Daly's cupboard. I knew if I didn't clear it out then, it would become more and more difficult to do so in the future. I did not have the courage for delayed encounters. Ruby helped me sort through the many business suits, shirts and ties – lined up in a wardrobe, spick and span as if they were board members waiting for an important meeting. They reminded us of long hours, periods of absence and stress, and they did not represent the O'Daly.

We made three piles; one for the Kenia clothing appeal, one for the yellow clothes bank outside the Silver Tankard, and one for a young boy who one day would be a man. The pile for safekeeping ended up in vacuum storage bags. We filled them and sucked the air out until they could stand in a row – like a dole queue on a weekday morning.

In the bag for Kenia we slipped the surplice and academic gown once used by Ruby at her posh school, and an Irish porcelain doll in a ludicrous shamrock green velvet dress. I couldn't help but imagine the faces when the bag was opened: a heap of things, somewhat random and out of place. A bag of possessions that once belonged to someone, and had since lost its meaning.

We bought paint and in a rush of enthusiasm painted the walls of the kitchen and bedrooms until there was no hint of yellow. In our flurry there was no time for preparing the walls – we were scared that if we put down the brushes for even a second we would lose the courage. So we painted over bits of spider webs and debris.

The O'Daly always took meticulous care in preparing surfaces before a paint job; I could see him watching over our eagerness, and I could feel him disapproving of our lack of preparation. Redecorating in the wake of loss was a painful process, but hugely cathartic as we laughed and cried through the many brush strokes. In our laughter we connected with the O'Daly – he had a most wicked sense of humour.

Unbeknown to us the dreaded bedbugs from Drumcondra made their way into our house at Headfort, and when the kids were covered in bites, I had no choice but to call pest control. The day the sales agent arrived in his marked van was a low point, a Job-of the Bible moment – a place from where there was nowhere more to fall. The agent was full of the chat as he stepped through the house, telling me that our situation was nowhere near as bad as homes in Dublin where they were faced with bedbugs and cockroaches. He did not know that our house had a hole and that the bugs were reminding us of our loss. He also did not know that I had no bandwidth for bedbugs.

We had to remove mattresses, skirting boards, duvets, pillows and clothes, and for a couple of days were not allowed in the house. I decided to change the carpets and the children's beds – the thought of an on-going infestation was not an option. I came close to leaving the house and walking away from it all. In some strange way the fumigation process helped with the process of stripping.

Soon only a few discreet reminders of the O'Daly were left in our house. We didn't need to be reminded of the excruciating gap by the constant stare of photos on walls, or shrines that emphasised the emptiness. There were a number of items with special meaning and O'Daly written all over them – in a song, the texture of a fabric, or in the colours of an artist's painting. And the little bag with his watch, ring and penknife; his hat; fly fishing fly collection; the Liquid Amber tree in the corner of our garden, and the deep places he holds within our hearts.

From the word go we included the O'Daly in our conversations, and we ignored social taboos and "no-go" areas. We did what felt right for us. For me the scenario was very clear – the O'Daly was no longer here, and picking up the pieces was going to be my task. Mine alone. I began to realise that I didn't need to understand why things happen, but to accept that they do. I began to focus on staying in the moment. From that point on I became sensitised to finding either the teacher or the blessing in every situation. And most of all, I surrendered to grace.

As Christmas approached I was faced with another decision to stay or go. In the top drawer were tickets to Jackson Hole in Wyoming, bought nearly 12 months earlier. We spent a memorable time there some eight years previously and fell in love with the place. So much so, that before cancer struck, the O'Daly went on a recce mission to that part of the world to explore relocation possibilities. We decided to go and I cancelled one ticket.

We landed at the small airport in Jackson's Hole this side of midnight. We were exhausted after a 24-hour journey but the excitement of retracing steps and memories made eight years ago kept us going. The pilot was at the door of the cockpit with a wave and big smile, and the moment we left the plane we stepped into the white of a -15°C night. The hairs in my nose froze and my hands nearly fell off as we slipped on our way to row 18 of the car park to find our rental car.

My brother and his wife joined us for our first week in Wyoming. They were making their own way there from London (via Chicago) and all we knew was that we were on separate flights into Jackson, about two hours apart. But synchronicity would determine that we ended up on the same flight - all seated in the same row of a full plane. Someone was looking after us. Having travel companions was a blessing as we soon discovered finding the condo in the pitch dark was a nightmare; something the kids and I would've struggled with on our own.

Stepping through the white days with the pair and catching up on memories and stories spanning a lifetime were delicious. The days had the same soft touch of rose quartz as it settled in the hollow of your hand. Our condo was nestled amongst trees at the base of the Teton Mountain range in the Aspens, a quiet resort community. Within walking distance were the Rocky Mountain Bank, small grocery store, Starbucks, a couple of restaurants and a ski bus stop at our front door. The condo felt like home: the whistle of a kettle on the stove; fire in the fireplace; freshly baked scones and buttermilk pancakes; choc-chip cookie dough in the fridge; the smell of coffee; and the luxury of being able to dip into the fridge first thing in the morning.

We spent 12 days suspended in a gentle white space where the heel of each day never touched the past – what was, and the toe never the future – what was ahead.

From the very first day all the familiar bits and pieces started to unfold in front of us like the clues in a treasure map: the road to Teton Village, Cowboy Café, Bridger Centre, Cody House, Mountain High Pizza Pie and Albertsons grocery store in Jackson. I was even expecting to hear Bob Seger's 'Against the wind" in the Casper mountain restaurant, but the moment never came.

For most of the first week jet lag caused our days to start at two in the morning with tea and chatter in warm beds, and then a struggle to reach beyond six p.m. for dinner.

There was a regular bus service between the Aspens and Teton Village, so sometimes we left the car under its snow blanket and took the grey Alltrans bus. Most of the grey line drivers were not your typical bus driver, but cowboys – complete with cowboy hats and pony tails. One such cowboy did his e-mail on a Dell notebook and mobile connection en-route while another left his bus idling at the bus stop while he popped into a saloon for a take-out pizza, and then proceeded to eat from the big box while driving the bus. Yet another did his admin, completed forms and filing while driving on the slippery roads. And then there was the new chap who was late on his first day because he had to take his girlfriend to the Jackson hospital with the dry heaves in the middle of the night and he got into trouble for not knowing the route or how to work the card scanner and for being late. The next day he was still trying to catch up and we got an update on the girlfriend and both of their irritated employers on later shifts. This was another world.

The snow and skiing were wonderful. Most days greeted us with a foot of fresh, fine powder snow that would crunch under the soles of our shoes, bury our car and keep the snow ploughs busy. Jackson Hole presented Ed with his first real attempt at skiing and he passed the Bear class, but never quite mastered the Moose to get to the Bronco group, which meant he never left the green slopes. This had nothing to do with fear, but rather his unconventional stopping technique as he could not resist ending in the powder bumps on the edges of the slopes. And when Ed's ski school finished, the African *meisie* who could barely hold her own on the more difficult terrain, became the ski instructor for the boy who went down the slopes in a pizza-wedge.

We love Jackson Hole: the place is unpretentious and the people gentle and friendly. Life in the Hole is simple, rustic and down-to-earth – a place you feel at home and a place that begs you to move in. At the foot of the mountain range wood, copper, aspens, rivers, creeks and winter log cabins rest in the beautiful valley.

The kids and I spent our last four evenings at the Teton Mountain Lodge. Here we could ski-in-ski-out and end the day in a hot tub in the snow along with others with their hairy bellies, marshmallow pink swimming trunks, foreign languages, and mountain stories. In the lodge breakfast consisted of oats porridge, waffles, maple syrup, Indian River ruby grapefruit, and on the slopes Lotus flower tea during breaks, and chilli vegetables, hamburgers or wraps for lunch. At night we would wake to the beep-beep of the snow groomers' engines in the dark, followed by the bang-bang-bang of the avalanche control mortar shells. When this happened the next day was only hours away.

The children looked on in silence as the families arrived with their suitcases, ski-gear, groceries, and wrapped presents. The more Christmas slipped into the valley the more they tried to pretend that the days were bog-standard, normal days. But as the snow quietened the land the white flakes also covered the last remaining specks of disbelief they had about their father: this was it - he was not going to come back.

On Christmas Eve we had to dig the car out from under the snow and crawl the few miles on the slippery road to the Roadhouse for dinner. This was a cool restaurant where there was a bucket of peanuts in shells at each table, and at the end of the evening all the shells ended up on the floor.

The three of us drove home in the magic of a snowy night with snowflakes twirling in the headlights, trees showing off their lovely fairy lights, and a soulful country and western voice singing 'Silent Night.' Back at the lodge we lined up on one bed and giggled as we uploaded photos of our stay; outside the mountain was mysterious and still with all the memories of the day locked under its white coat.

Christmas Day was glorious and blue. Santa Claus did not find his way to Jackson's Hole, but instead he detoured to Dublin to deposit Ed's presents. All day we kept active and busy. Ruby mastered double black diamond slopes with her snowboard and left the mountain on a high with labels such as "you rock," "hard core," "rad," "gnarly" and "totally awesome." For the first time in six months she was in her element.

At Jackson Airport a security woman found explosives on my trusted eight year old pair of Caterpillar boots. She disappeared with my shoes and when I enquired what was going on, all I could see was her walking around, talking to others with my shoes clutched to her bosom as if they were hers. Luckily further tests cleared my shoes from the serious allegation.

We were sad to leave Jackson; sad because we had to step out of the bubble of white and back into our lives back in Ireland. I was sad because the time had arrived to step out of the period of grace and full-steam back into business, busyness, and Ruby's preparation for her Leaving Certificate.

After four airports, three airlines, delays in London, lost suitcases, and a taxi strike in Dublin we arrived back in green. The moment we touched down in Ireland I wasn't sure if Jackson Hole had ever happened, and if the lovely days in the mountains were only a dream. We stepped out of this illusion into the back-end of a fairy-tale to collect the presents Santa left for his buddy at the apartment in Castleknock, and travelled to Headfort with one suitcase, a soft brown bear, huckleberry taffies and three expired ski lift tickets. At home we were greeted by a mountain of mail, Christmas cards addressed in my name alone and a grey school jumper split open on both sides.

Whereas the Himalayas tested my endurance, Jackson Hole tested my fear. I was skiing down slopes you would hardly walk down, alone, with no-one to lead. There was no-one to say "go for it, you'll be OK" when I got stuck and my legs froze with the fear; no-one to help me get up after a big tumble. By venturing into the scary places and going down the intimidating slopes I somehow knew I was going to be OK.

We were in Connemara when 2008 stepped over the count-down of ten and locked the O'Daly forever into an old year. When the New Year arrived it stretched out all the way from the Orange room; down the Shanbolard driveway; past the 12 Bens and Galway; Athlone and Kells; and the edge of the sea.

And as the first moments passed by I could feel the soft brush of a new day against my cheek.

Back to clay

No one ever tells you about the time that you will have to pack a green box with a nametag into your hand luggage for a journey. And when the name on the tag is that of your partner of 20 odd years you know the suitcase will not be big enough to fit all the memories. But then you squeeze in as many of them as you can, close the zipper, slip into a taxi as if you're going on a casual trip, face the cold scrutiny of security staff at airports, and return to a very special place: the Kalahari Desert.

A handful of us boarded the six o'clock flight from Johannesburg to Upington; it was a grey, wet day on the Highveld and after a miserable Irish winter we were desperate for sun. An hour-and-a-half later we landed in the sun and the heat and the endless open spaces of the Kalahari.

The town of Upington is from a bygone era and we stepped back into the charm of a place that was forgotten by time and where shops have names such as "*Babsie*" Hair Salon, "*Rafels*" ("threads") Sewing Shop, and Bears Furniture. We had a couple of hours to kill while waiting for the remaining members of our group to arrive by small plane. Our destination was a camp deep in the desert, about five hours away from civilization. There was nothing there so we had to load up all our own provisions for the couple of days. In the local Pick & Pay supermarket we stocked up two trolleys with an eclectic mix of food and drink: tins of baked beans, tuna, sweetcorn and "*chakalaka*" (a traditional tomato & onion sauce); flour for *mieliepap* (maize porridge); chutney, pepper and salt; eggs; mango's, papino's and pears; bread, potatoes, garlic, tomatoes and pasta; beers, bottles of Brutal Fruit and hundreds of litres of water. Our basic food menu was supplemented by surprise treats that appeared from duffle bags and suitcases.

We loaded our white minibus to the brim and took the straight road north to the Kgalagadi Transfrontier Park – the place where South Africa, Namibia and Botswana meet.

The drive to the gate of the park at Twee Rivieren took two and a half hours and it took us a further two and a half hours over a corrugated road to reach our tented camp near Mata Mata, on the border with Namibia. We were in the middle of nowhere, in a thirsty but very beautiful land; a sacred world where heaven tucks in around the seams of the desert to make one amazing big space. I loved being back under the African sun.

On our way to Kgalagadi we drove past the red dunes where once a blue quad bike rode. During the late eighties the O'Daly brought me to the Kalahari on our first holiday together – he couldn't wait to show me one of his all-time favourite spots in the world. He brought me to the Kalahari at the height of summer – not an ideal time to be visiting a desert. At the time we were penniless and could only afford to stay in a little two-man tent pitched at the side of a thorn tree. I remember the heat, the solitude, and the roar of lions at night, barely a few metres away from the camp fence. I remember the long drives in an air-conditioned car around midday to hide from the sun; and I remember how the O'Daly melted into his element in this beautiful place. For the O'Daly the Kalahari Desert was his spiritual home.

One of our mid-day drives was legendary; we were heading for a picnic spot and toilet stop some hours into the wilderness. Stops were few and far between. I was intrigued to know how they established where in the park to place these stops, but the O'Daly dismissed my curiosity with an "only a Capricorn can think of something as trivial as that." It did not take long for him to eat his words. As we pulled up to the designated picnic spot, a dozen or more lions were waiting for us; they were draped over the picnic table and lounging in front of the door to the toilet; they too needed to pause at the little oasis.

This time our drive through the wilderness was more subdued – this was no holiday, we were on an important mission. Our base for the next few days was a tent camp high up on a red sand dune, overlooking the ancient Auob River. There are no fences around the camp and after dark no one is allowed outside the confines of the tent. One of the tents became our communal kitchen and gathering point: here we concocted meals out of ingredients that were not made to fit. After dinner our own shuttle bus did the drop-offs back to each tent. A shared deck with trees and a swimming pool the size of a postage stamp offered some cool during the heat of the midday when the heat was even too much for a siesta. In the pool Ed got severe sunburn that worried me at night – we were a lifetime away from doctors – and made him shed his skin like a snake in pools and homes around Gauteng for days afterwards.

The Park greeted us with abundance and green - as if the landscape knew to prepare for the return of an Irishman. Every so often I had to pinch myself to believe that we were actually in a desert and not somewhere in the Bushveld. Here and there the soft red tops of dunes peeped out of the green to show its desert-ness. The game was plentiful, in excellent condition with loads of young, and big stretches of the landscape were covered with yellow and purple flowers.

At night under a private sky we tried to soften the edges of the hole left when four became three with recall and thoughts and tears and laughter. Under the watchful eye of Orion words came straight from the heart and darted the dark pauses like arrows.

We were surrounded by the smell of grass and sky; Camelthorn and thirst; and the sun and familiar places. Once the chatter finally stopped, all I could hear was the sounds of the night, the desert, and the silence.

The O'Daly's ceremony of light happened on a Wednesday, two days after St Patrick's Day. Until this day we saw herds of game, but on this morning – as if on cue – we saw a number of lions. They were draped on the roadside within spitting distance, striding on hilltops, and draped under the shade of thorn trees.

We left camp at the crack of dawn and travelled the hour-and-a-half journey to a special spot where no-one could disturb or find us; right in the heart of the land. The day was perfect: our thoughts were intense, the blue sky endless, and the memories raw. After a mango and water break we gathered in a circle, our bare feet in the soft of the sand, and a gentle breeze in our hair.

There was a message from Genesis; prayers in English and Hindi; a little cairn with stones from Headfort (they still had moss on them) and the Kalahari, pebbles with white marble lines from Diminio in Greece, and a single black rock from the base of Everest. The smell of incense mixed with the breeze and birdsong added the music – on this occasion we did not need the Kgalagadi tenors – we had the birds. We ended the ceremony with a tot of whiskey for each of us; and then we took our time to enjoy the view and feel the pulse of the earth.

I remember the ashes falling to the earth and leaving a highlight in the grass. I remember the ashes scattering on the soil until a white highway formed for the ants and other insects. And I remember the wind, the beauty of a sacred place, taste of salt, thorns in my feet, special camaraderie, and the empty green box. The O'Daly was home at last; back to clay.

On our way back to Upington we stopped at the sign that advertised dune rides. An inebriated local with toothless-gaps sold us on a "dune as high as the sky." He told us the dune was so high that once down it would take us forever to get back up, and for the same price we could stay all day if we wanted to. The dune turned out to be a little hump, but hey, there is something alluring about a dune, red sand and the fact that you can.

Behind the red dunes of the Kalahari one journey ended. In the night sky the mystery of one and two that became three and four, will forever be buried within the four bright corners of Orion; secure within its ancient heart.

We returned to Johannesburg to a width and depth of warmth and welcome that blew us away. It was a busy time re-connecting with friends and catching-up on the big gaps left by absence. We spent one precious week in the quiet and calm of Oubaai – where recharge happened with a view over the blue of the Indian Ocean.

During the last few years of his life the O'Daly discovered an uncanny luck while betting on horses. He did this for a bit of craic; only every now and then, and always with a Euro or two. He could never explain why, but he was typically compelled to veer off his normal course, go into the bookies, be drawn to some random horse, place his money minutes before the race would take place, and win every time. After the race he would take his spoils and leave the hard core betters completely flummoxed. Here was a man – like a fish-out-of-the-water - strolling in, placing a bet, winning and leaving as discreetly as he arrived. The O'Daly's betting antics were strange and made for compelling dinner stories and a good laugh.

Shortly after our return from the Kalahari I was on my way home from work one afternoon when I received a text from one of the O'Daly's close friends. It was the time of year for the races at Punchestown and simply said "bet on horse no seven in race number one." I was making my way along winding country roads and through annoying road works and did not feel like making a detour to the bookies. Besides, I had never been to bookies before and had no idea where to begin, so I did nothing with the information. The next morning there was an email in my inbox with the result: horse number seven in race one had won – his name was Kalahari King. A horse in Ireland with the name of a desert – this could be none other than a very big wink.

A chip off the old block

Ruby couldn't wait for the day she finished school. For her the whole school thing was a little tedious; she never really got into it, and of course school meant maths - theorems, integration and differentiation and she always used to say, "I love the idea of maths, but I just don't get it."

Her schooling experience was not exactly straightforward. She attended four different primary schools: two in Johannesburg, and one each in Athens and Kells. During her first couple of weeks at her new school in Athens I was absent; I was in Johannesburg tying up the last of the loose ends. On her first day she was dropped by the O'Daly – en-route to the airport for his flight to Beijing. Much later she told me about the memories of her blue and white candy-stripe school dress, sandals, long bus drives, and the anxiety that surrounded the foreignness of everything. By the time she had settled into the wonderful Mediterranean life we relocated to Ireland.

At Headfort it was my turn to drop her and a big holdall with her grey uniform, pyjamas and duvet into the eccentricity and strangeness of a Preparatory School as a weekly boarder. This was to be the beginning of name labels, clothing lists and laundry bags, tuck money, and exodus weekends. From weekly boarder she moved on to becoming a seven day boarder at a school on the outskirts of Dublin. I couldn't understand the O'Daly's obsession with boarding schools – the concept was foreign to me, and yet I was unable to challenge him on the matter. Boarding schools were one of those inexplicable things that were to be part and parcel of our life in Ireland.

As she struggled in an environment with established cliques and specific daily routines I was pre-occupied with setting up home in a foreign world while the O'Daly spent most of his time at airports and on airplanes.

Right from the start she hated boarding and on a Sunday afternoon when we had to take her back to school she would become withdrawn and reluctant. There were tears and upset but her father's view of "toughing it out" and "seeing things through" always won over; until her desperate cry for help finally echoed in the cuts on her arms and we could no longer ignore her voice. Somewhere during the period of settling into a new homeland I missed the signs of Ruby's unhappiness. She wrote her junior certificate under extremely difficult circumstances, but passed with flying colours.

We moved her to a day college in Dublin for her Leaving Certificate and she loved the freedom and independence of life in the city. Her commute was long and meant an early morning start and late finish. During her first week at her new school the O'Daly was diagnosed with terminal cancer, and when we responded by renting an apartment in Dublin to be close to the college and chemo, she stepped into the role of taking care of herself; making her own meals, doing her homework and getting to and from college. In the weeks when chemo happened she cared for the O'Daly after school; she was only sixteen.

On the eve of her Leaving Certificate exams we remembered the O'Daly with four candles, a song and a prayer; and the next day a young girl, very upset and still angry about the father that had abandoned her and "burdened" her with the responsibility of looking after her mother and brother, sat her exams.

When school was all over Ruby fell into a summer of chai lattés, berry crumble colours, pink scarves, sunglasses, shorts, cricket in the courtyard, home-made biscotti, creamy oats porridge and beach days.

One Wednesday morning her results came in a big brown envelope; her maths marks were not good and tainted her excellent overall performance. The Irish points system had decided her fate – she did not qualify for a radiotherapy course in Ireland. Suddenly there was disappointment in the air as the blip in maths muted any plans for full-sized congratulations. Suddenly we were faced with the possibility of parking her dream, repeating the year and extending the lease on the apartment in Dublin. I wasn't able to get my head around another year at school.

Then again, she is a chip off the old block, and in typical O'Daly style, she picked herself up and within one week had contacted Liverpool University, compiled a bio note-from-the heart, got the attention of the head of Radiation therapy who saw the person and not the points; got herself into the prerequisite of a day in a radiotherapy facility in a Dublin hospital; carried herself through a lengthy telephone interview; and got a place on the course.

Out came the champagne and the excitement: a fresher's year, her own college room, a new booklist, white coat, and a pottery mug and bowl with daisies. In Liverpool Ruby found her niche; here her world trebled as she joined the rowing and climbing clubs, and the societies for Afro-Caribbean and battle re-enactment; dissected ovaries and testicles; won the debate on ethics; charmed the Coronation Street actors and her examiners in a patient role-play; and got herself a Scouse accent.

At the same time she moved to Liverpool I travelled south on a very different mission. It felt like any old runway when the Boeing 747 screeched to a halt – as if the pilot had suddenly run out of tarmac. I left the plane, saw the mountains and smelled the air – there could be no doubt, I was in my heartland. The trip came after an intensive week-long NLP course in London; the sweat from rushing on the Piccadilly line to Heathrow, the colours of West Brompton Street, smell of curry and workshop words still fresh on my skin.

I was in Cape Town to place my father's ashes. He died on father's day and I was unable to attend his funeral. Who would have thought that I would become a widow before my mother? Who would have thought that I would lead the way when it came to collecting the remains of a partner? So we went to the undertakers in the Bellville city centre and collected the little wooden box. This time there were no garden gnomes, but a soulless street with cars and people doing their daily business. As we left the waiting room, I felt the box fit perfectly on my forearm; tucked in next to my heart. He was a big man.

It was a private, simple ceremony under the shadow of the big white 182 year old church in Durbanville; witnessed by the birds, the mass of purple vygies (Mesembs), and the blue of the sky. I couldn't help but think about a young boy in a boarding school in Ireland who now was the oldest male in his bloodline.

My visit to the Western Cape was over in a blink. When I returned to the red, gold, orange and yellow of autumn I fell into the empty spaces of a cold house. There was no-one to meet me with a "hello" – everything felt that much harder. When I stepped onto that Dublin pavement on that momentous day in June, I stepped into the new morning with the experience of a co-pilot. Now I had to fly solo – I was in fact the pilot, and I was already clocking up the hours.

During the first year-and-a-half into my new solo phase I came to experience a great ebb and flow of emotions. There was the rawness of withdrawal – when others pulled away and sometimes disappeared as if there was no past and there was not going to be a future. There was the jockeying for position; to be the helper, knight in shining armour, or rescuer. These were generous and much appreciated gestures, but when they were withheld, they left another gaping hole. I dropped off invitation lists and very soon became a non-entity. It was as if without the O'Daly, I was no-one. Much later I realised that the reaction was never about me, or us – but really about the needs of the other; and when those needs were no longer met, the friends who I thought were friends became absent. If only they could know how they left when I needed them most. Their absence highlighted the subject of entitlement – I realised I wasn't entitled to any of their company; that friendship is a gift. The experience taught me how friendships cannot thrive in the presence of conditions and unrealistic expectations; and it brought home the significance of generosity – generosity without the need for a reward. But ultimately I realised that the journey through loss can be none other than solitary; at its very core there is no space for another.

My journey through loss consisted of the pleasure and excitement of finding and meeting new people; betrayal and loyalty; egos and generosity; prejudice and acceptance; forgetting and remembering; closing and opening; and resentment and grace. Through the loss I faced boundaries, hurdles, surrender, flow and freedom.

While in the fire I found the soft space in between two moments – that place of blissful suspension where there is total silence and all I can hear is the absence of my breath.

New Delhi

She wouldn't show her full face from under a thick fog blanket - as if she wanted to say: "Look at my colours and my people; look at their doing; follow their steps; and see their prints." It was as if she wanted to keep her sky as a bonus.

Ed and I landed at Delhi airport around two in the morning, and it took another two hours to collect our cases, say our helloes, find our driver, enter the relative calm of the sleeping city, check into our accommodation and catch a few hours' sleep before we joined the day that was already underway.

I was venturing out far beyond the usual comfort zone. Right from the start there was a strange familiarity about the place – something I couldn't quite explain.

Our base in New Delhi was the India International Centre (IIC): a members-only-club and place with pedigree, both distinguished and down-to-earth; and busy meeting place for business people, academics, activists, Nobel Prize winners and politicians. The check-in procedure was lengthy and entry depended on a million questions. At the IIC people talked in muted tones. At times some debate over Kashmir, or blasts in Mumbai, or some other topical issue would overspill into the hushed environment and stir the order.

For the couple of days at either end of our visit to India the IIC became our haven in the city. The IIC overlooks the beautiful Lodhi gardens – a park spread over 90 acres, and in the 15th Century home to the Sayyid and Lodhi dynasties. Lodhi is home to the tombs of Mohammed Shah and Sikander Lodi; the Bara Gumbad and Sheesh Gumbad; beautiful trees and gardens; and a multitude of birds.

We landed with our feet moving and our first day took us around the gardens; to the book launch of *Songs of the Gurus* by Khushwant Singh - one of India's best-known writers/columnists – and into a room with the Sikh intellectual elite and the prime minister's wife Gursharan Kaur; to the vibrancy and busyness of the Khan market; and into Anokhi – a wonderful hand crafted textile shop. I was lucky to be at Khushwant Singh's book launch; very privileged to be tagging along someone with local connections and knowledge.

At the Khan market - rumoured to be the 24th costliest retail location in the world - Good Earth, Nike, Reebok, Beneton, KK Lee shoes, amazing bookstores and cramped little hardware, food, electronics, kitchenware shops all live side by side. Mr. Lee, the owner of the shop, was determined to see me leave with something: he and his three helpers had all their size seven sandals out of their boxes and every time I tried on a pair they egged me on by indicating with either a thumbs-up or thumbs-down. Back at base a wall of exhaustion prevented us from leaving our room to attend a house party somewhere in the city.

The ease with which we slipped straight from a raw Irish winter into the warmth of the Delhi days surprised me.

On a low-key Sunday a trip to the Cottage Industries – with everything from jewellery to furniture to bedspreads to crafts to camel saddles – left me bewildered and overwhelmed by sensory overload. After an evening of meetings between here and there; old school friends; a Fordham Business School professor; some of the cream of Delhi's activists; vegetarian 'thali', tandoori roti, dal, paneer and ghar ka khana; two singing Santas; and stories and laughter we were ready to commence our journey south.

Our first stop was Agra. Leaving with two cars, two drivers, a fair mountain of luggage and three families was not something that could happen without complication. Before every departure there was always the customary consensus via committee and some toing and froing – more so if the party consists of a headmaster of a school, an anthropologist, social scientist, two boys who could at any moment suffer from separation anxiety and a mother with a restless toddler. During the long drives there were animated debates about civilisations and the war on terror.

Leaving an Indian city is not easy. Indian cities go on and on forever – and it is very difficult to tell where or when a city begins and ends. You set off filled with anticipation of getting stuck into the journey, of seeing countryside, stopping for a picnic – but that of course doesn't happen for a couple of hours, until suddenly the chaos begins to thin out and open spaces begin to appear. Only when the green of fields and the yellow of mustard seed entered the landscape I knew we had left Delhi.

The sheer volume of traffic and movement on the roads was mind-blowing: a throng of mechanical and human traffic and the way it worked was a constant "beep-beep" followed by just go. Cows, water buffalo, camels, elephants, dogs, goats, humans, cars, bicycles, rickshaws, tractors and trucks all shared the same road. Somehow this chaos works – during all the miles we travelled I never saw an accident or one iota of road rage.

Stopping anywhere in India is also not easy as you get swamped by a multitude of beggars, touts and hangers-on. I was moved by the vastness of the need. During a small wait in a car at Kosi we were confronted by several persistent snake charmers and their cobras, a disabled man crawling on all-fours, monkeys, peacock feathers, necklaces, gemstones and other knick-knacks.

After a five hour drive we squeezed into Agra. It took us more than an hour's hard work through the city and its almost two million people to get to our hotel and in the process we missed a perfect sunset over the Taj Mahal.

Agra was founded in 1504 and the place has little other than the Taj Mahal to show and as we inched our way through the crowded streets I was struck by the unbelievable decay, squalor, pollution and rawness of life in her fold. I was relieved to leave that behind and retreat to our comfortable hotel for the night.

Over the years I have seen many pictures of the Taj Mahal, but nothing could've prepared me for my real encounter with this place. Our taxi driver dropped us at the site and a pulled rickshaw took us the last mile or so to the entrance of the complex. I felt such a surge of excitement and anticipation – not an inch of the monument was visible. I could barely wait to get there. We arrived in the impressive grounds of the large forecourt – once a large bustling, colourful bazaar. The forecourt is enclosed by a red sandstone wall which once housed 128 small shops, each one open to an arcaded veranda. From the forecourt we stepped through the Taj Ganj gatehouse, and here I got my first glimpse of the marble coated masterpiece. Suddenly the monument was in front of me and the sheer beauty took my breath away.

Shah Jahan built the Taj in loving memory of his wife Mumtaz Mahal and the monument took 22 years of hard labour and 20,000 workers, masons and jewellers to complete. The most prominent dome rises 24 meters over the building directly over the tombs of Mumtaz and Shah Jahan, and the entire inside and outside of the mausoleum is decorated with an inlaid design of flowers and calligraphy with precious gems such as agate and jasper. I felt small against the main archways carved with passages from the Koran, and from a distance the monument appeared to be floating in the air.

The complex is vast and the symmetry perfect. I battled to take everything in: the paradise gardens, celestial pool of abundance, red sandstone mosque and guesthouse at either side of the Taj, and the other palatial buildings. The day was blue, the crowds modest and Ed was in great demand to pose with total strangers as a prime example of Paddy-pale. I couldn't help but chuckle at the thought of an African-Irish boy's visit to India appearing in the photo albums of foreigners. In the early nineties the late Princess Diana posed for an iconic photo in front of the Taj Mahal. At the time the photo stirred me – there was something haunting about the paradox, the aloneness. I never imagined that some 17 years later I too would pose on that same bench, on my own.

From Agra we travelled the 35 km to Fatehpur Sikri, the City of Victory and capital of the Mughal Empire under Akbar's reign for some 12 years. Towards the end of the 16th Century Akbar selected Sikri as the seat of his government, believing the move to be a positive one, but when the water ran out he had to abandon the city. He experimented both with architecture and art and built a city expressing his ideals and vision. We entered the city via the Buland Darwaza loft gateway – made of red and buff sandstone and decorated with white and black marble inlays, and rumoured to be the highest gateway in the world. Inside the fortress the complex of monuments and temples are immaculately preserved, with the Jama Masjid one of the largest mosques in India. Today Fatehpur Sikri is a ghost town – deserted and left with an eerie silence within its walls.

We left the abandoned city in the late afternoon, not knowing we had a five and a half hour drive ahead of us to reach Jaipur. It was the 23rd of December and we were eager to get to our base and get stuck into Christmas.

At some stage in the journey the landscape changed from flat to hilly and a beautiful sunset spilled from the sky onto the Aravali hills and coloured them pink. The last three hours of our journey happened in the dark, on and off a highway under the heavy burden of construction. The drive was harrowing with vehicles travelling on the wrong side of the road, threatening to meet us head on. Some of the vehicles had headlights and some not. Through all of this our driver remained as cool as a cucumber.

It was after 9.30 p.m. when we arrived in Jaipur – a little the worse for wear. Baua and Babaji were there to welcome us with quiet and calm; big smiles and refreshments; Handel's Messiah; and one of cook Ganesh's signature meals. Baua and Babaji were there to step in as parents and grandparents. In Jaipur we said goodbye to our two drivers who spent many hours with us on the road – always in full control. And all I could do was fall into my bed at the General's Retreat next door.

On Christmas Eve I got an opportunity to visit the original Anokhi; and for a good hour or two was lost in a world filled with bold, striking, colourful textiles. The Anokhi brand is based on conservation and development, and the on-going revival of traditional textile skills. They still use hand block printing – with the hand block carved out of wood – and vegetable colours. Anokhi's creations embrace both skill and tradition – their fabrics come with the taste of pomegranate, forest, ocean, sandalwood, spices and sky.

Jaipur was founded in 1727 and is the royal capital city of Rajasthan and first planned city of India. The old city is painted in pink. Maharaja Jai Singh II consulted several books on architecture and architects before making the layout of Jaipur. He was a lover of mathematics and science and he focused on his scientific and cultural interest to make a brilliant city. The city is surrounded by huge walls with seven strong gates. Jaipur oozes calm and charm.

We had enough time in our one day to see the impressive Hawa Mahal and visit the City Palace in the heart of the old walled city; drive-by the water palace Jal Mahal and Amber fort; meet some beautifully decorated elephants on the road; and get close-up to a couple of baby elephants. Back at base we had the privilege of a personal showing of pashminas from Kashmir; the man had cycled for hours with the pashminas in a bundle on the back of his bike. He patiently opened each and every one in an attempt to entice. I couldn't help feeling empathy for the man and his load and he readily parted with a striking black one adorned with delicate embroidery.

We spent the eve of Christmas singing carols, listening to music, cutting Ed's well-travelled Christmas cake he had made at school, feasting at a fully laden table, and wrapping last minute presents.

After an early boy wake-up on Christmas morning we started the day with papaya, pomegranate, nuts, oats porridge, coffee and orange juice. The rest of the day was filled with visitors; a lunch feast with dahl, green chapattis, vegetables, atjar, Christmas pudding and mince pies; and a visit to a Dutch/Indian family on their smallholding on the outskirts of Jaipur.

After an early morning breakfast on St Stephen's day Ed and I got a pyjama send-off for our trip to Goa. As the Fiat with "RJS1" number plate took us to the airport I knew our stay in Jaipur was much, much too short and that I wanted to return sometime in the future. We had not even scratched the surface of Jaipur and Rajasthan.

Ed left Jaipur with a rash that started on his face and for the five days in Goa the big itch travelled down his body until on the last day it ended around his fingers and toes. Some nights the itching left him crying – but in the day the dreaded rash did not prevent him from swimming until his skin completely shrivelled up.

Our Goan days were fantastic: sun loungers; palm trees; coconuts; blue skies; sun; spoiling; sweet lime sodas; books; hiding; anonymity; ankle bracelets; sarongs; big smiles; spicy fish; colourful dancing; and an Ayurvedic massage by a medical practitioner that left me feeling complete weightless.

We were blissfully unaware that Goa was the next target after the Mumbai bombings; the place was extra quiet with loads of tourists cancelling their holidays. When we found out we decided to keep a low profile and avoid public places, and the small resort of Coconut Creek was the perfect hide-out: 12 houses nestled in a coconut grove; wooden and wicker furniture; slatted wood and lattice panels for fresh air; red-tiled roofs; earthy tones; hammocks; and lush bold green.

At night the fairy lights lit the grove and the smell of burning coconut hair to deter mosquitoes filled the sky. We always retired to our room with the mosquito nets tucked in around our beds like little nests.

After five days in paradise we were ready to leave the quiet and calm of Coconut Creek and connect up with our hosts; and go on an epic journey to an undisclosed destination somewhere in the jungle of central of India.

An epic journey

Our flight left Goa late and in Mumbai I realised only superhuman intervention could allow us to collect our baggage, transfer to another terminal a good distance away, and check in our luggage – all in the space of 40 minutes before take-off. As we ran between terminals two men spotted our urgency, scooped up Ed and his case; then me; bundled us into a scooter; drove like lunatics on the wrong side of the road; demanded a wad of US dollars for the five minute ride, no negotiation; and dropped us off at the door to the terminal. This time we were lucky and we were in time for our flight to Raipur.

On New Year's Eve we had a long journey ahead of us – an hour-and-a-half flight from Mumbai to Raipur, followed by a five hour drive to our destination in Madhya Pradesh, or so we thought. Our driver was there with his white cardboard sign and a smile to meet us; he had driven down from Tala to Raipur the day before. As we loaded the jeep with the customary toing and froing in order to reach consensus, I noticed a very smooth rear left tyre. The driver wasn't keen on suitcases on the roof so we ended up with the luggage in the back on the two jump seats and four of us (two moms and two boys) on the back seat. The car was a strange breed and every time the driver started the engine a stupid jingle would say in an American drawl: "Please buckle-up for a safe journey." I could never find the safety belts. The driver was very taken with this little gimmick and it never failed to raise a smile on his face.

We left the airport at midday, our spirits high in anticipation of the adventure that was about to unfold. We were also looking forward to a New Year's celebration upon our arrival in the jungle. However, what we did not know was that we had to work our way through Raipur with its six million inhabitants first – a lengthy process with the usual chaos and congestion. Our driver had to stop several times to ask for directions. The first leg of our journey took us through Chhattisgarh – the newest Indian state that was carved out of Uttar Pradesh as recently as 2000.

Raipur is known as the Rice bowl of India, and the place had become an industrial destination for coal, power, steel and aluminium industries. This meant trucks and trucks and more trucks – I have never seen so many trucks before. We travelled north on a straight road much too narrow, with no hard shoulder, and completely inadequate for such heavy traffic. Driving on the roads involved a game of constant ducking and diving to avoid both oncoming and same lane traffic; there were a million-and-one near misses.

As we travelled through Chhattisgarh and Madhya Pradesh I was able to experience every inch of the land: Acacia, Teak, Eucalyptus, Sal forests, rice/wheat fields, rivers, villages dotted at regular intervals, locals doing their daily living, trucks decorated in festive colours, cattle with painted horns, and even an oncoming bus with no front. We travelled through villages without names; struggled through godforsaken Bilaspur – a town with two million people and almost half the population of Ireland; and around four in the afternoon finally found a place quiet enough to open Ganesh's packed lunch of Perantha stuffed with fenugreek and chapattis for a roadside picnic. At this point our driver informed us that we had another five hours ahead of us. I think the driver was either too embarrassed to tell the truth about journey times or else he did not have a clue. This was a perfect case to practise "trusting the process" and "going with the flow."

In this part of the world road signs are few and far between and our driver had to stop and ask for directions another 15 times. At one place a local had used the only road sign as one of the supports for the walls of his shack. Nobody uses roadmaps; the notion of journey distance, travelling time, or even the names of towns and major junctions along the way were unimportant. This was not a place where mileage and milestones lived, but instead a place where you make things up as you go along. In this place only the moment counted.

The further we travelled the more remote the landscape, windier the roads, steeper ascends and descends, more severe the potholes, and denser the jungle became. For miles and miles I saw no sign of civilisation, only the frequent lights of oncoming trucks, or the sudden surprise of a dark broken-down truck right in the way of our vehicle. We travelled through sacred land: home to the aboriginal tribes of the Gonds, Behl and Baiga people; the Amarkantak plateau where the Vindhyas mountain range and Satpuras hills meet and the Narmada, Sone and Johila Rivers emerge; and the pilgrim town of Amarkantak where gods, celestial beings, demons, saints and sages are said to have all achieved great spiritual powers. The locals believe that whoever dies at Amarkantak is assured of a place in heaven.

At nine in the evening our driver stopped for a chai break under the bright lights of the busy village centre of Sihora. At this stage only the driver and myself were awake – we were in the middle of nowhere with no end in sight; and then the news of a flat tyre. For this hiccup fate not only brought us to a village, but the car stopped right under the guard of a light. There was a gentle unease in the night as the locals gathered around us in silent curiosity. We had to get out into the cold night and move the luggage from the boot to release the spare tyre; we were outnumbered by far. Barely three feet away were two food stalls frying someone's take-away food.

We were counting our progress in batches of hours and at half past eleven – within five miles of our destination – we came to a sudden halt with a second puncture. At this stage I began to think that we would never reach our destination and that the surprise would remain a mystery. A rescue car was sent, and we bundled everything into the fresh vehicle and travelled on the dirt road to arrive at the Junglemantra resort on the dot of midnight. We arrived in time for a New Year's feast with four other visitors from South Africa. We had travelled a long way to fetch the New Year – all of 11 hours and 500km.

But this epic journey delivered us into Bandhavgarh - a national tiger reserve and slice of paradise set among the Vindhya hills of Madhya Pradesh with the highest density of tigers in India; and into the home of Junglemantra.

British Asian nature photographer and wildlife artist Shailin Ramji and TV producer Rhea left their London life and relocated to India to create Junglemantra. They camped on site for eight months to ensure that the construction of the resort did not disturb the animal corridors. From time to time tigers appeared in the grass next to their main outdoor seating and dining area.

After a restless sleep the 5:30 a.m. wake-up call on New Year's day came much too soon. We loaded two open jeeps; hot water bottles in our laps; coats, breakfast picnic; and hardy, thick dog blankets. The blankets were not for cuddling, but were fit to form a ring around you. It was a short drive through Tala to the main gate where we collected our guide. And then into the jungle where the early rays of the sun transformed the trees and morning mist into magic. Once inside the park the excitement was palpable as we hoped and listened for the alarm call of a Langur or spotted dear warning us about the presence of a tiger.

Shortly before nine we were fortunate to join a number of other jeeps for a beautiful viewing of a young male tiger. Seeing the orange and black in nature was unreal; the moment almost too big to comprehend and when the tiger appeared, my fingers were unable to find the camera's focus or click buttons.

Once a tiger is spotted the bush races begin as every jeep scrambles, scuffles and jostles for position. The carry-on was both ridiculous and exhilarating, both appalling and hilarious as the jeeps raced each other to follow the tiger. The tiger was completely oblivious to these antics – not a great example of man's behaviour in another's habitat. But then again, the stakes are high and people with impressive camera lenses travel from far and wide to see a tiger in the wild. The guides would do almost anything to deliver on this quest – they would nearly kill themselves in the process.

On our second day we saw another tiger – this time from the vantage point of an elephant's back. This was altogether another story. Before sunrise the Mahouts (elephant drivers) take their elephants and track the tigers. As soon as the tiger is tracked, wireless messages are beamed around and the Tiger Show gets underway. No-one knows until shortly before the gates close for lunchtime whether or not such a show will happen. This means that all the jeeps have to race to the main gate; guides scramble to get a place in the queue and hopefully secure tickets for their charges; jeeps race back to where the tiger was spotted; and then wait in a line until it is your turn. Getting a ticket is a lottery – and then there is the added risk that while you are waiting in the queue the tiger may decide to move on.

We were lucky and saw her high on a ledge where she was resting after an earlier catch. Wow – the once in a lifetime experience of coming eye to eye with a tigress in her natural habitat.

Bandhavgarh covers an area of 437sq kilometres and holds 32 hills, overhanging cliffs, grassy swamps, sheltered valleys covered by evergreen Sal forests, and plains interspersed with meadows. Dense tracts of bamboo and orchids are scattered throughout the valleys. The reserve is a natural habitat for gaur (Indian bison), sloth bear, leopard, porcupine, wild boar, Royal Bangal tiger, sambar (deer) and spotted deer.

At the centre of this place – on top of a hill 811m above sea level - is the amazing Bandhavgarh Fort. The fort is believed to be 2000 years old and we made it up and down the steep 300m ascend in an open 'jeep'. The drive was extreme to say the least, and on our way up we stopped several times to follow fresh pug marks of a tigress and her cubs in the neighbourhood. Through the imposing gateway are 560 acres of grassland; a big lake, three small 12th Century temples; avatars – a statue of half-man-half-lion Narsimhan towers almost 22 feet above the grass; and rock paintings. Kabir Das, the celebrated 16th Century saint, once lived and preached here.

The views from the natural ramparts were breath-taking. There was the additional thrill of finding these monuments in the jungle, unspoilt and unexploited. After a picnic lunch on the temple steps I returned to Junglemantra for a lazy afternoon on the lounger in a sunny corner of the outdoor deck, a good book, and the bush as company. I stayed there until the neighbouring cows started on a long line home; and for a spectacular sunset to colour the sky. In the distance I could hear the alarm of a spotted dear. As dinner time got closer, the smell of basmati and spices filled the air. I could equally have been somewhere in Africa.

At night we re-told stories around the open fireplace. The cold night sky held the smell of teak and mahogany on the fire, and the sounds of the jungle and some distant drumming.

All too soon it was time to go and on our last morning a 4:30 a.m. wake-up call started our day: we had a four hour drive of about 200 km to the nearest airport at Jabalpur. Our driver was there to collect us with a big smile and two new tyres. We rattled and shook all the way to Jabalpur through farming and forestry land; spotting the odd wild boar, wild dogs, jackals, scarecrows, a line of women attending to their morning toilet at the roadside, and a man wheeling his food stall in the road.

We arrived two hours early for our flight and due to fog in Delhi had an additional four hours' delay at Jabalpur airport with no services. When we were completely desperate and demanded to be looked after the Air India marketing manager offered to share his lunch box with us in his cramped little office.

A two-and-a-half hour flight from Jabalpur via Gwalior landed us straight into the fog chaos at Delhi airport's new domestic terminal. We were glad to be back at the IIC where we were reunited with Baua, Babaji and our red suitcase.

While in India our care was so thorough that I was not allowed to go anywhere near fresh root vegetables or fruit without their skins. I must be one of a small handful of travellers who moved through India constipated; back in Delhi I couldn't hold out anymore and overdosed on bean sprout salads, tomatoes and sweet pink carrots. The raw vegetables tasted like manna from heaven.

Back at base we fell straight into a large family reunion and on our last day I took an INR400 4-hour taxi to Fabindia, a shop with showcase Indian handloom textiles. My red suitcase was already filled to the brim with curtains, shawls, scarves, kurtas, silk, cotton, sandalwood and colours so I avoided Anokhi. We met with a prominent MIT and Yale educated graphic designer and cultural activist in his cupboard sized office where he treated us to spicy food from Andhra Pradesh. When I thought no-one else could fit in the small space, a brave journalist flanked by her heavily armed security guards, arrived to join us. At the time she was involved in a controversial and high profile court case involving terror and human rights.

I loved New Delhi: the eco-friendly busses, yellow and green scooters, Ambassador cars, feather light Idlis (South Indian rice cakes), mango ice-cream, and the people. I loved her space, colours, ease, and vibrant melting pot. New Delhi is a happening place.

The city was built as the imperial capital of India by the British, while rambunctious Old Delhi served as capital of Islamic India. Unfortunately our brief stay meant that we never made it to Old Delhi.

India was incredible: and yes, there are many people, men urinating and spitting everywhere, dust, dirt and decay. But I found her authentic, light, inspiring and magical. I loved the fact that she has no fashion rules – none of this 'tartan is big this winter' or 'purple is the colour this season'. There were no high-street shops with rows of the same clothes. Instead the colours were rich and individual – and the outfits beautiful. Even in the midst of a shanty town the bright colours of a saree brought beauty to the squalor. At times the sarees revealed a glimpse of gold or splendour.

As I moved through India I couldn't help but think of the O'Daly – he had such a longstanding dream to visit the place; to be on elephant back; to go tiger tracking; to enjoy the food; and to see the desert of Rajasthan. For a brief moment I wondered if I was living his dream.

On our last night we fell into the warm welcome of a house party and as the evening unfolded impromptu singing slowly but surely filled the crowded space: anti-war songs; soulful ballads lamenting the past and Irish rebel James Connolly; and a Kerala boat song. The singing was beautiful – I desperately wanted to join in but as hard as I tried could not remember any of the words. The music stirred the night and I struggled to remain on the side line.

The next morning Baua and Babaji were there to see us off. As the black taxi car drove us to the airport in dense fog I felt a little sad; sad because in the short time we were there the place felt like home. India received us so openly and graciously: we were in the safe fold of family and she even gave us a glimpse of her amazing soul.

Back in Ireland we found the 5-and-a-half hours we lost on our trip to America– unscratched and open to receive our new prints.

Whereas the Himalayas tested my endurance, the ski-slopes of Jackson Hole my fear, India brought me face-to-face with surrender. I had no choice but to step right into the heart of each moment – and finding there an incredible lightness of being.

Catching balls

When the O'Daly departed he left a good number of balls in the air – a business, fledgling charitable foundation, apartment in Greece, as well as a couple of prickly pears. It was as if the O'Daly planned ahead with a devilish grin and a "this will keep her busy for a while." Numerous times I felt so overwhelmed by the many balls I was trying to juggle, and I got close to turning my back on them and leaving them to drop from the sky. During these moments, anger and resentment overtook me.

I became the custodian of the vision of creating "a place of quiet and counsel" where others could come to reconnect with a deeper sense of soul, self and balance. From the word go I experienced the project as a labour of honour and passion, but in the process of creation and growth I discovered a road fraught with egos and private agendas. I was shocked by the ugly selfishness that could attach to the beauty and purity of this dream. Shortly before the O'Daly's death we were on our way to Navan when, out-of-the-blue, the he said: "I will never leave you alone with the Foundation." Trying to bring this vision to life became a difficult journey, and at times I was barely able to hold on to the dream. I felt guided as I stepped through the highs and agonising lows; one day at a time.

The changes in my life brought with them a thirst to explore my own being. This longing came from deep within and urged me to search far and dig deep. I found myself in places like Findhorn in Scotland, Omega in Rhinebeck, New York, Kripalu in the Berkshires of western Massachusetts,

Dunderry in County Meath, and the centre of London. Some of these places I had never heard of before – they simply landed on my path. And I found myself in the presence of amazing teachers. As I stepped through this process of discovery I gathered invaluable wisdom. The solitary process of discovery and peeling had begun – little did I know that the process had all the ingredients to result in a journey of profound proportions.

Rainbow Easter

Easter is always a good time to visit South Africa; the days are still sunny and warm without the crowding that goes with the peak summer months. Ed and I packed for our annual pilgrimage to the southern tip of Africa – this was our first trip back after we brought the O'Daly's ashes to the bosom of the Kalahari. On this occasion it was like stepping into the heart of a brown river, and its flowing carried me through familiar landscapes to corners, colours and people in my heartland. We landed in a late-summer South Africa – and for almost three weeks we were on a wonderful adventure in a place that still remembers our footprints. A place that gently guards our roots.

This trip was about reconnecting. The bittersweet joy of finding friends we lost touch with more than a decade ago when we left for Greece and our journeys diverged. The pleasure of being able to step through the past, and arriving at a new place filled with possibility; of meeting strapping lads who were once toddlers; of finding wisdom where before there was inexperience; and still finding the same soul and energy that connected us in the first place.

Shortly before our trip noises of a thirty year school reunion began to appear on the pages of Facebook. In the fuss I reconnected with four old classmates, and without any explanation we formed a virtual group that spanned the US, Canada, Ireland and South Africa. A virtual family that simply dropped from the sky.

Never friends at school, the wonder of synchronicity brought the six of us together like keys on a key-ring; diverse, each with an individual story, yet sharing the safety of the same circle. After 30 years these five strangers stepped into my life and filled the void at a time when I felt at my most vulnerable; and they brought with them compassion, friendship and support. I often wonder how life's journey can cheat us out of the many years in between the points of separation and re-connection. How was life for each of them during the thirty years? What marks did the highs and lows leave on their hearts? And yet, somehow the timing to re-connect was perfect.

Everything about the circle is extraordinary: piano notes, standing ovations, tours and fine dining; camera lenses, bicycles, elegance and adventure; laws, animal farm shenanigans, lakes and swimming; computers, millions, school runs and bravery; town plans, sense of humour, scrapbooks and bows and arrows. We unpacked memories from the sixties, seventies and eighties as if we were unwrapping a present during a game of pass-the-parcel. Contemporaries in the same boat facing the same challenges; children from the same streets and school colours, and 30 years later like characters in a book eager to see how each of our various plots were unfolding. While in my heartland I was able to meet up with two of the group of five; straight from the pages of a faded high school yearbook.

With being in South Africa comes the delight of being able to communicate in my mother tongue: of remembering, sharing and laughing in Afrikaans. And of making bucket lists with words that have become un-oiled because they were stored in drawers and cupboards for so long. How I've longed to taste the sound of these expressive words in my mouth.

On the banks of the Vaal River in Parys we discovered the gem *Hoi Polloi* – a place where the well-heeled travel from Johannesburg to experience unexpected fine-dining. In the main street opposite a Fishing-and-Hairdressing shop, above a tyre-and-clutch shop, the steepest narrow steel staircase that wouldn't pass the Irish health and safety test leads to the front door. The restaurant welcomed us like a best friend. Inside the space oozed charm and the aromas hinted at garden-fresh ingredients. On each of the tables fresh roses in silver trophies softened the conventional settings of cutlery and glasses. At the door to the toilets a small wooden table with a collection of perfumes and hand creams extended an invitation to explore and top-up on fine fragrances.

We were on a whirlwind through Johannesburg, with just enough time to experience the rhythm, beads, art and fare of the Rosebank rooftop market. Here we met the creator of a wire baobab tree: I could not resist his big white smile and bought his handiwork for Ruby. I imagined this baobab tree filled with her jewellery bits and pieces, and then spent the next couple of minutes wondering how I was going to make this awkward shape fit into my hand luggage.

In the suburb of Morningside we visited one of my first bosses: a home where spoil leaks out of every seam. We connected with a godfather and a godmother; stocked up on hand-made jewellery and visited homes away from home where the furniture knows our contours. There was a tense moment when an armed would-be robber left a racket in his wake at a supermarket in Lonehill and left cold shivers down my back. Our trip involved a merry-go-round of travelling west-east-south-and-north; getting lost on highways I once knew so well; and long, long conversations where the many words kept on clogging up the open spaces.

In the Western Cape we stayed in the colourful village of De Waterkant, cradled in between the city and the V&A Waterfront. The village of semi-detached cottages and cobbled streets date back to the 1760s; here we paused in the presence of history, character and spices. We explored the coffee shops, wireless spots, sushi and pedicures in the old slave quarters; enjoyed the famous home-made yoghurt ice-cream of the area; decadent papaya and mango breakfasts; Cape Malay dishes; and pink sunsets over Camps bay. Days of bed-heads; two boys who talked like old men; and a scary crawl up to and slide down from the Noon Gun restaurant perched on the side of Signal Hill. We were accompanied by first-timers to South Africa and I loved the thrill of reliving my heartland through first-time eyes.

We spent a couple of flawless days in the coastal town of Hermanus where blue stretched from one end of the day to the next. Here Ed announced to us all that he was 100% African. He loved the feeling and detail of his background.

At the Spier Wine Estate cheetah sanctuary there was big excitement when Ed lined up to meet and pat cheetah Khaya. However, a last minute change of plan made the handler turn into another enclosure and a wonderful moment of synchronicity gave Ed a close-up encounter with a cheetah named Joseph – his dad's name. A look of pure joy filled his face like an encore after a fine performance. Ed received a certificate as proof of his encounter with Joseph. This was another wink – thinking about the chances of finding a cheetah with the name Joseph in the Cape when it was really meant to be Khaya made me smile.

The motherland took great care of us and as usual we found a welcome that stretched as far and wide as to the moon and back. As ever our days were much, much too short.

While in South Africa we had a special mission to fulfil. In order to create something more permanent in the O'Daly's memory our dream was to create a prize for the top academic student at Headfort School. I knew this would mean a lot to Ed – he never did manage to complete the little wooden cross in our garden. So on our way through South Africa we collected a Carrol Boyes pewter vase for this mission. Back in Ireland we found a carpenter with a chunk of Headfort yew timber, and we combined the Carrol Boyes piece with the yew. The yew had special meaning for us because it was from the place where the O'Daly spent the last years in his homeland. In addition the yew Tree has an incredible life span: the tree can tolerate harsh conditions, has evergreen foliage and is able to layer itself. For this reason the yew has been considered a symbol of immortality through the ages.

On the last day of the school term the O'Daly trophy was awarded for the first time - holding within the piece the beauty of creative lines; the strength of metal; the connection between Africa and Ireland; the wisdom of an ancient tree; and the memory of a special man.

Flow

I was grateful when Ruby and Ed discovered their own flow. From the word go I became aware of the need to untie myself from the children, to make room for their independence. I could not explain this – injecting distance went against my core and ideas of motherhood. Yet, there was this urge to let them fly – as young as they were – because losing the O'Daly made me very aware of the fact that I could not guarantee to be there forever. My decisions regarding the children raised eyebrows in the community – it was unheard of, and appeared non-caring to others. Did they even know how difficult it was to make these decisions? At a transpersonal level I knew I was making decisions regarding the children for their sake and not mine; it was as if someone else was in control.

Instead of becoming one of the world's best bass players at a young age, Ruby embarked on a career working with cancer. Nothing could deter her from achieving her goal of becoming a radiotherapist. Not even the early days of working with terminally ill patients where dignity had been scrubbed from the walls, or working a demanding week with seven-to-seven shifts cleaning vomit and changing soiled sheets could change her mind. She had on her heart the desire to make a difference. Ed settled into life at boarding school and blossomed into an eager student. One day I overheard him during a telephone conversation with his sister say: "I don't know why, but really good things are starting to happen to me." I smiled. We had all been touched by the gold dust of grace.

One day an email slipped into my inbox and its jingle unlocked the notion of dating to me. The last time I came close to dating was more than 23 years ago when a part-timer on our MBA course took a fancy to me; pursued me all the way down to Cape Town where I was going on holiday; presented me with a limited edition box-set of Bruce Springsteen for Christmas; and then tried to introduce me to his parents in East London on a roundabout way home to Johannesburg. This was before the O'Daly stepped in. I kept him at arm's length and we were both bowled over when geeky paddy O'Daly arrived back from a trip to New York and Ireland and popped the big question out-of-the-blue. I found out much later that during this trip the O'Daly announced to his family that he had found his life partner – before I knew. Thinking back, everything about our connection felt right; the endless hours spent chatting; sharing of music and mountains; metaphors and dreams; helping each other through dissertations; and the valuable learning of a three month letter-writing-separation when I worked in Italy. In the space of only a few months the O'Daly managed to sneak into my heart from right under my nose.

Our non-dating partnership worked because of a soul-connection; friendship; yin and yang; the balance between visionary and organiser; and the continuous dance between the-sky-is-no-limit and how-do-we-get-there? There on a shelf are the volumes of our 20 years – like books lined up between two bookends – held upright by a wedding song in February at the one end, and a funeral song in June at the other end.

After losing a life-partner, where does one go to meet men? This is not something you ever think of when starting your adult life. The email in my inbox came with an invitation to the unfamiliar world of online dating. I subscribed to a suitable site, entered my search criteria, waited for the faces to pop up, and then sifted through the portfolio. However, this was not going to be a straightforward process – I could not get into the swing of things. It took only two weeks of finding photos of men with "meet Bob, Alan, John" in my inbox every morning before I unsubscribed. My gut told me that I was not going to meet someone in this way.

Next I considered lunchtime dating, where you pay an impressive sum to an organisation and they organise lunch dates with suitable candidates. I attended the interview in Dublin; filled in a lengthy questionnaire and picked qualities like I was ordering from a menu; had my photograph taken as if I was renewing my passport; and on my way home decided "no, this is not for me." I resigned myself to the belief that if I must meet someone, it will happen when it happens.

I longed for someone to share my life with. There are the practical aspects of lugging heavy suitcases down staircases and into trunks of cars; of trying to find the right screwdriver for the job; and of fixing toilet seats and pop-up sink stoppers that no longer work. Being alone after 20 years meant that there was never anyone to meet me at an airport, to say "hello" when I arrived home from being out, or to make me a cup of tea.

The O'Daly's death triggered a strange occurrence: the life crisis hit a switch and from that moment on I started to live my life backwards. As an undergraduate at university I was a little prissy – as if I was a forty year old in the body of a twenty year old. Here I was in my middle ages and feeling like a twenty year old – young and alive; and all in the aftermath of a life changing trauma. Somewhere in the rubble cluttering my soul I found the precious gift of a new life.

One day, when I had enough courage, I moved the O'Daly's favourite monster fridge out of our small kitchen and out of our home. A difficult forceps birth was required before the fridge finally fell into the night and left on the back of a trailer on its way to the heaven for oversized appliances. To give the concept of new wings a test and the universe a wink, I placed our house on the market.

I continued the process of shedding and every week Midland Waste Recycling collected the endless supply of stuff I dumped in our black and blue bins. I always wheeled the bins out after dark – like someone who has something to hide; as if the stuff I was moving out wouldn't be able to see who was abandoning them. At the end of the driveway I placed our bins with the other bins where they were waiting for their early morning collection as if they were a line of commuters waiting for their bus to work. Each mum about the secrets they held inside.

We hired Skippy bags and filled them with bits and pieces collected over the years: wooden birds, funky birds, rag dolls, crimplene and wet-look Barbie and Ken dolls' clothes from the sixties; suitcases; chairs; soft toys and sewing machine bits. All I could manage was to oversee the process – I did not have the courage to throw anything into the bag. I asked Ed and Ruby to cover the bag from the rain; to provide dignity to the possessions on the last part of their journey. As the bag filled up the kids in the courtyard appeared as if from nowhere, eager to root through the Aladdin's cave, and parts of our past ended up in other homes in the courtyard like adopted orphans.

The last thing I tackled was the green shed. I hired a skip, took a deep breath, and stepped inside the dark, musty space. On the rusty shelves were several tins of paint – all our attempts to bring new life to tired walls; paint brushes that had gone hard; a yellow level measuring tool; rake and shovel; a depleted toolbox; a pair of wellington boots with a big scary spider in one; a pair of old number plates; a spare door; three boxes of business files; Christmas lights not used in three years; and a collection of man things.

In the time following the loss I became to appreciate transience: the impermanence of everything except for that which I am. I have come to let go of most of my attachments to people, places, things or time. Instead I try to strive to be open to the moment and whatever the moment may bring. It is a constant effort – one that requires a decision to do so every single morning.

I have experienced first-hand the wonderful freedom that comes with letting go and moving on. In the split-second when I touch transience, I can only smile as I feel its weightlessness against my hand.

Fall and four gems

I returned to New York one more time for a reunion with school classmates, a workshop with American author and mystic, Caroline Myss, and to visit friends in Boston. This was my first journey back to the Big Apple after that difficult time three years before. Flying over the Atlantic felt so smooth – we were suspended in the endless sky. I closed my eyes and imagined we were gliding on the tail feathers of the sun; away from the night and further into the day.

Earlier my stomach was in a knot as I said a quick goodbye to Ed at Headfort School. While I was talking he stared past the grey walls into the distance because he too had memories of New York. I never anticipated his tenseness around the place and for a moment it looked as if he was going to unravel like a garment when a loose thread is pulled. I could see him trying to be brave; trying to cling to the hours between here and there. In his mind he was already calculating the difference in time to see when he could make his first phone call.

When we landed in New York I struggled to remember the details of our last visit – as if to try and retrace my moves during a game of chess. The last time I walked the pavements of Manhattan's Upper East Side I was combing the shops to find something the O'Daly could stomach. I could not help but wonder if the busy pavements remembered my footprints; and if the streets could remember my pain.

I caught glimpses of landmarks that looked familiar, and felt sick to the core when I sensed that I was in the vicinity of the Sloan Kettering Hospital. The move through New York was swift and before long I was on a bus to Rhinebeck with a super-size peppermint ice cream in my hands. I was heading into unknown territory; sailing on unchartered waters.

By the time I arrived at my room in Number 41a of the retreat centre her stuff was already settled into the top four of the six drawers, and her clothes were hanging in neat lines in the thin cupboard. In the bathroom two shower caps were balanced on top of two white towels; her washing bag took up half the basin and a bag full of brushes, cosmetics, pots, colours and promises was carefully balanced on the towel hook.

She had long silver-grey braids – the longest ones reached all the way down to the small of her back. Before we were scheduled to start our different workshops she slipped into the bathroom and stayed there for a long time – as if a long teal green coat adorned with large orange beads and silver braids in your hair gave one an automatic privilege to go first.

At night when I returned from my session she was already settled in her bed – a retired African American musician from NYC and re-programmer of DNA. I listened as she told me how her music used to move people in inexplicable ways, and how when she touched people the electro-magnetic field around her caused extra-ordinary things to happen. She was a wise woman.

At night she slipped into her caftan with the same ease a performer changes outfits in between scene changes. For two nights we became sisters. I was a long way from home. On the two mornings in Dutchess County her alarm called her at 4.57 a.m. for a ritual of absolutions and prayers she directed to the north-east-south-west and ended in a deep "ohm."

She was on a workshop called "How to communicate with animals." At the end of the first day she arrived back at our room completely mortified: some of the participants on the course brought their dogs, cats and birds, and during the afternoon session a big husky came over to her and licked her on the face, on her lips and then proceeded to lick the make-up off her right eye. She could not believe how the owner of the husky could simply sit and watch the dog without intervening. In Rhinebeck I discovered sisterhood; I discovered the beauty and wisdom of my tribe.

From Rhinebeck I took the bus back to New York City for my flight to Boston; and a couple of days with longstanding friends in their elegant home on the shore of Lake Winnipesaukee. These were colleagues of the O'Daly and this visit was the first since four became three. In the welcome of this slice of paradise we re-traced steps, remembered days gone by, and made new memories.

We explored the lake in two kayaks, one orange and one yellow; and at night we took the two faithful boxers for a walk. A canopy tour along the treetops of the White Mountains in New Hampshire allowed me to let go of my fear – I surrendered to the open spaces where free flow carried me. According to the foliage tracker we were ahead of the peak period, but even so, the trees were covered in vibrant autumn colours. Zipping across the tips of the magnificent trees felt liberating; it was OK to fall into the precipice. The zip-lining experience was both spectacular and exhilarating, and the feeling of freedom transported me back to a time when I was carefree and full of life – a time of handstands and cartwheels. Across the valley Mount Washington watched on in silence.

On the way back we slipped the car's soft top down and sang along with the CD player at full volume; our voices filled the evening. At the home next to Lake Winnipesaukee I experienced a special healing – there was no doubt this stop was meant to be on my journey.

From New Hampshire I took a bus to Boston and a flight to YFK airport for my transfer to Ithaca. When I arrived at the airport the official at the check-in desk asked me "Who on earth wants to go to Ithaca?" I responded with: "Me." Long before I even knew of the existence of this place, the name "Ithaca" appeared in my awareness from a number of random sources; three times in short succession, bang-bang-bang, just like that. The coincidence was so weird and inexplicable that the synchronicity rattled me.

At Ithaca airport an old school classmate fetched me in her yellow Volkswagen beetle; we last saw each other thirty years ago. There was big excitement as we prepared for the reunion with a couple of other classmates at Windgarth House on the shore of Cayuga Lake.

In the warmth of the white and blue house we filled every minute with chatter, food, and catch-up. We were teenagers once again. We went for long walks; kayaked on the lake; roasted marshmallows over an open fire; took turns to make South African meals; and in the evenings paged through old school yearbooks. During one of the nights, when no-one was looking, I pocketed a piece of the beautiful moon.

Meeting Ithaca head-on required big bold steps. Joining a reunion with classmates with whom I never had a close connection was pretty random. No-one could have prepared me for the revelations that surfaced. For the first time I heard how others saw me back then – out of the mouths of youths. I realised how disconnected I was during my high school years, and how I missed out on those school friendships which seem so important to many others. At night when alone in my bed, I re-visited those years, and I recognised the little seeds planted back then which would shape my beliefs and choices for years to come. That part of my childhood needed to be healed, and it took Windgarth and Cayuga Lake to provide the healing space.

Late one afternoon I stepped out to inhale the sunset over the lake. Muted shades coloured the landscape – the water a mirror reflecting the trees, silhouettes, and the sky. I was surrounded by pure silence and I felt joy. As I got closer to the pier I saw a young girl, about twelve years old; her fine blonde hair tied into two ponytails, her eyes full of dreams, and her smile innocent. I recognised her in an instant – a younger version of myself. And I knew I was home.

Wings

The O'Daly's death was the impetus for change – his leaving had given me the opportunity of a new beginning. Instead of dwelling in the disbelief and agony that accompany bereavement, I was filled with an inexplicable urge to move forward. I experienced a deep knowing that this chance was a gift, and that I had to treat the opportunity with appreciation instead of pity. After all, an opportunity for rebirth does not come around too often. With this new beginning came the invitation to re-connect with my purpose on this earth, and to do so in an authentic way. Second chances leave little or no room for procrastination, or self-pity. Such a call to action requires self-belief, courage and a good dollop of faith.

Upon reflection I realised that my resentment towards the O'Daly for having given up my career to follow him on his expeditions, was undue. Unbeknown to me, I tucked in alongside him as he led me on my journey to Ithaca. He fetched me in Johannesburg and brought me to a place where I could never have dreamed of finding on my own. At the appropriate time he turned to me as if to say: "Here now, off with you! This is your time to fly." The O'Daly gave me a huge, unselfish gift.

When I got notice of a fixed term project in Johannesburg, the time felt right to make a move and I decided to give the project a go. I had to satisfy the pull I felt to return to my heartland, so I packed a couple of big bags, made arrangements for a rental apartment in Sandton, and tucked in a protective net of support around Ed's life in his boarding school at Headfort. I felt a strong compulsion to go.

The plane landed in Johannesburg on a blue spring day – the month for Jacaranda, Bougainvillea and Petrea blooms. It was almost nine years to the month since I left South Africa, and yet it felt like the other day when I last stepped into the Highveld air.

I picked up my Avis car from the OR Tambo International Airport and as I left the boom at the parking garage I knew the N3 would be waiting for me, three lanes still choked with morning traffic. On the Highveld a brand new day was unfolding.

ABOUT THE AUTHOR

Ria Wiid is a business mentor and founder member of The Tamhnach Foundation, a charity with the aim of promoting a healthy work life balance. She has spent the best part of the past decade on a journey of self-discovery; a process that is ongoing.

Ria moves between Worcestershire in the UK, and County Meath in Ireland. Wherever she finds herself, she provides a harbour for her Cavan man, her two children – a teen and a twenty-something, and her extended family.

She is committed to living her life from a place of heart, and remains curious about the process of unfolding. During her spare time she loves to travel to interesting places. Ria is well into her next book project.

Printed in Great Britain
by Amazon